PRAISE FOR
America the Beautiful?

"*America the Beautiful?* is so funny and special and illuminating that it makes even me, a person who cannot tolerate trees or weather, wish I could've tagged along in the back seat."

—Samantha Irby, author of
Wow, No Thank You., and *We Are Never Meeting in Real Life.*

"This hilarious, thoughtful, and bighearted book will have you packing for a journey, whether it's a road trip or just a deep-dive into your own psyche. Either way, bring toilet paper."

—Emily Flake, author of *That Was Awkward* and *Mama Tried*

"Blythe is such a funny writer that I would read about her going to the toilet, never mind going on a great American road trip! She writes about these national parks with a joy and a wonder that makes you lust for adventure, but that doesn't protect their often villainous history from her lucidly honest and deliciously salt-coated writing. This book is a revelation for anyone who has ever driven on a road in America."

—Will McPhail, author of *Love & Vermin*

"Blythe invites you into her world with ease, and you're all too happy to stay awhile, so you can laugh, think, and feel. Also, my Black behind is *way* too scared to ever road trip it alone, so thank goodness for this book so I could live vicariously through her. Brave woman. Fantastic writer!"

—Phoebe Robinson, author of *You Can't Touch My Hair*

"So relentlessly funny, smart, and inspiring that it made me question my rule of only sleeping in places with a lobby. I wolfed down this book like a tub of car-temp hummus—one of Blythe's trusty road staples and a food I'd happily live on if it meant sitting next to her a little longer for more irreverent, seriously fascinating hilarity."

—Jen Spyra, author of *Big Time*

"Blythe perfectly captures the beauty of solo travel—the relentless horniness, the existential spiraling. Basically, she's the ideal travel companion!"

—Catherine Cohen, author of
God I Feel Modern Tonight and host of *Seek Treatment* podcast

ALSO BY BLYTHE ROBERSON

How to Date Men When You Hate Men

AMERICA THE Beautiful?

ONE WOMAN
IN A BORROWED PRIUS
ON THE ROAD MOST TRAVELED

BLYTHE ROBERSON

HARPER ● PERENNIAL

NEW YORK ● LONDON ● TORONTO ● SYDNEY ● NEW DELHI ● AUCKLAND

HARPER ● PERENNIAL

HarperCollins books may be purchased for educational, business, or sales promotional use. For information, please email the Special Markets Department at SPsales@harpercollins.com.

FIRST EDITION

Library of Congress Cataloging-in-Publication Data has been applied for.

ISBN 978-0-06-311551-4 (pbk.)
ISBN 978-0-06-327340-5 (library edition)

23 24 25 26 27 LBC 7 6 5 4 3

For everyone who helped me on my way

Names and identifying details of the individuals I met in my travels were changed to protect their privacy.

CONTENTS

INTRODUCTION

It's a Free Country

THERE ARE ONLY SO MANY POEMS YOU CAN READ ABOUT being free, only so many times you can listen to Joni Mitchell's travel album, *Hejira*, before something inside you snaps. On January 17, 2019, Mary Oliver died, and I sat at my office desk ignoring my work to read her poem "Moments," about actually living your life when you're alive, about how the lamest thing you can possibly do is be cautious.

Fuck, I thought. *I gotta quit my job.*

That was the moment I decided, and two months later I did. And then, as you legally must after quitting your job, I went on a Great American Road Trip.

For years I had fantasized about going on a huge road trip, but of course I never could. Those were the years when I began to credibly claim that Google Maps was my favorite website, since "for fun" I would plan elaborate road trips that never came to fruition. Usually I designed my theoretical trips with the idea of writing something about them. Early on, I envisioned doing a road trip where I visited every man I had ever had feelings for, in order to "interview them" (make out). This idea stemmed less from the belief that this would make an interesting book than from the realization that my crushes had spread out across the country in a way that would make for an interesting drive.

Then it struck me: even though I am a Puritan bitch who can't justify having fun unless I assign myself some homework to go along with it, I *was* allowed to take a road trip without writing about it. And so I spent the next three and a half years taking road trips whenever I had time off work. Over those years of traveling I thought about why I wanted so badly to drive a car across America, why I once developed a crush on a guy just because he told me about a road trip he had been on. I thought about the canonical American travel narratives that made a road trip seem like the epitome of freedom. And I wondered why there were so few canonical American travel narratives written by women and what that meant for me, a woman who wanted to go on the road.

So, after my brain's attachment to a steady salary and employer-linked health insurance was thoroughly eroded, after I decided it would be sane and in fact very good to quit my job to focus on writing and, uh, being free, I decided that I wanted to write a female American travel narrative. My book would answer the question: what if Bill Bryson got his period? (I didn't need to know what would happen if Jack Kerouac got his period: he would have freaked out and quit his road trip. It would have ended the Beat Generation.)

I WOULD GO on the road and write about it. But . . . where would I go? A trip long enough to merit serious thought requires an organizing principle. Mine was a modified version of an "optimized" national parks road trip. Over the years I had seen various articles about people who had run the numbers and figured out the mathematically best way to visit every national park in the contiguous forty-eight states. I wasn't sure which parks I'd end up camping at, which I'd just hike around in for a few hours, and which I'd skip altogether, but I knew I wanted to use one of these algorithm-generated supermaps as my general guide.

I wasn't choosing to spend months on end camping and hiking as some personal dare. It wouldn't be a trial by fire, in which seeing if I could lug a backpack up a mountain or sleep outside would teach me something about myself. Hiking had already taught me things about myself. For example: if I exercise for more than five minutes, my entire face and body turn hot pink and stay that way for the entire rest of the day (I am Irish.). But being in nature feels comfortable to me, and right; I'm an outdoors person. Hiking is one of maybe three things I truly love doing, along with playing tennis and watching network dramas about high-achieving women who drink too much.

My love of camping and hiking can be traced back to a childhood visit to Devil's Lake, a state park in Wisconsin about a three-hour drive from where I grew up. Devil's Lake is bordered by 500-foot quartzite bluffs on either shore, which, for kids who grew up surrounded by the monotony of flat cornfields, qualified as thrilling. One summer day my stepdad, TB—whose real name is Tom Brandes but whom my friends and I at some point dubbed TB Ice because that's the kind of thing we did in the early 2000s—sardined every child from our neighborhood into the back of his white kidnapper van and drove us to Devil's Lake for a camping trip, not a seatbelt among us. In retrospect, maybe he chose Devil's Lake as a destination less for its majestic bluffs and more for the fact that three hours is about as long as you can drive with a bunch of loose kids in the back of your van and not reasonably expect to be charged with a felony.

On the second day of our trip, TB took the, in my memory, dozen kids to a ranger-led nature hike. At the end of the hike, the ranger described a rock formation that anyone who was interested could find by hiking just a tenth of a mile farther. After about a half hour we started to suspect that we had gone a bit more than 0.1 miles. In fact, we had no idea where we were. TB, fulfilling his role as the only adult among us, told us we would be turning back and retracing our steps. But we twenty-five rowdy preteens were having too much fun. "No!" we screamed. "We want to keep going!" Tom reiterated that we were lost and needed to turn around. "It's a free country! Let's put it to a vote!" we demanded, and the children outvoted the adult, forty to one.

And so we hiked further into the woods. We hiked past a cleave in a giant block of quartzite and, drunk with power, named this rock formation TB's Buttcrack. We imagined ourselves lost forever, even though in retrospect we likely hiked past at least one map. We hiked down a scree field that we didn't think could possibly be part of the trail but which definitely was.

It felt as if anything could happen; it was maybe the first time I felt like I was experiencing every moment as it occurred. I felt awake. And it wasn't just me. That trip instilled in all the 400 kids present a love of sleeping on dirt. Twenty years later, those neighborhood kids and I still go camping together. We hike up mountains and don't shower for a week, trying, every time, to get ourselves lost.

THE DIFFERENCE BETWEEN those trips I regularly took with my friends and the trip I was about to embark on all alone was that I would be traveling not for a week but for months. And, crucially, I had no real idea of how many months I would be traveling. I had a list of parks and an order in which to visit them, and as far as planning goes I had nothing else. This uncertainty, for me, was far more uncomfortable than sleeping on the hard ground in the middle of the desert or, as I ended up doing just as often, sleeping in my stepdad's Prius in the middle of the desert because I felt too lazy to set up my tent. I am a planner by nature. I am "high strung." I am a person who makes an eight-page Google Doc for a one-week trip. But in the case of this trip, I flew out on a Tuesday and had no idea where I'd be sleeping on Wednesday. Trying to exert my will on the universe for one week was one thing. Expecting the trip to bend to my will for months on end seemed so futile that I didn't even attempt it. Studies say that half the enjoyment of a trip comes from the planning of the trip; in this case, I guess, half the enjoyment came from seeing if I could go with the flow for one summer, ever.

Here's what I did know: I would start with the national parks optimized trip and modify it slightly to include only parks where I had not yet acquired a Junior Ranger badge—essentially a small plastic pin earned by completing a children's education booklet. I've been obsessed with them ever since I got my first at Devil's Lake, a "Wisconsin Explorer" badge decorated with a mushroom. It's aged incredibly well, in that it is a hit with all my friends who either love hallucinogens or follow mushroom foraging accounts on Instagram (together, this accounts for 100 percent of my friends).

THE ONLY REASON I could plausibly get away with having no set plan for where my journey would take me was that, because doing this trip meant not having a source of income, I planned to free-camp every night. Only a few years before I'd learned from a friend that you're allowed to camp for free anywhere in a national forest or on Bureau of Land Management land. There was a website, too, that aggregated some preferred campsites, though my friend told me not to spread the word and risk the campsites becoming too popular. The website interface seemed to be in on the secret: it was visually discombobulating and difficult to navigate. It looked like it was last updated before the internet was invented.

Free-camping means no access to nice bathrooms—you're lucky if you find a pit toilet, which, as its name suggests, is just a toilet seat over a big hole in the ground. There's never any running water. Showers are obviously out of the question. But, very importantly: it's free. And, since free-camping often requires driving deep into protected land, it can mean sleeping in staggeringly beautiful wilderness.

The remoteness of most free campsites meant I would often lose access to Wi-Fi—which was, of course, part of the point of visiting natural and wild places. The years I worked as a researcher on *The Late Show with Stephen Colbert* overlapped with the years that Donald Trump ran for and was elected president, then proceeded to overload the news cycle with a psychotic amount of horrible decisions and statements and scandals, thanks partly to his narcissistic personality disorder and partly to a Steve Bannon–designed psy-op to desensitize Americans to misery. So, for years, my job involved always knowing what Trump and his cronies were up to. I was excited to get the chance, on this trip, to experience the freedom of not being constantly online. As is true of so many Americans, I feel bad about the amount of time I spend looking at screens, but I also love hiking up a mountain, sitting at a beautiful vista, and checking my email.

Still, I hoped I would be able to surrender myself to this trip. I hoped that for a few months I could stop missing my friends and my drama, could ignore my Pavlovian instinct to refresh Instagram 400 times a day, long enough to really experience being on the road. I suspected and hoped that if I let myself be truly present, something alchemical might happen, that what I was doing might transcend being just an obscenely long vacation and that I would get to the center of something. For the first time in my life I was giving myself permission to be free and permission to be a full-time writer, and I wanted to write about being free.

My mind was made up: I knew I wanted to take a Great American Road Trip. I knew a few questions I wanted to think about while I did it, though many more hadn't yet occurred to me—questions about the parks' place in the shady history that is the history of America, about the sheer number of people visiting the parks, about how many weeks straight one woman can drive alone in a car before she becomes very irritated or very horny or very both. I knew I had to accept, as much as I get stress hives anytime my plans are foiled, that this trip would be the boss of me and not the other way around. And so, one day in the middle of spring 2019, I booked a plane ticket to Chicago.

The Plains

1

Hermergency

A JOURNEY OF A THOUSAND MILES BEGINS WITH A SINGLE step, they say, but they're wrong: a journey of a thousand miles begins with figuring out what you're going to pack.

How does one pack for an open-ended trip across a continent? I'd be gone for a spring and a summer, visiting both snowy mountains and deserts. I wanted to bring clothes that made me look hot and made me feel like myself, but I'd also be living out of a duffel bag and going for long stretches without showering. I'd be hiking and swimming and getting caught in the rain; I couldn't bring anything that couldn't get wet or dirty. It was a tall order; I can barely throw together a coherent outfit on days I have access to my full closet.

Every choice was fraught. Like: which of my baseball hats would not mark me as an East Coast elitist? A *New Yorker* hat was an obvious no. My Yankees hat marked me a little less obviously as a New Yorker, or at least marked me a New Yorker who enjoyed "Sports" instead of "Long Articles by Jill

Lepore." I had a Harry Styles hat, a simple black cap that just said "Harry"—this could have gone either way if not for the fact that people who saw me in this hat uniformly assumed it referred to Harry Connick Jr. Though I wasn't sure what kind of chaotic energy these people were picking up on when they came to that conclusion, it wasn't the energy I wanted to lead with during my trip.

The question I asked of each thing I packed was: will this item of clothing get me killed? When I told people I was about to drive around America alone, the first thing each person told me was that I was going to get murdered. Sometimes, very occasionally, they wouldn't tell me I was going to get murdered and would instead give me a tip for not getting murdered. They became even more sure of my eventual demise when I told them I planned to mostly free-camp in the middle of nowhere. They were convinced that this would lead to headlines like "Woman Murdered While Free-Camping"; or "Body of Missing Woman Finally Found, Murdered, after Detectives Asked Themselves Where the Dumbest Place to Camp Would Be and Then Checked There"; or "New Details: Murdered Camper Clearly Hadn't Shaved Legs in Weeks."

Among the "Blythe gonna get murdered" truthers was TB, who spent the weeks before I flew into Chicago to start my trip trying to convince me not to borrow his old black Prius. This wasn't because he was afraid I'd hit something with it (that I would eventually hit something with it was just assumed). It was because he believed the Prius would not sufficiently protect me from getting myself killed.

TB is obsessed with murder; predicting my death is something of a hobby for him. He is the kind of person for whom multiple children independently decided to buy *I'll Be Gone in the Dark* as a Christmas gift. On the phone TB told me that I should take the motor home he had somehow recently acquired.

"Don't take the motor home," my mom interrupted. "It's disgusting, and the mileage is bad."

"It's not disgusting, it's very nice inside," TB protested. "It gets twelve miles a gallon."

Ideally I would have made the trip in something compact and easy to maneuver, something I could drive through rough terrain and that got good gas mileage. It would be a plus if the car would instantly inform all the strangers I'd encounter that I was, in fact, cool. Had I my druthers, I'd road-trip in a Jeep or maybe a Geo Tracker, a car I knew almost nothing about except that it looked like a Jeep and that the impossibly hip purple-haired woman who cut my hair had one. But the thing about my druthers is I never get them, and I was willing to settle for "easy to maneuver," "gas mileage above twelve miles per gallon," and if not "able to drive through rough terrain without harming car," at least "already beat up enough that you can gently run into a couple boulders and it won't look the worse for wear." To this end my stepdad's Prius, which had visibly survived a hailstorm and at least one collision with a car-shaped object, was exactly what I needed.

SOMETHING ABOUT THE fact that I would be a woman alone, going on the road for months, made everyone I talked to— friends, coworkers, randos—think of violent death. And these people were seemingly normal! They could not, as TB could, hear a GPS coordinate and tell you about a young woman much like yourself who was recently killed within a ten-mile radius. But they all agreed: I would be alone, I would be unsafe,

I would be killed. Unless! I bought any number of incredible products designed to prevent that exact thing. Just as we give women tips for not getting raped instead of giving men tips for not raping women, people not only deluged me with tips for not getting murdered, they introduced me to the "don't get murdered" industry.

One major category of the Don't Get Murdered Industrial Complex is location-tracking devices. Almost everyone I told about my trip recommended some sort of location tracker to me. Letting everyone in the world track me like a Domino's pizza would, of course, not prevent me from getting murdered. At best, it would let them figure out that I had been murdered as quickly as possible.

Then there were the products that would prevent me from getting murdered, or at least make murdering me slightly more inconvenient. When I described my trip to two women over drinks, one told me about a website called Damsel in Defense, from which her mother had bought her a pastel-hued stun gun. I pulled up the website; for seventy dollars you could buy a stun gun that, photographed in soft lighting and nestled on a couch next to an array of throw pillows, looked exactly like a sex toy. You could buy rape whistles or, as the website called them, "hermergency necklaces." They also sold a striking tool with a baby blue body and sleek silver tip. I turned my phone screen to the women to show them.

"Sorry," I said. "I'm not supposed to put this in my butt?"

Constant predictions of one's impending violent death are not only an emotional strain that men don't have to deal with before going on the road. They're a financial strain as well. Men aren't told they're going to be murdered on their solo trips, so they don't have to spend seventy dollars on a stun gun. They don't stock up on Mace. They bring things to protect them from the wilderness—a knife or a canister of bear spray (a kind of pepper spray used to deter bears, *not*, critically, something you apply to your body like bug spray)—but not to protect them from other men. I don't have a single male friend who owns a stun gun or a rape whistle, or whose family suggested they get those things before setting off on solo trips. Certainly I don't have any with stepdads who, like TB did to me, offered to get them a gun. I decided that I wouldn't spend any money on any of those things men wouldn't have to spend money on. Bear spray would be enough to keep me safe.

Ultimately I forgot to pack bear spray.

I KNEW THAT I would not get murdered on my trip. It was obvious to me! At the same time, it's hard to overstate how at peace I was with the idea that I could die on this trip: I could get in a car crash, I could fall off the side of a cliff, a deer. . . . . could kill me. Or I could get murdered, sure. It took a lot of time to grow comfortable with the idea that the trip would be planned only a few days at a time in advance; after that, accepting my own mortality was easy. Everyone has to die sometime! If a deer feels the need to kill me, we should respect the wishes of the deer.

Some people assumed that I would be riding the rails or hitchhiking across America, both of which admittedly are more dangerous than going on a long drive; I wasn't doing either of those things. That I had access to a car I could borrow and money to pay for gas was a privilege. I wasn't going to make things harder on myself just to try to seem more legit; I long ago came to terms with the fact that I am not legit. I didn't want to perform authenticity like that type of man who feels so weird about his trust fund that he hitchhikes into the wilderness to die. I don't have a trust fund, but if I did I would simply use it to buy a Geo Tracker.

But it wasn't like the world was really so dangerous. The murder rate in the United States was falling—at least before covid made us throw the social contract out the window. It was just that the murder shows my mom and dad and friends would quote to me, while explaining exactly how I would get dismembered, made it seem like we were in more danger than ever before. "We" meaning a very specific slice of the population; as my friend Madelyn put it to me once, when all my other friends were convinced I would be murdered going on an out-of-town hiking-centric first date: "The true-crime industrial complex wants white women to fear everything."

Being a woman entails certain risks, but I had learned ways to look out for myself, and I couldn't see why those risks would be greater on a mountain in the middle of nowhere, surrounded by no one, than they are in my normal life in the middle of Brooklyn, surrounded by drunk men of all ages who stand in front of my apartment talking all day and talking *loudly* all night. Our culture is just as invested in the idea that cities are dangerous for women on their own as it is in the idea that the road is dangerous for women on their own. If I had beat the odds on one for so long, could the other really be as dire as society made it out to be?

ON THE FIRST morning of my Great American Road Trip, my mom picked me up from Chicago's O'Hare Airport and drove me to Wisconsin to pick up the Prius. On the second morning of my Great American Road Trip, I still had no concrete plans for actually hitting the road and heading anywhere. And so I went to a café, poured iced coffee directly into my brain, and Googled "how to get to Isle Royale National Park."

If you have never heard of Isle Royale, you're not alone. The year before my trip only 18,479 people visited the main island, making Isle Royale the least visited national park in the contiguous United States. 18,479 might sound like a lot of people if you, unlike me, have never lived in one Brooklyn apartment with 18,479 other people. But look at it this way: in 2019 the most visited national park was Great Smoky Mountains National Park, with 12.5 million visitors. To the Great Smoky Mountains 18,479 is just a rounding error.

Isle Royale is a forty-five-mile long, nine-mile wide island in Lake Superior, lying closest to Canada and the tip of Minnesota but technically part of Michigan. That island, as well as 450 smaller surrounding islands, accessible via seaplane and a few ferries, make up Isle Royale National Park.

As I sat in a café trying to buy a ferry ticket, I didn't know any of this. At the time I knew two things about the park, both of which TB had told me. The first was that TB knew someone whose brother had lived year round on Isle Royale until he had just recently died of . . . botulism? . . . from exclusively eating expired canned goods. This story seemed suspect to me for a number of reasons, the first being the official year-round population of Isle Royale is zero, and due to the park's relatively small size and to the existence of planes, it seemed likely that if a random man was surreptitiously living on the island, someone would eventually figure it out. On the other hand, if any country was going to have a guy whose idea of freedom was living illegally and uncomfortably on public land while owning the libs by ignoring "best by" dates on Campbell's soup, that country would definitely be America. So: who knows?

The second thing I knew was, to quote TB, "They're trying to introduce wolves because the moose population is running amok." It's true! The park is known for its moose population: in 2019, there were 2,060 moose in the park. But moose had come to Isle Royale fairly recently—they arrived in the first decade of the 1900s, after swimming to the island from the mainland, on a dare. Wolves followed about forty years later by walking over an ice bridge from Canada, which I won't even make a joke about because it is, simply, too metal.

In the decades that both species have been on Isle Royale, their populations have generally fluctuated in concert. This is essential because, while we all as a culture may be obsessed with the idea of seeing a moose, there is such a thing as "too many moose on one island" (which is of course the premise of my hit sitcom, *Moose Island*). The moose eat and perhaps stomp on all the trees and plants that birds and mammals and insects depend on. It's true what they say: if you give a moose a muffin, it will devastate the ecosystem of Isle Royale National Park. And over the past fifteen years, this is exactly what had happened. In 2005 there were thirty wolves and 385 moose in the park. Then the wolf population started to thin due to inbreeding, since climate change meant that ice bridges formed less often, so new wolves couldn't get to Isle Royale to replenish the gene pool. By 2017 there were only two wolves left on the main island—and there were 1,600 moose. The moose, as TB so aptly put it, were running amok.

The big question became: should the National Park Service, as stewards of Isle Royale, act to replenish the wolf population? According to the Wilderness Act of 1964—and Isle Royale is a federally designated wilderness area—the guiding principle is not to intervene. But, according to a *New York*

Times op-ed written by the three scientists in charge of deciding whether or not to reintroduce wolves to the park, it's disingenuous to hold nonintervention above all, because humans have already intervened in even the wildest parts of the planet, through climate change. Ultimately they decided to send the wolves. And so, just like me, in 2019 twelve wolves were about to take an unforeseen trip to Isle Royale National Park.

I LOOKED INTO ferry schedules and decided to make a day trip of it: I'd camp on the remote tip of Michigan's Upper Peninsula, take a three-hour-ish ferry ride over to Isle Royale early in the morning, and ride back later that afternoon. The man who answered the ferry company's phone told me that daytrip tickets were still available and asked me where I would be staying. Instinctively—wary of letting these ferry perverts learn where I was camping so they could come kill me in my sleep—I lied.

"At . . . my . . . stepdad's house," I said.

"Okay," the man from the ferry company said. "Check-in is at seven a.m." Of course they wanted to know I'd be staying in close enough proximity to make it to the early-morning ferry. *This guy doesn't want to murder you*, I realized. *Don't flatter yourself.*

THE FIRST LEG of my trip saw me driving due north, but because of the fluke of geography that is the Upper Peninsula, I would be reentering the Eastern Time Zone. All borders are violent and colonialist and arbitrary, but it seems particularly arbitrary to me that the UP belongs to Michigan and not to Wisconsin. It touches exactly one of these states, and, surprise: it's not Michigan. But I am alone on this hill, and, in fact, it is not a hill anyone considers an interesting topic of conversation. So I thought about it silently while driving on deserted back roads through pine forests in upper Wisconsin, trying to make it to Isle Royale's mainland visitor center in Houghton by six p.m. Eastern Time.

And despite losing an hour just because some 183-year-old treaty said I was "in Michigan" (sure), I did make it to the visitor center in time. I grabbed my Junior Ranger booklet and sat in my car looking at every app I had so studiously ignored in the sixty minutes since I had last stopped to pee. "You're about to go into some real pretty roads," texted a friend who had spent some time in Copper Harbor, where I'd be catching the ferry the next day. He was right: the final hour of my drive, into less and less populated land, was like driving through a painting in my dad's living room. The road gently curved through thick birch forests until all of a sudden it ended at the shore of Lake Superior.

I drove up the local "mountain" (big hill) to get a better view: evergreens as far as the eye could see, on the mainland and on a couple small islands running parallel to the shore. It was charming to a level that was, frankly, psychotic.

I WAS AT the ferry dock by seven a.m. the next morning, and yes, that is a brag. My time between waking up and driving to the dock was expedited by the fact that the night before, as I tried to set up my idyllic little campsite, I discovered that the tent TB had loaned me was fully inoperable, missing poles and ripped. After calling TB to get his permission to throw out the "tent," I instead spent my first night alone on the road curled up in the passenger seat of the Prius. Being five-foot-two: it's a hack.

I checked in for the Isle Royale ferry and headed over to a picnic table to, in a long tradition of people with nothing else to do, stare at the water and think about my life until the ferry started to board. Leading the boarding process, I am sorry to tell you, was a man who looked like Steve Bannon, if Steve Bannon were 50 percent healthier and also hanging out in Michigan's UP instead of making tiny baby Hitlers all over Europe. "Before we begin, here's a factoid," Healthy Bannon said. He gestured to the ferry and a four-foot-tall staircase we had to climb to get to the deck. "Seven years ago, the deck was level with the dock. You just stepped off the dock onto the boat. That's how much the water level of Lake Superior has risen." I blinked and wondered if this man had mixed up the word *factoid* with the words *chilling reminder of the imminent death of our planet*. "Okay! Let's board!"

Inside the ferry I sat at a table across from two women and spent the next three hours talking to them. This may sound like hell to you, as it would have sounded to me, a person who famously hates talking to strangers. But it was, instead, lovely. The women introduced themselves as Debbie and Meg, a mother and daughter from Green Bay, who were going to Isle Royale together because Debbie had gone as a young woman and had always dreamed of returning one day with her daughters. We talked about Wisconsin and Timothée Chalamet (who I, at the time, cared about because I had not yet turned thirty) and about travel. After two hours it occurred to me: "I think you are the first people who haven't told me I'm going to get murdered on my trip."

"Oh, you won't get murdered," Debbie said. "If you can survive in New York City, you'll be fine."

It's true, of course, that women can get murdered in cities

and on the road. This is what Adrienne Rich calls "the role of male violence in keeping all women subordinate." If being in these places means that you as a woman are at risk, you can never be fully exuberant there; part of your attention is always being drained.

But statistically the people who should be afraid to take road trips or move to New York aren't women: according to the United Nations, approximately 80 percent of homicide victims worldwide are men. The same is true for the United States and has been true for decades. More to the point: men are more likely to be victimized in public and by a stranger. Women are more likely to be victimized by someone they know, in the exact place we are supposed to see as our one safe option: our home or the home of someone we know. The domestic sphere might be both bereft of adventure and actually the *most* dangerous place for us to be, but the true-crime industrial complex and the culture at large try to convince women to stay there because, coincidentally, it's where women can perform the unpaid labor necessary to keep our very poorly designed economy afloat.

The narratives we tell about women being unsafe on the road exacerbate the problem: when women feel unsafe going on the road, that almost certainly keeps some women from doing it, so there are fewer women walking around telling their friends about their great road trip where they weren't murdered. Do you think people were telling Jack Kerouac not to go on the road? No, they were probably like, "By all means, be my guest, drive away for a couple months, leave me the hell alone."

AS SOON AS I spotted the first small islands surrounding Isle Royale, my eyes filled with tears. I'd just gone on hormonal birth control a few months earlier, and now, well, everything was just too beautiful.

We disembarked, and I had no time to lose. I waved goodbye to Meg and Debbie, who were checking into Isle Royale's Rock Harbor Lodge, and set out to find a trailhead. The day before, at the visitor center in Houghton, I had explained to the ranger on duty that I was planning to be on Isle Royale just for the afternoon and asked what he thought I should do in that time. He gave me a map and recommended a four-mile trail on a narrow peninsula, from Rock Harbor to something called Scoville Point. I had just over three hours to do it, which the ranger assured me was possible, though it had been a year since I had seriously hiked and I couldn't remember if I was actually capable of hiking that fast. I rushed around the harbor, found a trail that seemed like the right one, and plunged into the woods.

I don't want you to get your hopes up, so I will tell you right now: I did not see any of the 2,060 totally amok moose when I was on Isle Royale. And of course I didn't see one of the now fourteen wolves on the island, who were busy getting used to their new home and clocking in at their "eating moose" day jobs. (As I write this, the wolf population has doubled since 2019, and the moose population roughly halved.) But it didn't matter. I was thrilled to be hiking, dropped into a new landscape and learning about it through walking around. I was doing my absolute favorite thing, and since it was cold enough to wear a jaunty red beanie, I even got to look like a hot Steve Zissou while doing it. I hauled ass down the trail, completing my Junior Ranger activities along the way, listening to the sounds of nature and looking at plants and writing about my experience.

Everything around me was, I'm sorry, stunning! Lake Superior is slept on, or maybe it's so far north that I had always thought of it as not worth a visit, or maybe Lake Michigan has always seemed to me "meh" at best, and "don't touch that water, you'll get hepatitis" at worst, and so I had assumed all the Great Lakes were the same. But I was completely unprepared for Lake Superior's majesty. The pine forest would suddenly open to a craggy shoreline and choppy sapphire water to the horizon. Every so often I'd have to hike over planks, traversing bits of land where soil gathered in depressions of rock, where water could never fully drain, and where swampy plants like marsh marigold thrived. When I finally got to Scoville Point, I peered out toward the horizon, miles and miles of lake between me and any mainland. It made me realize, damn: I can't believe moose swam here. Those guys are maniacs.

BACK ON THE ferry for the return trip, I settled into a seat—I had a whole four-top table to myself. And then. Halfway through the journey back, a man appeared out of nowhere and asked if he could sit with me. Anyone who suddenly needs a place to sit two hours into a boat ride is bad news, and he had a frayed energy that set off the alarms I've developed over years of trying not to get murdered in New York. But because I was socialized female and as such taught to be polite and accommodating, and because I did, after all, have an entire table to myself, I let him sit. He slumped onto the bench across from me and got down to the business of any man sitting next to any woman he doesn't know: the business of annoying me.

"What are you reading?" he asked.

I showed him the cover of my book: *Yes Means Yes: Visions*

of Sexual Power and a World Without Rape. It was the one book no man can turn into a flirt.

But, somehow, he tried. For a full hour he kept asking me question after question, as I clearly refused to engage. When it finally became clear that annoying me would not help him to achieve his goal (getting my phone number? distracting me from learning about rape culture?), he decided to devote his remaining time to making me as uncomfortable as possible. Over the last hour of the trip, he incrementally shifted his legs toward me into my space and then began to spread his legs apart, until there was nowhere left under the table for me to put my own body. And for that entire hour, I put up with it. On the Isle Royale ferry, cornered by a creepy dude's manspread, I wondered how far into the process of murdering me someone would have to be before I asked them to please not.

We were almost back in Copper Harbor by the time I asked the man to move his legs, but when I finally did, I was weirdly proud of myself. I was strong! I was overcoming my societal programming to be deferential and standing up for my bodily autonomy! I was a woman on the road!

And then I grabbed my backpack, got off the boat, and sat next to the ferry office for thirty minutes, until I was sure the man was gone and couldn't follow me back to my campsite.

2

Somewhat Complex Flesh Machine

THE THING ABOUT SLEEPING OUTDOORS IS THAT YOU wake up very early. You can spend years carefully constructing an urban identity as an artist who goes to bed at three and sleeps until noon and still find yourself, two days into an extended camping trip, exhausted at nine p.m. and not only awake but kicking and punching and ready to hike at five-thirty in the morning. Waking up at the same time as octogenarians do, or as Ben Franklin lied and said he did, is frankly embarrassing. But I did, and then spent the entire day driving west across the Upper Peninsula and the Northwoods of Wisconsin.

By the time I made it to Duluth, Minnesota, that afternoon, it had been thirty-two hours since I had had coffee, and I was ready to commit a felony. I parked at a kitschy diner that Yelp swore up and down had good food and ordered lunch and a cold brew as big as my torso. I drove to a second location to drink more coffee, drove to a third location to eat coffee-flavored ice cream, went to Walmart to buy a tent, and spent the night at a KOA. (Kampgrounds of America, popularly known as KOA, is a privately owned chain with sites across the United States and Canada, though the fact that they spell "campground" with a "K" is so tacky that I feel certain the idea must have originated in the USA.) The sounds of young people around me having fun, and the sensation of every single stick in the forest poking me through my cheap tent, lulled me to sleep. The next morning I hit the road to Voyageurs National Park.

VOYAGEURS WAS ANOTHER park I knew almost nothing about. The only reason I was even aware something called "Voyageurs" existed was because it had been included in a national parks calendar a friend had given me a couple years before. I flipped to June and all of a sudden there was a moose standing in a lake under the word *Voyagers*, except spelled how it would be in the group text I'm on with a bunch of people who have British passports and multiple fur hats each, all of whom write random words in French for fun. I stared at the calendar page and the French moose. *This exists in America?* I thought. *Now I've heard it all.*

The park is located in remote northern Minnesota on the border with Canada, and consists of a labyrinth of connected lakes. From the late 1600s until the late 1800s, these connected lakes were used by beaver-pelt-trading, canoe-paddling French Canadian teenagers called *voyageurs*. These voyageurs, according to the 1971 legislation enabling the creation of the park, "contributed significantly to the opening of the northwestern United States." It's like they say: all it takes to change the world is a dream and a canoe.

It was chilly and raining and too early in the season to be busy when I arrived at Voyageurs. The ranger manning the desk at the Ash River Visitor Center was a woman who appeared to be in her sixties. She looked like the kind of serious-minded woman who started working for the National Park Service as a way to give back to the earth and as a way to teach young children about natural beauty. She did not look like the kind of woman who would be amused when a twenty-eight-year-old adult flew in from New York City and asked to participate in the Junior Ranger program.

ACQUIRING JUNIOR RANGER badges was the organizing principle of my trip. So what exactly are they? The Junior Ranger program is available in not only national parks but also at national monuments and other sites run by the National Park Service. Participants are given an educational workbook which, after a certain number of activities are completed, can be exchanged for a badge. These badges are made out of wood or cloth or cheap plastic, and I thirsted for them. I would do as many word searches containing names of animals endemic to the park as I needed to; I would go on as long a hike as necessary to get bingo on a grid of things I might see ("insect," "scat"); I would attend whatever ranger program was happening that day: I was going to get my Junior Ranger badge from every park I visited. Crucially, while the program is designed and intended for children, it is open to people of all ages.

Sometimes when I ask for a booklet, rangers will tell me about just recently having given a booklet or a badge to an extremely ancient person. (Presumably they do this to make me feel better about the embarrassing thing I am doing by asking to participate in a children's program.) When I visited Petrified

Forest on a road trip around the Southwest, the ranger there told me she had just awarded a Petrified Forest Junior Ranger badge to a 103-year-old man. "He said that it was the last remaining national park Junior Ranger badge he needed to get," she said.

"Ah," I responded. "So now he could die." The ranger did not laugh.

Why did I plan my trip around acquiring these badges? Well, I love to do vacation homework. Traveling only to national parks where I had not yet earned a badge seemed like a good way to visit a lot of beautiful places I hadn't seen before. Ultimately, the most primal reason was that it gave my trip a structure; and a structure—any structure—was essential to this open-ended trip I was taking immediately after quitting my job.

I would never, in the two or three months I was giving myself to go wild, be able to see all the natural beauty America has to offer, experience all the disparate cultures, go antique shopping in all the small towns, have coffee in identical indie cafés with white subway tiles and a lot of green plants in every city across the country. But getting a Junior Ranger badge from every chosen park was within my grasp. It was a finite task made up of dozens of smaller tasks, each of which would give me the satisfaction of having really experienced something. If I got Junior Ranger badges from every park, legally I became secretary of the interior. And as an added bonus, it wasn't difficult, because it was designed for 12-year-olds.

BOOKLET IN (ADULT) hand, I sat in the Prius at the Voyageurs Visitor Center and completed as many activities as I could, hoping to wait out the worst of the rain. One activity invited me to compare the clothing of an 1800s-era voyageur to a modern-day sixteen-year-old. Both were described as "young men"—though as you and I both know, any cis male under the age of thirty-five is not a man but a child. I drew lines from the voyageur, standing tall in his chemise and little Santa cap, to his twenty-first-century equivalent, slouching in a hoodie and trucker hat. The activity felt like a passive-aggressive own on all teens, but it also felt like a missed opportunity to imagine that, two hundred years after "the opening of the northwestern United States," a different-looking person could experience this land. I was used to large institutions making at least a stab at performative diversity, but the Voyageurs Junior Ranger book was committed to imagining adventure only for white, able-bodied "men" (teens).

In reality, the visitors to national parks do skew heavily white: according to 2011 National Park Service surveys, only 21 percent of visitors were people of color. Black people, especially, are underrepresented in parks: 14 percent of Americans are Black, but only 7 percent of national park visitors are. The fact that national park visitorship is so white is a complex issue with a lot of causes, but one of those is probably representation in the parks. I'm not just talking about teens illustrated in kids' booklets: according to a report by the nonprofit Partnership for Public Service, white people make up 80 percent of park employees.

The whiteness of national parks also has to do with geography: the areas where most parks are clustered, in the West, tend to be predominantly white. In fact, according to a 2018 NPS survey, distance to the national parks and lack of transportation options to get there are two of the reasons most cited by BIPOC (Black, Indigenous, and people of color) respondents for not visiting NPS units. "Tom Brandes' 2015 Toyota Prius" was, I could see, an individual solution to a systemic problem. If the National Park Service and its supporters agreed with Wallace Stegner that the parks were America's "best idea," I wonder why they didn't make a bigger effort to make sure that idea was accessible to all Americans.

IF I HAD actually planned my road trip before setting out, I would have learned that Voyageurs was best experienced by boat and that boat tours didn't start for another week or two, when spring finally reached northern Minnesota. So I was alone and feeling somewhat stupid as I hiked through the woods toward something called Beaver Pond Overlook. I picked my way over slippery, moss-covered rocks, and when I found my footing and looked up, there was a massive deer thirty feet away, just above me on a small ridge. For five full minutes the deer and I stood considering each other; it reminded me of Cheryl Strayed and the fox in *Wild*, but instead of seeing the deer as a physical manifestation of my mom, I was just hoping it would move two feet so I could get a better photo.

After that hike, I set off on another and then another: it may have been the wrong time of year to properly see Voyageurs, but I was still enthralled by the simple pleasure of going on a walk in a place I'd never been before. I scrambled around shorelines, I nearly stepped in a porcupine carcass, and as the rain turned into a mist I got my second Junior Ranger badge of the trip.

THE DRIVE WESTWARD from Duluth the next morning was ominous, and not because of the moment at a gas station when

I caught my reflection in my car window and realized that, in my flannel and my camo Waffle House hat, I was only seven days into my trip and already looked like a long-haul trucker. No, what was ominous was the sudden ubiquity of antiabortion billboards.

Mile after mile, I passed billboards picturing white or very light-skinned babies next to absolutely bonkers lies about fetuses having a heartbeat after eighteen days. "It's not true, first of all, and also eighteen days is before you would have missed your period!" I ranted to my mom on speakerphone as I drove. (I come from a family where "ranting about politics on speakerphone" is an acceptable way to kill time while driving.) "You wouldn't even know you're pregnant yet!"

"Yes, sweetie, that's why they're saying that. Because then they've got you."

I couldn't believe I was running into these billboards so early on my trip. I was in *Minnesota*. It's literally the only state that didn't go for Reagan in 1984, that's how blue Minnesota is. I thought I'd have at least another five hours of driving before I was reminded that much of the country viewed me not as a person but as a uterus surrounded by a somewhat complex flesh machine. It was the kind of disbelief that comes from living for a decade in East Coast cities, where everyone agrees that abortion is health care and we all listen to the same Carly Rae Jepsen album at the same time. Most of what felt to me like settled reality was, to most of the country, up for debate. This was obvious to me during my childhood in Illinois, another blue state, where most adults I knew loved George W. Bush and—despite my efforts to convince them otherwise—knew for a fact that global warming was a hoax. As I drove west through Minnesota, I tried to tell myself that there were a lot of people around who *did* support abortion access, who had just decided to put their billboard money toward actually helping people get abortions. But it was clear that a lot of the people around me did not support abortion, did not support women, did not support me.

BEFORE HEADING TO the next national park on my list, I had to swing north on a pilgrimage: I was going to Lake Itasca, the headwaters of the Mississippi River. How do I say this, and not sound very, very stupid: I had always known that the Mississippi headwaters existed, but they also seemed somewhat mythical to me. Like, "somewhere" in the northern woods there is a house made of candy where a witch lives, eating children. Also, "somewhere" in the northern woods there is an unassuming stream that eventually becomes the fourth-largest river in the world. *Sure.* No, sure! Sounds great.

I pulled into the visitor center parking lot at Itasca State Park. The park and the eponymous lake, I would learn, are actually named after their claim to fame: they are a horrible portmanteau of ver*itas* (Latin for "true") and *ca*put (Latin for "head"). Though there are arguments to be made that the Mississippi's headwaters lie elsewhere—off longer tributaries or those that contribute more flow—Lake Itasca is the culturally accepted source. And why not? Are humans really meant to understand exactly how rivers work? (Scientists are like, "yes.")

Within seconds of walking from the parking lot, I reached a bridge over a small stream with steps leading down to the water on either side. *THE HEADWATERS!!!!!!!* I thought. I marveled at the fact that the source of such a giant and culturally significant river was so unassuming, so uncrowded, so largely unheralded. As I considered this, I took some selfies on one side of the bridge and then the other. And then a mother and her son walked past. He tried to head down the steps, but his mom told him, "Wait until we get to the headwaters."

After taking a couple more selfies—now deep in character as "woman who is just happy to be photographed with any random creek,"—I walked a few minutes further. And there they were: the headwaters. (!!!!!) They were unmistakable: for one thing, they were marked by a tree-trunk-turned-obelisk, engraved with the words, "Here 1475 ft above the ocean the mighty Mississippi begins to flow on its winding way 2552 miles to the Gulf of Mexico." For another, they were packed with people of all ages, showing the Mississippi who's boss by casually wading across it. And so I slid off my Vans and did the same. Carefully I walked along the slick rocks that marked the border between Lake Itasca and the Mississippi River. As I waded in the water, only a foot and a half deep and eighteen feet from one bank to the other, I thought about the many times I'd crossed the Mississippi on almost mile-long bridges, suspended over a massive river rushing below. I couldn't believe that this stream became that mighty river, that we lived in a country big enough for that to be true. And on top of it all, I couldn't believe I was here—that I really had a life now where I could drive on a lark to finally see a place that had felt to me more like a rumor than a location. It was a Monday, and back in New York my friends were in an office building looking at Google Docs. Meanwhile, I was in the most random part of Minnesota, where I changed from pants to shorts in the middle of a parking lot and then waded across a stream, just because I was curious and wanted to. I felt like I had lived more in the past thirty minutes than I did in some full weeks back home. What other unexpected, serendipitous places would my trip take me to in the weeks and months to come?

As I daydreamed, I noticed a little boy near me squat down into the river to pee. There, 1,475 feet above the ocean, a little boy's pee began to flow on its winding way to the Gulf of Mexico.

FARGO SHONE IN its role of "cute Midwestern city" when I stopped in for lunch and a quick wander. At a Seattle-themed café—what will they think of next?—I ordered an iced coffee. It wasn't until the barista handed it to me that I realized just how far out of the liberal bubble I had driven. Not only was I given a plastic straw, but the straw was inexplicably a full foot long. Fully caffeinated and now responsible for the future death of a sea turtle, I set off on the last leg of that day's journey: a nearly five-hour drive straight west on I-94, from Fargo, on the eastern border of North Dakota, until I was just 20 minutes away from its western border, at Theodore Roosevelt National Park.

The drive was supremely uneventful. Because I refuse to listen to podcasts despite the best efforts of every man I have ever gone on a date with—who, in response to me saying I don't listen to podcasts, proceeds to recommend a podcast to me while I dissociate—I had a lot of time to think. I listened to Joni Mitchell sing about leaving her man at a North Dakota junction (oh my God, I was in North Dakota!), going to New York to buy a mandolin, and brilliantly spiraling out after seeing a wedding dress in a store window, and I meditated on what I saw as the most insidious deterrent keeping women from doing what Joni and I had done in going on the road. While I wasn't worried by the warnings that I would get murdered—I should *be* so lucky!—and I wasn't bothered by the reality that my IUD meant I would cry every time I saw a big tree, I *was* very concerned by the idea that it is easier for men to go on the road because they are less hampered by things like marriage and parenthood.

Joni's album *Hejira*, which I was listening to that day, is an album about what I have come to accept are, for better or worse, my two favorite hobbies: driving around the country, and thinking very deeply about men. The life she describes over the course of *Hejira* seemed to me, in the months before I quit my job, like exactly the kind of life I wanted to live. How, I wondered, could I live a life that had space to travel and to think and to make art about it all? Other than not having a job that involved going to an office every weekday, I suspected that having this kind of space in one's life had a lot to do with the fact that when Joni was doing those things she was not married or raising a child. I wasn't either, so all should have been fine, except for the fact that as much as I envied Joni's 1970s lifestyle, I feared ending up like 2010s Joni, romantically alone and with a disease that made it feel like I had bugs under my skin.

Not until that summer did I begin to understand that enjoying men and always having at least one in my life did not mean I wouldn't, in fifty years, end up without anyone to love me or care for me or advocate for my burial wishes after I die (throw my raw corpse in a shallow hole in the ground). I felt especially at risk of this due to the fact that I am shy, lazy, and have a bad personality. Evidently I would need to invest in a relationship to make it last beyond the "manic flirting" and "criminal horniness" phases, and I wondered if that kind of investment was entirely contradictory with picking up and going on a random road trip, with being free, which, to me, was a moral imperative. As much as magazines have spent decades asking if women could have it all, it's obvious that they can't because so many things appear to me to be direct opposites, "freedom" and "companionship" chief among them.

Married men in our society are allowed to fuck off on adventures much more than married women. To hear that a father went on a two-month road trip is mildly interesting; to hear that a mother did the same sounds like the start of a movie about a woman leaving her husband, Charpt, and blowing up her entire life. We may be past the years when hotels refused female travelers who tried to check in alone after dark. But there are still not enough cultural scripts in which women can have adventures and not need a psych evaluation.

And so I have a Rolodex in my mind of women who wrote new scripts: Gloria Steinem never had kids. Stevie Nicks never had kids. Annie Oakley never had kids—not that I'm dying to spend my life getting good at shooting guns, but still. Joni Mitchell gave up a daughter for adoption and left a bad marriage, all before she turned twenty-five; during the years she made so many of my favorite albums, she really was a woman of heart and mind with no child to raise. I had never felt a strong pull to be a mother, so that element of it didn't feel like a big sacrifice. But as I drove farther and farther away from anyone I had ever kissed, I hoped that being able to have adventures didn't mean I had to choose not to experience love and partnership. And that the time I was spending driving and writing wasn't making the choice for me.

NORTH DAKOTA SPREAD out interminably before me as I thought about all this. For hours I drove through a monotonous expanse, only occasionally enlivened by a towering scrap-metal sculpture of, say, a bunch of geese. The road was completely flat and completely straight: hell to drive through, less an "interstate" than a "torturous exploration of the concept of 'time.'"

Hours after leaving Fargo, I reached the exit that would take me into the miniscule town of Medora, which sits at the entrance to Theodore Roosevelt National Park. The sun was low in the sky; I had arrived before the last of the campsites was claimed; my picnic table gave me a view of a stand of cottonwoods and, across a meadow, the rolling, striated badlands. I was, in a word, stoked. With the last bit of light I set up my tiny, one-person tent, made the disgusting food I love to eat—a bagel with sliced avocado and a heaping, oily pile of sun-dried tomatoes—and began reading the pamphlet and newsletter I was given upon entering the park.

Theodore Roosevelt National Park is unique in that it is the only national park named after one dude. All the parks gesture at natural beauty and invite you to *check this shit out*, but Theodore Roosevelt National Park is the only one that invites you to imagine you are a certain person while you do it. The park was established not only to protect the North Dakota badlands and their wildlife but also to protect the land where Theodore Roosevelt lived and ran a cattle ranch in his twenties. ("It was here the romance of my life began," he later wrote.) Imagine: a national park dedicated to anything you did in your twenties! A nightmare. (Come to beautiful Chicago to visit Blythe Roberson's Long-Form Improv Phase National Park!)

Theodore Roosevelt created the US Forest Service, signed the 1906 Antiquities Act into law, and during his presidency established 150 national forests, five national parks, eighteen national monuments, four federal wildlife preserves, and fifty-one federal bird preserves. This amounted to 230 million acres of protected land. As a fan of land, I have to say: nice. That legacy of conservation alone—to say nothing of his trust busting—explains why some people consider him a president worthy of having his name slapped on parks or his likeness dynamited into the side of a mountain. But the more I learned about Roosevelt, as is so often true when I learn about any historical man basically ever, the more I realized how much of what he did was both racist and sexist.

As a person who grew up in a predominantly white area and whose only sustained engagement with American history had been to absorb what I was taught in a way most likely to earn me a 5 on the AP test, I only started to learn about Roosevelt's genocidal and colonialist legacy over the past few years. That legacy was in the news in 2017, when protestors splashed fake blood onto a statue of Roosevelt at the American Museum of Natural History. The statue is clearly racist—it depicts a hierarchical scene of Roosevelt on horseback with a Native American man standing on one side and a Black man on the other—but it wasn't until the civil rights uprising of summer 2020 that the museum announced that the statue would be removed. In the meantime it was placed under police protection, and as a compensatory gesture to Roosevelt's legacy, the museum's Hall of Biodiversity was renamed in his honor—despite the fact that the museum already had the Theodore Roosevelt Memorial Hall, the Theodore Roosevelt Rotunda, and, just outside, Theodore Roosevelt Park. Reading all this, I wondered: does the board of the museum realize Theodore Roosevelt is dead? *You're allowed to say something critical of him, my dudes. He can't hear you.*

THE SUN SET over the Badlands as I zipped myself into my sarcophagus-sized tent and kept reading through the park materials. I opened the glossy, foldout map and noticed a quote from Roosevelt: "I have always said I never would have been President if it had not been for my experiences in North Dakota."

For a while I'd been thinking about Teddy and the freedom he'd had in going out west. It started one day at work. My boss walked into the office to chat, and the conversation quickly turned, as conversations are wont to do when your boss has seemingly read every book on the planet, to the life and legacy of Theodore Roosevelt. Until that day I hadn't heard Roosevelt's backstory: his mother and wife died on the same day, his mother from a fever and his wife shortly after giving birth to a healthy baby. Emotionally wrecked, Roosevelt headed west. As my boss poetically characterized it, Roosevelt went where the rugged, unforgiving landscape matched his grief. His connection to that landscape would make him a lifelong conservationist.

I nodded for a second. "Wait," I said. "So who raised his kid?"

My boss didn't know. I obviously didn't know. My friend Cami, another researcher who happened to be reading an enormous biography of Roosevelt at the time, also didn't know and in fact was very mad that our boss had spoiled the "wife and mom die on the same day" plot point for her.

Roosevelt and his sacks of gold coins were able to go west, to get in bar fights and learn how to rope cattle, as a direct result of his ability to pawn off the consequences of his choice to have a child. It's especially cruel, then, that he spent his political life working to control other people's reproductive choices. He supported eugenics and advocated for the sterilization of poor people and people with intellectual disabilities. At the same time, as immigration to the United States increased, he encouraged white women to have more children so as not to commit "race suicide." Roosevelt wrote that "[t]he man or woman who deliberately avoids marriage . . . is in effect a criminal against the race and should be an object of contemptuous abhorrence by all healthy people." Encountering this line felt like Roosevelt was peering directly at me. I peered back: *Hi, you white supremacist dickhead!* I wished he could see me, IUD firmly in place, my most fertile years quickly waning with no husband on any horizon, going out west where the landscape was rugged and where I could reinvent myself as "a person who writes about how Teddy Roosevelt was a racist villain."

I folded up the map and set an alarm on my phone for an hour before the park's visitor center opened. Two women in neighboring campsites talked loudly about car-camping hacks they'd found on Pinterest and about how they'd rather pee on the side of the road than in bathrooms, because "bathrooms are disgusting." (Interesting. . . . . take. . . . .) As quietly as I could, I texted my crushes until I fell asleep.

ISLE ROYALE AND Voyageurs were lovely parks, and I do not mean to insult them when I say that it was in Theodore Roosevelt National Park that my trip felt like it had finally started. For the first time since I had left Milwaukee, I was in a place geographically distinct from the lakes and the more or less flat forests where I had grown up.

The south unit of the park, the unit I was visiting, sprawls over forty-six thousand acres. As is true of a shocking number of national parks, TRNP was designed to be experienced by car. (Fifty percent of the park's visitors, I was told, do not plan to visit but just notice a sign on the interstate and say, "Eh, what the hell.") That morning I backtracked to the visitor center for a Junior Ranger booklet and some recommendations, and then set out on the park's scenic loop drive.

As I rounded a curve, I saw a strange animal hanging out right by the side of the road. It was tan and roughly a foot long; it looked a bit like a groundhog, but sexy and with a better personality. I was instantly struck with a tender feeling for this little animal, who lacked the self-preservation instinct to get out of the road when a car was coming. Through my open windows I heard the animal make a little chirp. *Goodbye, tiny weirdo*, I saluted, and I sped up and rounded the rest of the curve. Before me lay an open field, covered in dozens of that tiny weirdo's relatives, popping up and scurrying around. It hit me all at once: I was in a prairie dog town.

These were black-footed prairie dogs, one of five species of prairie dog in the United States and the only species found in the park. They ran around their town, which to my eye looked just like a field of short grass but which consisted mainly of subterranean tunnels and rooms where genetically related families of prairie dogs lived together. (Celebrities: they're just like us!) The prairie dogs interacted, flirting and gossiping and chirping—the technical term is "barking"—as I tried to take a picture in which they looked like prairie dogs and not just white dots in the distance.

I didn't succeed, because as a general rule, visitors are meant to stay twenty-five yards away from all wildlife. This is the animals' home and it's common courtesy, of course, but the rule is also for visitors' protection. Prairie dogs might look adorable, but they can bite, and perhaps more worrisome, they can be infected with bubonic plague—yes, *that* bubonic plague—which can be transmitted to humans via their fleas. Sure, we have treatments for the bubonic plague now. But if I caught a disease that once killed half the world's population, my friends would never let my peasant ass live it down. I posted a photo of the dots to Instagram, with one circled. "These are prairie dogs."

BACK AT THE visitor center where my day had started, my final agenda item in the park was a ranger lecture at the cabin where Teddy Roosevelt had lived. I attended not out of intellectual curiosity or any desire to congregate with other humans but solely because it was a requirement to earn my badge. A toddler sat near me scribbling in her Junior Ranger book; at the end of the day we would both be awarded the same pin.

Roosevelt's life in North Dakota, as the ranger described it, was a master class in being a poser. (The ranger did not characterize it this way.) His parents were very wealthy; when he first visited North Dakota to hunt bison, he was horrible at it and forced his guides to prolong their trip until he felt satisfied. Roosevelt essentially faked it until he made it: we were shown a photo of him dressed in outdoorsy clothes and toting a gun, in what at first glance looked like a forest. In fact, he was posed in front of a backdrop; as the ranger told us, the gun and the buckskin outfit were rented. It reminded me of an amusement park close to where I grew up, where tourists could purchase sepia-toned souvenir photos of themselves in Old West costume: cowboys for the men and "person in corset" for the women. When Roosevelt did acquire his own western outfits, they were those of an East Coast elitist: his knife was made by Tiffany. He bought himself a cattle ranch and worked it for a couple of years, until the ranch went bankrupt. And then he simply returned to his life and his wealth in New York, and within fifteen years he became president. Needless to say, I was not shocked that a wealthy New Yorker could go bankrupt, evade all consequences, and become president: there is no limit to how high men can fail upward.

At the end of the presentation, the ranger asked us if we had any questions.

"Yes," I said. "Who raised Roosevelt's daughter?"

It was his sister, Bamie.

SO MUCH OF a full life, of "having it all," of a functioning economy under capitalism, relies on the unpaid laborers we call "wives" (or, in Teddy's case, "sisters"). While it's a hampering force for women, it's a life hack for men. I once asked my dad a question about whether he saved plastic grocery bags—an extremely basic question, it seemed to me—and he replied, "Why would you ask me that? How am I supposed to know that? I'm busy. I have to work." I chided him that I, too, had a career, despite not having a wife to know whether or not I kept plastic bags.

"I am my own wife," I told him. He laughed. The realization felt exactly the same as when, after working as a personal assistant, I found myself doing the same tasks for myself, and it struck me that I was my own personal assistant. Assistant, wife: synonyms.

AM I GOING to flex on my haters (white supremacist patriarchy, the ghost of Theodore Roosevelt) by never getting married or having kids and instead driving around the country until I get canceled for burning too much gas? Ultimately this was a question I was delaying answering, waiting to grapple with the gendered trade-offs until I met a person worth grappling for. But I was beginning to see that delaying answering quickly becomes an answer in itself. Again I thought of Joni: she may be romantically alone now, but she wasn't alone at the time she made *Hejira*. In fact, she was sleeping with both the drummer and the bass player. I was also in what can be thought of as the "sleeping with both the drummer and the bass player" period of my life, but to what end? During the centuries before I had sex and the subsequent centuries when I was having very little, I assumed that having a steady stream of men in one's life would naturally be a sort of progress toward marriage. But I felt no closer to marriage than before. I wasn't alone: in 1960, 59 percent of Americans aged eighteen to thirty-four were married, according to the US Census Bureau, but in 2018 only 39 percent were. The longer I went without marrying, was I getting more settled in a life and personality built around the absence of marriage—focused on, to quote a famous pig: *moi?*

The possibility that I'd have a kid seemed even more uncertain. The world was burning, the country I lived in and its economy and its health-care system were broken, my apartment was small, and my villain neighbor was addicted to blasting music at three a.m. To bring a baby into all that was a weighty thing!

For years I thought Joni Mitchell was alone because she insisted on having space in her life for love and adventure. Then I read a Joni biography and learned that she is alone because—and I say this with only pure, shining love in my heart—she is an absolute dick to almost everyone she meets. (Certainly she has earned that right, and perhaps I too would be rude to everyone I know if I were a genius or more focused on my art and less on sleeping nine hours a night.) Commitment to art takes up a lot of time that can't, then, be spent on meeting guys. Traveling takes you away from all the guys you might meet because, simply, there are no men in the middle of the desert. But art and travel and adventure are not in and of themselves incompatible with love and partnership.

It was difficult to guess how my life would go; there are so few good narratives about what it means to be a woman who is free that it was hard to generalize. What I know now that I didn't know then, at Theodore Roosevelt National Park, as I gently spun out over all this, is that while Joni may or may not have a lover, she's not alone. She's surrounded by friends, constantly popping up on Brandi Carlile's Instagram in the middle of a circle of people, men and women, great artists themselves, who adore her.

BACK AT THE campsite the bugs were biting, so I got comfy in the Prius's passenger seat and tried to catch a strong enough signal to post a photo of a feral horse to Insta Stories. One had been blocking the outbound lane of traffic when I drove back to the campground. (Feral horses are descendants of horses that escaped from homesteads hundreds of years ago, which is why they're called "feral" and not "wild." But saying that feral horses couldn't drag you away just doesn't sound as poetic.) Some noise outside broke my concentration, and I looked up to see a bison chomping some grass while standing inches away from my fender.

I don't find bison particularly thrilling. Out west they're abundant and, much like feral horses, they're descended from stock from zoos or farms—only the bison in Yellowstone are descended from ancestors that were always wild. Nevertheless, from somewhere ancient inside me, my instincts kicked in. *Click.* Without thinking I took a photo. The bison stopped chewing his cud, raised his enormous head, and stared me straight in the eye. It was in this split second I remembered: the bison is the largest mammal on the continent. Bison can weigh more than a ton and stand six or more feet tall. They can run forty miles an hour and jump fifteen feet. The bison is, to quote the Theodore Roosevelt National Park literature, "the most ferocious animal in North America." (Laughing, but respectfully.)

Feet away from, the bison stared me dead in the eye and I stared back, realizing how scared I should be. If it wanted to, it could have easily flipped my car. I tried to make meaningful interspecies eye contact in a way that communicated contrition for being a weird fan and taking a photo without asking first. It must have worked: the bison shot me one more dirty look, then walked away.

3

This One's Hard

THERE'S NO FEELING QUITE AS SOOTHING AS WHEN YOUR GPS tells you your destination is five hours away. A chunk of driving like that is akin to a Temple Grandin machine in the space-time continuum, an interlude in which you are allowed to focus on accomplishing the very simple task of getting somewhere. Decades later, it carries the emotional residue of being a kid settled into the back seat as my mom drove to my aunt and uncle's house: for the next seemingly endless thirty minutes, nothing was expected of me. As an adult, simply operating a motor vehicle while trying to go exactly nine miles over the speed limit—fast enough to feel alive but not so fast that I'd get a ticket, I reasoned—was the mental equivalent of being a kid and doing nothing. Responsibilities couldn't reach me because I was driving and not supposed to be looking at my phone (had bad service).

Five hours at the wheel is what I had before me as I pulled out of my campsite at seven a.m. I was itching to not be in

North Dakota anymore and so gladly hauled ass to . . . South Dakota. I hoped, if I could swing it, to sleep in Denver that night. It would entail eleven hours of driving all told, roughly equivalent to the amount of time I spend conscious in one day when I am feeling seasonally depressed. But I could do it, and I was energized by the realization that I would not have to drive through Nebraska.

Around noon I stopped for lunch at a lake in South Dakota's Paha Sapa, or Black Hills. Though I was near Mount Rushmore, I had decided not to go to there on my trip for two main reasons: it's deeply problematic, and I had just been there. After eating a PB&J and walking around the lake to remind my legs they existed, I climbed back in the Prius and sped toward the southeastern corner of the state and my next national park: Wind Cave.

At just over 33,000 acres, Wind Cave is one of the smallest national parks, consisting most notably of, well, a big cave. As such it can only be experienced via a ticketed, ranger-led tour, which left at timed intervals throughout the day. As it was 1:35 p.m., Wind Cave was thirty-four minutes away, and the next tour left at 2:20, I figured I could just about make it. I drove past rolling grassland and mountains covered in Ponderosa pine; from a distance they merge into a dark mass that gave the Black Hills their name. A random herd of bison and elk on the side of the road didn't help my schedule—despite my professed indifference to the most ferocious animal in North America, I submitted to fundamental human nature and pulled over to take photos—but I made up time by speeding through the small-town streets Google Maps saw fit to send me down.

It was 2:16 when I threw the Prius into park in the crowded Wind Cave parking lot, so you can imagine how fast I ran to the doors of the visitor center. "Can I have one ticket for the 2:20 tour?" I asked the man at the information desk, *not* panting from exertion, in fact, because I am very fit.

"Afraid it's sold out, actually," he told me. "You'll have to wait for the 3:40. And you have to buy the ticket over there." He pointed to a small line of people waiting to talk to a woman at a second information desk.

"In the meantime, can I have a Junior Ranger booklet?" I asked, doing my best impression of a person asking a normal question.

"Well, which do you want?" he responded. "There are two."

It turned out that, in addition to the Wind Cave National Park–specific book, there was also a book shared across all cave-related national parks, which explored the cave ecosystem with a bit more advanced science. The news that I would be able to do twice the amount of homework came as a very welcome surprise: I started flipping through the activities as I stood in the second line for my tour tickets.

"One for the 3:40 tour, please," I said when I finally reached the desk.

"Just you?" the woman responded. As I so often have to do in my life, I confirmed that I was friendless and alone in this world. "Ah, I wish you had come two minutes sooner. We just sent off the 2:20 tour with one spot left."

ANGELA CARTER WRITES in *The Sadeian Woman* that caves are a symbol of the womb: "those dark, sequestered places where initiation and revelation take place." In my opinion, they are purely big dark holes in the ground where there may be treasure. I love a cave! I'll go into a cave any day of the week. I think it must be some hardwired human thing to see a cave and think, I gotta get inside that.

And you can't get much more "cave" than Wind Cave, the first to be designated a national park. It's the third-longest cave in the United States and is either the sixth- or seventh-longest in the world, depending on who you ask. Wind Cave has some of the strongest airflow speeds of any cave in the world, over 75 mph at the walk-in entrance. Why is this important and not just terrifying? Because the speed of a cave's barometric winds indicate how large that cave is. Based on Wind Cave's barometric winds, scientists suspect that only 2 to 5 percent of the cave has been discovered. (Before you start thinking about how much treasure could be hidden in that 95 to 98 percent, know that a significant portion of the cave is probably inaccessible to humans, either because the rock is too crumbly to hold weight or because the passages are, much like my ice-cold heart, too small.)

These are not things I pulled up to Wind Cave National Park knowing. These are all examples of things one can learn from Junior Ranger booklets (supplemented by the Wind Cave website). When I parked my car at 2:16 p.m. I was like, "I stan a large hole in the ground," and by 2:45 p.m. I was like, "The technical term for cave decorations is *speleothem*, and Wind Cave has an amount of boxwork unequaled in the world." Wind Cave, the booklets told me, had decorations called "soda straws" (basically hollow stalactites); "popcorn" (small, knobby balls); and "flowstone," described variously as "melting cake icing" or "cave bacon." What I took from all this is that someone needed to tell speleologists to stop naming cave formations when they were hungry. And of course Wind

Cave had boxwork—95 percent of the world's boxwork, in fact. The word was coined at Wind Cave, and refers to the fact that this type of speleothem looks like post office boxes, if you have a very loose interpretation of the phrase "looks like."

After an hour spent perched precariously on a tall ledge without falling backward into a ravine (brag), I finished the cave-based booklet and waltzed inside the Visitor Center to claim my Cave Scientist badge. The ranger on duty, a man in his sixties or seventies, smiled. "I'm impressed you did the cave book!" he said. "This one's hard." He signed the booklet and handed over a small wooden badge, which I immediately pinned to my denim jacket. By now it was 3:30—time to make my way down to the cave entrance.

Once inside the cave my tour group formed a single-file line as we followed the ranger deeper and deeper. Every so often the narrow trail would widen, and the ranger would stop and point out cave decorations that I, an accredited Cave Scientist, could already easily identify. We were sternly told not to touch the cave, an instruction promptly ignored by the rude white male children who surrounded me on all sides. Their disrespect for the formations that took hundreds of years to form filled me with annoyance, yes, but also with bone-deep relief that I was not the parent of any of them.

As we went along, the ranger told us the history of Wind Cave. It all started, he said, in 1881, when a settler named Jesse Bingham noticed grass waving around a hole in the ground. When he came close to investigate, the wind blowing out of that hole was so strong that it blew the hat off his head. His immediate reaction was to go find his brothers so they could take turns putting their hats on the hole, the lesson here being: men are strange. A while later Bingham again tried the trick with the hat, but this time the hole sucked his hat *in*. This, legend has it, is how Wind Cave was discovered.

There's nothing worth mining in Wind Cave, so it wasn't long before entrepreneurial-minded settlers started marketing the cave as a tourist destination. A man named Jesse D. McDonald (lots of Jesses in the late 1800s) and his family decided to explore the cave, make some bigger passageways, and add some ladders, so they could make money both from leading tours and from (trigger warning) selling mineral formations snapped off the walls of the cave.

In order to give their tours, the McDonald family filed a homestead claim on the cave entrance. (You can't file a homestead claim on a cave, but if you file a homestead claim on the one known entrance, you've basically filed a claim on the cave.) The idea of filing a homestead claim on Wind Cave like you'd call dibs on the last slice of cake is especially shameful because, as the ranger informed us, the cave is sacred to the Lakota people. One emergence story holds that the Lakota people first came to the surface of the earth through Wind Cave. On one hand: the beliefs of an entire nation of people. On the other: the tens of dollars one white family could make from breaking off stalactites and selling them to random passersby.

While this wasn't mentioned on the ninety-minute tour I took of Wind Cave, the land within the park is important to many other communities; it's the place of origin for dozens of Indigenous peoples, and more than fifty nations have relationships with and claims to the Black Hills. To some, Wind Cave was sacred and culturally significant; other nations traveled in and out of the surrounding area. All these people knew about the cave, of course. It wasn't "discovered" in 1881.

That's just the first recorded instance of anyone entering it. And I have to say: when I hear that an activity I enjoy (like going into Wind Cave) was first done by a white male colonialist settler, it makes me wonder if what I'm doing is in fact morally bankrupt.

BEFORE I SET out on my road trip, I already knew this: the reason we have *any* national park is the same reason we have any land in America at all. White settlers and the United States government violently dispossessed Indigenous people of the land they had lived on for thousands of years, which they knew deeply and to which they had a spiritual connection. Various Indigenous peoples had pushed each other out in the past—the Lakota arrived from the Lake Superior area in the mid-1700s, displacing the Crow, Cheyenne, Kiowa, and Arapaho among others—but when Anglo settlers came, they came in enormous numbers and devastated the Indigenous population. Crucial to the government's genocidal campaign was the slaughter of bison, the animal that provided everything Native peoples of the plains needed to live.

It's estimated that when English colonists arrived in Virginia in the 1600s, there were up to seventy-five million bison in North America; by the 1840s, when white settlers arrived in the Great Plains, that number was down to twenty million. (If you're thinking that still sounds like a huge number of bison, you're right.) Bison were not only sacred to the Plains Indians, they were critical to the peoples' survival. So, when the United States government decided that genocidal removal of the Plains Indians was necessary to westward expansion and when that expansion was met with fierce resistance—as Christopher Ketcham writes in *This Land*, "by the 1870s the

U.S. Army was losing twenty-five men for every Indian it killed"—the government decided it would be easier to kill bison, thereby starving the people who depended on them to live. The government began killing bison en masse and by policy, encouraging private citizens to kill bison as well. Railroad companies, wanting to expand westward, put bounties on bison, which passengers often shot from train windows. An angry metal train charging across the landscape, full of men leaning out of windows frantically shooting, hoping to make a quick buck: has there ever been a more apt metaphor for America? According to Ketcham, "The figures are uncertain, but it's said that by 1900 there were fewer than a thousand buffalo in the wild." With the bison gone, the US government eventually succeeded in stealing the Plains Indians' land.

So that's why Jesse Bingham was swanning around the Black Hills in 1881 within stumbling distance of the entrance to Wind Cave—because his government had waged a genocidal campaign against the people who already lived there. That's why the area was "uninhabited" enough that one family felt like they could file a land claim on a cave. Considering this, was it indefensible to visit the national parks?

Parks were established around the country for the benefit of European American tourists, and the Native Americans who exercised their treaty rights by hunting, gathering, and setting prescribed fires on those sites were forcibly removed. That's why today we can drive in and visit Wind Cave for a couple hours on our way to somewhere else, maybe to the big mountain we've punished with dynamite until it looks like four presidents.

NATIONAL PARKS EXIST to preserve natural wonders but also to teach visitors about our nation's history. This much was obvious, as I had just come from a park whose existence hinged on a phase Theodore Roosevelt went through in his twenties. But in the parks I had visited so far on my trip, the history that was being taught was almost entirely Eurocentric, bordering on Manifest Destiny propaganda. Park literature and signage either ignored the fact that the land existed before white people saw it, or acknowledged the existence of Indigenous people in a gauzy, "prehistory" way. There was no mention of the fact that this "wilderness" had been inhabited before the people who depended on it for food, medicine, and culture, were denied access to it so that it could be an untouched paradise for Anglo vacationers.

The glancing mentions of Indigenous people on signs, on tours, and in Junior Ranger books reminded me of an 1896 painting of Yosemite Valley by Thomas Hill. I saw it years ago in an exhibition at the Milwaukee Art Museum, *the* spot to visit in Wisconsin to get cultured while inside a building that looks like a sailboat but also a dead whale but also like every other structure Santiago Calatrava has ever designed. Hill's painting hung next to a plaque that explained: "Although Yosemite had long been a travel destination for the middle class, Hill's inclusion of Native Americans in the foreground assured potential sightseers that the area retained its authenticity and was not entirely overrun with tourists." Just as bison coats became stylish at the exact moment the interests of the United States government were served by eradicating bison, Native Americans are seen as authentic set dressing, instead of actual humans and inhabitants of a place, at the moment the United States government wants to colonize a land, and profit off it, via tourism.

In recent decades the National Park Service has begun to

do better. The parks have started to allow affiliated Indigenous nations to exercise their treaty rights and gather plants from park sites. They've put traditional place names back on maps, which benefits all visitors, because in a case of parallel thinking, white male settlers across the continent always seemed to name any mountain "Fran's Nipple." Some parks have hired Native American rangers, who can tell a more balanced story which acknowledges that national park sites have histories that go back long before European settlers arrived and got their hats blown off by barometric wind.

There's no one reason for these changes. They surely stem from the civil rights movements of the twentieth century, including the American Indian Movement, and that of the past decade. They stem from a 1999 Supreme Court decision overturning a nineteenth-century ruling that the establishment of a national park nullifies any treaty rights. They stem from the fact that, in a first for both positions, the current secretary of the interior, Deb Haaland, and head of the National Park Service, Charles F. Sams III, are both Native Americans. And they likely stem from the increasingly visible effects of climate change, and the realization that the land was much healthier when Indigenous people were stewarding it. (This doesn't mean that now all Indigenous people will get what they want, or agree on public land policy. When the Biden administration suspended new oil and gas leasing on public land in 2021, the Ute Native American Tribe complained, noting that fossil fuel extraction is one of their community's main revenue sources.)

None of this is settled history. The Black Hills today are one of the most visible sites in the world of sustained efforts to return land to Indigenous people. The Oceti Sakowin, or

Sioux Nation, have been in an ongoing dispute with the US government over the return of the Black Hills since the government violated a treaty in 1874, only six years after signing said treaty. In 1973 hundreds of Oglala Sioux occupied Wounded Knee, the site of an 1890 massacre of hundreds of Lakota by the US Army, demanding a return of the Black Hills. In 1980 the Supreme Court ruled that the US government owed the Oceti Sakowin millions of dollars for violating the Sioux Treaty of 1868, writing, "A more ripe and rank case of dishonorable dealings will never, in all probability, be found in our history." Today, with interest, the amount owed is almost two billion dollars. But the Oceti Sakowin has refused the payoff, saying that the Black Hills are not for sale. For them, land is not money; it is something more sacred than that. Groups like the NDN Collective and their LANDBACK movement continue the fight today.

I knew none of this when setting out on my road trip; I learned it after visiting the parks and then educating myself. Just as any part of an environment—the grasses, the bison, the elk hanging out with the bison because apparently they are friends now—can't be separated from the rest of the ecosystem, the natural environment of a place can't be separated from its human history. I wish I had learned more of that history from the parks themselves. Maybe some of the reticence to address it comes from being overwhelmed by the horrific events this country and these parks were built on. It's easy to be paralyzed by guilt and to feel like visiting the parks is indefensible. But that doesn't help anyone. Instead of worrying whether it's okay to visit the parks, we should work toward returning control of the parks to Native Americans. This wouldn't mean that the parks wouldn't be open to all in the same way they currently are, just that the land would be stewarded and administered by Indigenous people. A similar return of public parks to Native control is already happening in other parts of the world. It works. And it's the right thing to do.

ON MY TOUR of Wind Cave, I didn't know about the 1980 Supreme Court ruling and I didn't know about the NDN Collective fighting for the return of the Black Hills. I knew how to identify approximately fifteen types of cave decorations and that was about it. As the tour concluded, the park ranger opened it up for questions. I raised my hand. "Have the Lakota ever sued the government to reclaim ownership of the cave?"

The ranger said yes and didn't elaborate.

We left the cave, dramatically wiping our shoes on a bat mat. I redeemed my second booklet and got into my car, on my way to somewhere else.

4

Leaves of Gas, Grass, or Ass

KEROUAC STOPS IN DENVER REPEATEDLY IN *ON THE ROAD*, stumbling along "with the most wicked grin of joy in the world, among the bums and beat cowboys of Larimer Street." Ginsberg moved to the city for a while to pursue Neal Cassady, an unhinged move (which I unfortunately have nearly done myself for multiple men in multiple cities), and later wrote in *Howl* about the greatest minds of his generation journeying to Denver, brooding and waiting there, watching over Denver and dying there, too. There was a frisson running through Denver, or at least there had been seventy years ago. After a week of driving mainly through broad expanses of nothingness, I couldn't wait to see it.

I had decided to spend two nights in Denver for the simple reasons that I missed my friend Molly, who lived in Denver with her daughters; I had no idea where exactly I was going next; and I thought it might be nice for other people if I took a shower for the first time in nearly a week. Molly and I grew up across the street from one another, and as she was one of the kids who got lost around Devil's Lake that fateful day in the early 2000s, she too was a nature lover, what Whitman calls "enamoured of growing outdoors." A couple years earlier Molly had moved to the edge of the mountains so her daughters could be enamored of growing outdoors too.

My plan for the first morning was to drive to Sputnik, a dimly lit, vaguely sixties-themed combination dive bar and diner, which happened to serve a mean tofu scramble. The charm of driving into Denver under cover of darkness, as I had the night before, is that you almost forget the mountains are there. Seeing them the next day, looming against the skyline, they seem even more unlikely and majestic. Given the proximity of mountains to tofu-based amenities, it's no wonder that between 2010 and 2020 Denver's population grew 21 percent—part of a larger wave of rapid population growth in the South and West that shows no sign of stopping. Millennials make up more than half the in-migration in some years; as we can decreasingly afford to live in New York or go on fancy vacations, it makes sense to move to a cheaper city close to public land, where for little or no money you can spend your vacation days walking up and down a mountain.

I finished my bougie breakfast and set off to run some errands. The first stop was Denver's flagship REI, ninety thousand square feet of shopping, climbing walls, and biking trails. It could be described as a cathedral of nature-based spirituality but only if you're brainwashed by capitalism and completely missing the point, which, let's face it, a lot of people are. Inside I walked past $450 backpacks and past coolers boasting the latest technology for only $1,300—an admittedly reasonable price if you can find a way to live inside a cooler. I needed a sleeping pad, because while I may have identified as low-key and at one with nature, I'd discovered that my spine was not at one with all the sharp rocks on the ground. Nonchalant smile glued to my face, I circled the sleeping pads until I found the cheapest option, something made of foam that did *not* purport to be extremely comfortable but *did* purport to be $39.99. It was the color of a sinus infection, which I assumed was meant to punish me for refusing to spend more money, but my will was stronger than the aesthetic assault.

THE DENVER OF 2019 was quite different from the Denver experienced by the Beats. The dive bars where they hung out have been torn down or gentrified past recognition. My experience of being a young person on the road in America was in some ways unrecognizable, too, from the canonical travel narratives I had read.

The canon I had in mind started with the first distinctly "American" writing, from the nineteenth century, and followed from there. Some of the books that inspired my trip were about travel and some were about nature, but they were all about finding freedom and, not to be lame, transcendence.

The first among these, their spiritual granddaddy, is *Walden*. Henry David Thoreau and the rest of the transcendentalists were inspired by the Romantics of Europe, but in writing about finding "an original relation to the universe," they were basically creating the first truly American literary tradition, inspired by the landscape of the United States. *Walden* isn't about travel, but it speaks to a desire to retreat from mass culture, to rely on oneself, and to live intentionally. Thoreau is the hero of many of my heroes; though I may find Walden as a whole a little, shall we say, "extremely boring," I find so much worth in what he wrote and I think about certain lines constantly. "I wanted to live deep and suck out all the marrow of life"—same! "I was rich, if not in money, in sunny hours and summer days, and spent them lavishly." These are the sentiments that sent me on the road.

Then there was the man most precious to me in all the canon: Walt Whitman. He was a contemporary of Thoreau and kind of a transcendentalist for the extrovert set. Whitman's "Song of the Open Road" was published thirty years before anything resembling an automobile was ever manufactured but is still the best piece of writing about travel I have ever read. "Afoot and light-hearted I take to the open road," it begins:

> Healthy, free, the world before me,
> The long brown path before me leading me wherever
>   I choose.
>
> Henceforth I ask not good-fortune, I myself am good-
>   fortune
> Henceforth I whimper no more, postpone no more,
>   need nothing,
> Done with indoor complaints, libraries, querulous
>   criticisms,
> Strong and content I travel the open road.

Being Whitman, of course, it goes on about 220 more lines from there. It's a perfect poem. I love it. I once sent this poem to a crush and he responded "He's good with rhymes," but whatever, you can lead a crush to water, but you can't make him thrill to the experience of being alive via reading poetry. There are lines in "Song of the Open Road" that perfectly capture the best of what I feel when I'm driving somewhere beautiful. Those lines don't feel any more remote to me just because they were written by a man who lived 180 years before I did. (I would realize halfway through the trip that 2019 marked the two-hundredth anniversary of Whitman's birth and wondered if I could retcon my Great American Road Trip into a celebration of Whitman's bicentennial. "I'll call the book *Leaves of Gas, Grass, or Ass: No One Rides for Free!*" I said, before being told that in no world was I allowed to publish a book with "ass" in the title.)

In 2019 it wouldn't be unheard of to see an outdoorsman—a real dudely dude in a Toyota Tacoma, a guy who knows enough about living off the land to idly consider applying to be on the show *Alone*—reading Whitman or Thoreau. But more likely you'd see them reading the work of Edward Abbey, a former ranger at Arches National Monument and author of *Desert Solitaire* and *The Monkey Wrench Gang*.

I found Abbey popular with a certain strain of guy, the ones who hated authority and thought most people were doing the whole "being in nature" thing wrong. While I can only aspire to be as bristly and misanthropic as those men, I too am skeptical of authority and was beginning to suspect many people *are*, in fact, doing nature wrong (for example, spending $500 million on a new "great outdoors"-themed fit by North Face x Online Ceramics so you can look the most drippy to take the same photo at the same overvisited location as everyone else on Instagram—FOR EXAMPLE). So I bought a copy of *Desert Solitaire* and began to educate myself on Abbey. Aspects of his writing were certainly compelling, like his resistance to "industrial tourism." But I couldn't get over Abbey's "I'm kind of a weird guy" energy—that brand of man who seeks to set himself apart and imply that he's better than others by faux-humbly pointing out that he's a little different, a little *weird*. "Most of my wandering in the desert I've done alone," Abbey writes. "Not so much from choice as from necessity—I generally prefer to go into places where no one else wants to go." *Sure.* Reading his popular but also racist and misogynist work—if it's possible to write about unsustainable population growth without sounding like a eugenicist, Abbey didn't know it—I felt more estranged from outdoors culture than I did before I started.

The book most foundational to my road trip was *On the Road*. It sparked in me a lifelong, burning desire to drive across the United States repeatedly until I got bored of it, burned out, or turned it into a book. *On the Road* wasn't just the book that launched a billion road trips; it taught generations of Americans how to be cool, if being cool involves writing poetry and rolling your cigarettes up in your shirt sleeve, which, obviously, it does.

WHEN KEROUAC HITCHHIKED across the country in 1947, it wasn't thought of as romantic or adventurous but instead reminded people of the itinerant unemployed who caught freight trains across the country during the Great Depression. But he set off on the assumption that "there'd be girls, visions, everything; somewhere along the line the pearl would be handed to me." When he handed the pearl to the world with the 1957 publication of *On the Road*, it created an entirely new context for American travel, and young people inspired by the book went on the road in huge numbers. Except that not every person who found inspiration in Kerouac's writing could follow his example.

The height of the Beat Generation directly corresponded with the peak of the male-breadwinner nuclear family, a time when women were more likely to get married, and to marry younger, than ever before in American history. (We forget that what I describe as a "hellish worst-case scenario" and what conservatives describe as "the traditional family" does not have a long history; in fact, it only predominated for fifteen years in the middle of the past century.) This coincidence meant that much of what the Beats were about was inaccessible to women of the time. As Joyce Johnson—a writer who was dating Kerouac when *On the Road* was published—notes in the introduction to *Minor Characters*, her book about that time, "Experience, adventure—these were not for young women." Adventure would mean exposure to sex, which could ruin a woman's life. Women were meant to inspire and appreciate art, not pursue experiences that would allow them to create art. Plus, in a movement that frowned on having a straight job and making money, someone had to work so these destructive male geniuses could eat while they put words on the page. And as girlfriends had no artistic reputation to lose, that ended up being the girlfriends. (I can't imagine a *New York Times* bestseller called *On the Job* by Jack Kerouac's mommy-lovers.)

Women have written fewer books about being free on the road or in nature for the obvious reason that women are less free than men are. A woman born in Thoreau's time couldn't have spent two years at her friend Ralph Waldo Emerson's property, hanging out in a cabin and dicking around. The female equivalent of Whitman was Emily Dickinson, who instead of taking to the open road was able to center her life around art only by famously never going outside, forever earning a reputation as a giant bitch who probably had a mood disorder. Society's functioning relied on women marrying, having children, and working in the home, which meant that women were less able to dip out in search of their own adventures, *and* that society was seen as tame and somewhat feminine. As Annie Dillard noted in her journal while she was in the process of writing a book about American nature, *Pilgrim at Tinker Creek*, "It's impossible to imagine another situation where you can't write a book 'cause you weren't born with a penis. Except maybe *Life with My Penis*."

Things have changed rapidly for women since 1957, and by the time I was alive and had a driver's license it was much easier for young women to go on the road. We had bestselling books about travel and about nature written by women, like Cheryl Strayed's *Wild* and Elizabeth Gilbert's *Eat, Pray, Love*. I hope that in the future we'll get more books where women set off on adventure without the justification of needing to heal from trauma (Gilbert from her divorce and Strayed from her mother's death). But over the first chunk of my trip it had become apparent to me that, even though my trip was different than it would have been if I were writing *Life on the Road with My Penis*, going on the road was pretty accessible for women who looked like me.

I WANTED TO drive around America and see wild places and write about it because I think that the more narratives we have about women doing those things, the easier it is for other women to imagine doing the same, and the safer it is for them to do it (or at least the less likely that their stepdad will try to buy them a gun first). But even if actually getting on the road wasn't as easy for anyone who didn't look exactly like

Jack Kerouac (white, youngish, square head), this particular American mode of adventure was alive and well.

I ate one more vegan breakfast on my way out of Denver, and noticed a sticker for an upcoming referendum to decriminalize magic mushrooms. It had been sixty-two years since *On the Road* was published, and even if Jack Kerouac might laugh at my tofu eggs, I could see a line from him to the hundreds of thousands of people who had moved to Colorado in pursuit of adventure and freedom. As I headed to the famous national parks of Utah, I was about to see exactly how alive and well the American road trip really was.

The Intermountain West

5

A Weird Cactus Doing Really Well for Itself

HERE'S THE THING ABOUT THE JUNIOR RANGER PROGRAM: it's not just a way for children and kooky adults to acquire pins through the diligent completion of word searches. The booklets are honestly a great way to learn about a park. I didn't realize the truth of this until a few years before my trip, when a (real) park ranger at Rocky Mountain National Park told me that when on vacation she did Junior Ranger books too, because it was the quickest way to get a good sense of the park she was visiting. In retrospect, I'd gone on trips with friends where I was the only person to do the booklet, and a couple days in I invariably found myself answering my friends' questions about elk or weird plants or park history. The Junior Ranger program allowed me to "meet" the local bioregion, which Jenny Odell describes in *How to Do Nothing* as "walking around, observing what grows there, and learning something about the indigenous history of the place (which, in all too many places, is the last record of people engaging in any meaningful way with the bioregion.)" The next park on my trip would have me meeting a bioregion of, uh, "sand."

As I drove the four hours from Denver toward Great Sand Dunes National Park, I had low expectations. Frankly? I do not care about sand. Sand is boring to me. "But this sand is white!" you protest. I'm sorry to tell you that you are thinking of White Sands, which is a different place, in southern New Mexico, and didn't become a national park until five months after my trip, which I *do* find annoying and which is only one of many reasons I am currently attempting to overthrow the United States government.

No, this was going to be just normal sand, and candidly? I've seen sand before.

But when I pulled around a mountain and saw the dunes, my brain reacted like a horse does in a movie when it encounters the villain: it startled, maybe even neighed a little. It's not just that these dunes were giant, though they absolutely are: they're 750 feet tall and cover thirty square miles. It's that these giant dunes are flanked by, on one side, absolutely nothing and on the other, the rocky peaks of the Sangre de Cristo Mountains. The dunes looked like aliens had left them there as a prank. Once again I felt the geographic immensity of the United States. It's not just that the same country could have the flat cornfields where I grew up and also giant sand dunes next to a mountain range. It's that it can have such a weird place, and *I had never even heard of it.*

So I sped to the visitor center, eager to learn the *how* and the *to what end* of these sand dunes. I asked the ranger at the information desk if he could kindly give me a Junior Ranger packet and advise me how best to [gestures duneward] get all up on that sand. Unfortunately the answer to the latter was "You absolutely can't." Having done no research before pulling up to Great Sand Dunes, I had managed to arrive at the worst time of day. The wind was too high and the chance of lightning too great for me to climb the dunes without either getting sandburn or getting zapped on the head. And so I stepped onto the visitor center's patio, found a seat where I could gaze at the dunes as the strong wind attempted to blow me into the sandy grassland, and opened my booklet.

First of all I had to learn how exactly these sand piles even got here. The basic idea is this: the Sangre de Cristo Mountains were pushed upward via plate tectonics. Many miles west, volcanic activity created the San Juan Mountains. Long story short, sediments from the mountains filled the valley between the two ranges, and the predominant southwest winds blew this sand into a curve in the Sangre de Cristo Mountains. But crucially! Sometimes storms caused the sand to blow back toward the valley, which led to the vertical growth of the dunes. Nowadays there is enough plant life on the valley floor and enough moisture in the dunes that the dune field is mostly stable. This is an extremely abridged version; I've left out an entire saga of a giant ancient lake that dried up a long time ago. But if you're looking to grow your own 750-foot sand dunes at home, that is the basic recipe.

At some more geologically recent time, humans arrived. Nomadic hunter-gatherers were first. Many modern Indigenous peoples were familiar with, sometimes lived in, or considered the area sacred, including the Ute, the Diné (Navajo) people, and the Jicarilla Apaches. Four hundred years ago, Spaniards arrived. In 1807 Zebulon Pike of "Pike's Peak" fame wrote about the Great Sand Dunes in his journals—the first known writings about the dunes. I mention this only because, *honestly*: imagine being named Zebulon. What was wrong with his parents? How is it possible that a man named Zebulon lived in 1807 and not in the year 5477, on a spaceship orbiting the solar system until Earth is one day habitable again?

After finishing a few activities, I decided to explore the Sand Sheet Loop Trail, which had a view of the dunes and seemed as good a place as any to complete a game of Junior Ranger bingo. Could I find dune grass? Check. Cactus? Check. Mule deer? Check. I had frankly seen more deer in the first two weeks of my trip than I could shake a stick at, though, as a staunch environmentalist, I would never shake a stick at a deer.

And then, in the upper right-hand square of the bingo card, was a drawing of a plant I had seen all over the place but never known the name of. I had first really noticed it the preceding year on a southwestern road trip with my friend Emmy. We were at the Grand Canyon, the giant hole in the ground that seems like it must be overrated but is instead that miraculous thing: a place that is massively hyped but still, somehow, the accurate amount of hyped. The full moon shone so brightly the night before that we had barely slept, so we arrived at the visitor center an hour before it even opened. After eating PB&Js, filling our water bottles, avoiding bees, changing our tampons, reading a little, and slathering on sunscreen, we still had thirty minutes to pretty much sit and look around. A plant caught our eye, a ball of green spikes like a huge, photosynthetic sea urchin with a tall, flowered stalk shooting up out of the middle. "Look at that thing," I said to Emmy.

"What do you think it is?"

Mortifyingly, I said I thought it was "a weird cactus that is doing really well for itself."

It turns out, the Great Sand Dunes Junior Ranger booklet informed me, that what we had seen and what I was seeing around the Sand Sheet Loop Trail was yucca. It isn't even a type of cactus—it belongs to the asparagus family. (Embarrassing for yucca, but moving on.) Yucca is an entire genus, which I didn't know at the time, but even knowing that the sea urchin plant was a yucca burst my brain right open like a party popper. I was able to look at a thing I had never known the name for and say, "That's a yucca." I felt so much like a person alive on this planet.

It felt good to observe and appreciate even one small thing about nature, as a massive apology to everything humankind has done to it since the Industrial Revolution. And it was easy and exciting to observe nature in an environment so different from where I grew up and from the city where I now lived. There is a strange weight to learning the names of animals and plants in the age of mass extinction. Am I in the last generation that will learn the name of, say, the Mexican spotted owl? Of yucca? Of deer??? If people knew the name of yucca, would they be more motivated to ensure its continued existence?

An insect scurrying amid the Indian ricegrass gave me bingo, and I swung back inside the visitor center long enough to turn in my Junior Ranger booklet. The dunes were still too dangerous to hike, but I decided to head down to at least get a closer look at them. Getting to the giant sand piles from the parking lot involved picking my way through a stand of cottonwood trees, then crossing the wide, shallow Medano Creek. The creek, made up of snowpack runoff from the Sangre de Cristos, doesn't exist for most of the year, but through absolutely no fault of my own I had lucked into visiting not only during the window when the creek existed, but at its peak. I took my shoes off and stepped in. I gasped. It was like ice, which shocked me until I remembered the creek had woken up that morning as snow.

I'd spent years hanging out in nature without knowing the names of so much of what I looked at—I'd even spent my childhood eating wild berries I couldn't name, which in retrospect seems less like a "charming detail" and more like a "cause of death." But as I ran around the creek and looked at the dunes, it made my experience so much richer to know the names of even a few plants and have a fifth-grade-science-level understanding of how the sand got there. I could see the edges of how things worked together, how intertwined everything is on this crazy planet with its asparagus cactus and its alien-prank dunes. I was happy to be so wrong about the entertainment value of sand.

THE NEXT MORNING I went to step outside the KOA cabin in Cortez, Colorado, where I had slept and almost trampled a small lizard. After ten days on the road, I had finally made it to the "small-lizard bioregion." This was southwestern Colorado, firmly in the Four Corners area of the United States: if I stood on high ground, I could see New Mexico, Arizona, and Utah from here.

The KOA I was staying at was owned by my Aunt Chris and Uncle John, who had left their careers five years earlier to run a KOA outside of Bryce Canyon. They had bought the Cortez KOA just weeks before I arrived. The benefit of Cortez, and the reason I was staying there, was that it was a ten-minute drive from Mesa Verde National Park.

If you haven't heard of Mesa Verde—or if you have but,

like my dad, you barely know anything about it and pronounce it "Messy Verdi,"—Mesa Verde is a national park dedicated to preserving the cultural history of the Ancestral Pueblo (or Anasazi) people. These people, from whom twenty-six modern nations are descended, lived at Mesa Verde for more than seven centuries, first in pit houses, then in aboveground houses atop the cliffs, and later, in the twelfth century, in extraordinary dwellings built into alcoves in the cliffs themselves.

After buying tickets for two cliff dwelling tours, I sat outside the Mesa Verde Visitor Center eating trail mix and doing my activity book. I flipped to one of the required worksheets, called "Being a Good Steward." *To become a Junior Ranger we need to be good stewards,* the book explained. *A steward is someone who helps take care of something that belongs to everyone.* The activity presented an illustrated scene and required me to circle which illustrated children were being bad, by sitting on the archeological sites, or picking flowers, or apparently holding out some interesting sticks for a mule deer to smell. (If there is one thing you take away from this book, I hope it is to NOT let the DEER smell the STICKS!!!) Another activity encouraged me to protect the environment by turning off the water while I brush my teeth; I was shocked to remember there was a time when this seemed like an adequate thing to save the planet. Whether we can fault the authors of the Junior Ranger book for failing to encourage children to blow up fossil fuel infrastructure is a question each of us must answer for ourselves.

I headed to the park museum, an old, squat building constructed with Cliff House Sandstone, the same material used by the Ancestral Puebloans. I wandered to the information desk to swap my book for a badge. There, Ranger Cameron had me raise my right hand and repeat the standard Junior Ranger pledge. And then he started to freestyle. "I promise I will floss . . ." he said.

"I promise I will floss . . ." I repeated.

". . . and I won't argue with anyone in the car."

"Well, I'm alone in the car. So that will be easy." Like an FCC delay, it took several seconds after hearing myself loudly announce that I was traveling alone before I realized, ah, *this* is how I get myself murdered.

ON THE MESA Top Loop road I learned about the history of the Ancestral Puebloans, who started moving into the Four Corners region in the sixth century. They did seem to be among the last people to engage deeply with the bioregion, living off only what the area had to offer. They gathered food—pinyon pine nuts, prickly pear cactus pads, grains from ricegrass. They hunted animals including deer, elk, and rabbits, and they farmed corn, beans, and squash—three crops that grow extremely well together—on the mesa top. The Ancestral Puebloans also domesticated animals: turkeys (first for feathers and bones, later for meat) and dogs (for unconditional love and internet content). They constructed reservoirs and farming terraces to collect water for their crops and to prevent soil erosion.

These were not people who passed through the land living lightly and making no mark; they were people who deeply understood their environment, interacted with it, and shaped it. Knowing and respecting their bioregion didn't stop the Ancestral Puebloans from trying to change it, but the way they lived was more sustainable than what I saw now: vegetables and consumer goods and tourists shipped in across state and country lines, burning fossil fuels to do so. Water being used willy-nilly, in the Southwest, in a drought. The mass of men walking around not even knowing what a yucca is. Being in nature and learning about traditional lifeways always made me yearn for a simpler, more connected life. But I was only learning about those things, I realized, because I was part of the problem.

THE TOUR FOR the cliff dwelling called Balcony House starts on the mesa top and then descends into the canyon. As is true of most national park tours and of my life, the tour group was plagued by annoying young white men. We proceeded down the trail single file, and I overheard the teen in front of me telling his mom that he wasn't impressed, he could have easily lived in a cliff dwelling, he could free-solo to the mesa top, no problem.

"No, you couldn't, Kyle," his mom responded. "You don't have the upper-body strength."

My second tour was of Cliff Palace, and our guide was none other than Ranger Cameron. Drizzle fell as he gave the tour group an introduction. Whereas Balcony House had thirty-eight rooms and probably housed thirty people, Cliff Palace had 150 rooms and a likely population of 100. It was used for ceremonies and was a social and administrative center. It was, in other words, the place for you and your domesticated turkeys to see and be seen.

The drizzle continued as we descended the trail to Cliff Palace, which was even bigger than I had expected. Moments after the last straggler had shuffled into the cliff dwelling's courtyard, the skies opened. It was an instant demonstration of why the Ancestral Pueblo people would have wanted to live under the cliffs in the first place: we stayed bone dry while three feet away a sheet of rain poured down. "I feel like we're in a Rainforest Cafe," I said. Only one woman laughed.

The main rooms of Cliff Palace were either closed or inaccessible during the storm, so Ranger Cameron stood in the courtyard giving his practiced spiel about the dwelling. And then, after a few minutes, he ran out of things to say. He looked out at the rain, now falling even harder than before. "Does anyone have any questions for me?" he asked, and for about five minutes people did, until we ran out. It was still raining. For fifteen minutes after that, with nothing better to do, we racked our brains for something—anything—to ask Ranger Cam while we waited out the storm. "What was . . . uh . . . the . . . average life expectancy?" asked one generous tour member.

"Well, actually," Ranger Cam said, making a meal of it, "*average* is a bad measure of this kind of thing. It was about twenty-eight, but only because childbirth was so dangerous for mother and infant." I, twenty-eight at the time, nodded. I understood what it was to be twenty-eight, a crone, and ready for death. "But if you survived that," Ranger Cam continued, "you could live to eighty or ninety."

I should stress here that none of the numbers Ranger Cam threw at us that day are supported by information on the Mesa Verde website, which put average life expectancy at thirty-two to thirty-four with an upper range in the fifties and sixties. But it got me thinking: if all a lady had to do to live to the ripe old age of ninety (sounds like a nightmare but okay) was survive having kids, couldn't she just . . . not have kids? So—and in my defense we were entering minute 25 or 30 of being stuck standing in this courtyard—I raised my hand.

"Did the Ancestral Puebloans practice"—and it was about here that I realized I was asking this question while surrounded by children—"Agh, any form of *family planning*?"

Ranger Cam looked at me with the wide eyes of a man who has either been scandalized by your question or is about to pull an answer out of his ass, or maybe both. "Yes," he said. "Matricide." Thunder clapped (it didn't). "But it's very sad and I'll tell you more about it later." The rain softened, and our group followed the trail up to the mesa top. I waited for Ranger Cam for ten minutes, but he failed to appear.

NO ONE KNOWS for sure why the Ancestral Puebloans started moving south soon after they moved into their cliff dwellings around 1200 BCE, but within a generation or two they had completely abandoned Mesa Verde. It might have been that, after living in the region for seven hundred years, they had finally depleted the forests, overhunted the deer and elk and bighorn sheep, and farmed until the soil was stripped of its nutrients. It might have been that everyone just got on everyone else's nerves—that social conflict made it more attractive to pack up and go live with family in New Mexico. It might have been the great drought of the 1270s to 1290s—though the current decades-long drought in the Southwest is already much worse than the one that may have caused twenty thousand people to abandon their cliff mansions.

If living in this region was unsustainable for a culture that did a pretty good job of paying attention to the actual ecosystem they were living in, I felt a looming sense of dread for what that meant for our culture, which does its best to ignore the ecosystem at every turn. (To be fair, "feeling a looming sense of dread" is kind of baseline in the twenty-first century.) As I so often do while learning about climate change, I felt in equal parts urgently called to action and completely paralyzed by the immensity of it all.

Why Isn't This Rock Famous?

THE DRIVE TO CAPITOL REEF NATIONAL PARK IS A DESO-late, astonishing road through the desert with only two downsides: you are guaranteed to lose phone service, and at some point your GPS may tell you to drive directly up the side of a cliff. If the latter happens, my condolences: you have encountered the Moki Dugway.

When you Google the Moki Dugway, the People Also Ask suggestions include "Is Moki Dugway safe?" "Is Moki Dugway scary?" and "What is the steepest road in Utah?" Who needs answers when you have questions like these! But to Google the Moki Dugway assumes you have foreknowledge of the Moki Dugway which, when I encountered the "road" on a trip the year before, I absolutely did not.

Emmy and I had been driving through Utah, mildly lost, when a cliff came into view on the horizon. Idly I wondered when Google Maps was going to direct me around the cliff. Fifteen minutes later, I was at its base. "Now drive up it, bitch,"

Siri told me. Thus commenced the most harrowing thirty minutes of my life.

The road before me was a series of steep switchbacks. It was unpaved. It had no guardrails. It was one lane. (It claims, I would later learn, to be wide enough for two cars, but whoever claimed that forgot that there are no guardrails and *it's on the side of a cliff*.) The sun had almost set, it had been fifteen minutes since we had even passed another road, and for reasons having to do with the problematic nature of being alive in the twenty-first century, I do whatever my phone tells me to do, so I began inching up the dirt road. I have never been more sure I was about to die.

When enough months had passed that I could think about it without retraumatizing myself, I learned that the Moki (from *moqui*, the Spanish colonizers' term for the Indians they encountered) Dugway (from the fact that they done dug the road out of the freaking cliffside), was constructed in 1958 to transport uranium ore from Happy Jack Mine to the town of Mexican Hat. Reviews online say the road has fantastic views, which is probably true if you are able to gaze objectively upon the abyss into which you are about to fall to your death. Signs posted just before the Dugway recommend that you take the switchbacks at 5 miles per hour. I recommend that you do not take them at all!

At the KOA, when I told Aunt Chris and Uncle John where I was headed, they made sure I planned a route that did not include the Moki Dugway. "Make sure this is saved to your phone," Aunt Chris said, "because you're going to lose service." They encouraged me to make it to that night's campground before darkness fell, to ensure that I did not blindly drive off the side of a cliff as is my wont. "And text us when you get to Capitol Reef!"

On my way out of the campground, I called my dad to share the happy news that I had not yet been murdered. Glad to hear it, he asked me where I was going that day.

"Capitol Reef?" he repeated. "That's the one that Trump made not a national park anymore, right?"

"Nah, you're thinking of Bears Ears National Monument, or Grand Staircase–Escalante," I corrected him, proud of how informed I was on the topic. I then immediately walked into the corner of a roof I had also walked into the night before.

Creating a national park like Capitol Reef requires an act of Congress, and so revoking one—which has never happened—would as well. Creating a national monument like Bears Ears or Grand Staircase–Escalante requires only an executive order, and so revoking one requires only a presidential signature.

Grand Staircase–Escalante refers to the "staircase" of cliffs and plateaus that rise from the Grand Canyon in Arizona to Utah's Bryce Canyon and beyond. It includes not only canyons and cliffs but hoodoos and rivers and forests. Bill Clinton established the 1.87 million–acre (that's almost two Delawares) monument in 1996, and in 1999 the Bureau of Land Management announced a plan dedicating the monument, home to an imposing amount of "biological, geological, paleontological, and archeological objects," to science and research. As you may assume from context clues about the United States, dedicating a portion of land this big to the concept of science had never previously been done.

Nearby Bears Ears, on the other hand, was preserved not for the scientific value of its canyons and mesas and pinyon and juniper but for the equally essential reason that the land is sacred to the Diné, Hopi, Ute, Mountain Ute, and Zuni Nations. Indigenous people have lived in the region for thousands of years, praying and holding ceremonies and stewarding the land. For decades Indigenous leaders campaigned for federal protection for Bears Ears, and finally in December of 2016 Barack Obama established the 1.2 million–acre monument. Donald Trump was inaugurated a month later, and in April 2017 he directed the Department of the Interior to investigate the legality and legitimacy of national monuments established since 1996. This action was true to his one and only cogent worldview: that anything Barack Obama ever did was wrong and ruined, somehow, the United States of America.

The public overwhelmingly opposed the reduction of the monuments, according to a poll of voters in western states and to millions of comments submitted to the Department of the Interior. Nevertheless, in December 2017 Trump signed an order reducing Bears Ears National Monument by 85 percent and Grand Staircase–Escalante by 50 percent. Though it seems like the word applies to every single thing that has happened since 2016, this reduction of public land protections was—say it with me—unprecedented. In reducing just these two national monuments, Trump removed protection from almost two million acres, opening the land to oil and gas drilling and other extractive industries. By the following September, according to a Wilderness Society study, Trump and the Republican-controlled Congress had removed protection of some kind from over 150 million acres of public land and water. That's 154 publicly owned Delawares, open to timber and mining and drilling and grazing, defacing sacred land and doing grotesque things to our environment, for the grand purpose of annoying Barack Obama.

The thought that what little protected land we had hung so precariously on the whims of our (often chaotic evil) elected officials deflated me. But what in the news didn't? I said goodbye to my dad and drove off toward some of the protected land we had left.

UTAH IS FUCKED up. I'm sorry! There's no other way to put it. It's too beautiful. Maybe it was the altitude, maybe it was the fact that I had hit my head on a roof twice in the past twenty-four hours and felt mildly concussed, maybe it was the cold brew I was chugging at a medically worrisome pace, but everything I drove past from the moment I crossed the Colorado border was the most physically perfect thing I had seen yet on my trip. Every rock looked like it should be famous. I occasionally encountered signs of humans—I drove past a DIY billboard that shouted THE GOAL OF SOCIALISM IS COMMUNISM—VLADIMIR LENIN—and when I did, I wondered why this land, more beautiful than most in the country, didn't warrant congressional protection.

The rocky, alien landscape gave way to a canyon that cut through striated rock, with a fertile green stretch in between: this was Capitol Reef. I joined a long line at the visitor center information desk, behind a white guy with blonde dreads and a pair of Crocs that appeared to have been buried underground for a thousand years. When I reached the desk, the man working it welcomed me warmly to Capitol Reef, "where we have all the beauty of Utah's national parks with none of the congestion." He was wrong, of course—I had just waited twenty minutes to use the restroom—but it was a nice thought.

Junior Ranger book acquired, I stood on a wooden boardwalk a mile from the visitor center, staring at a cliff wall covered in petroglyphs. They had been carved by the Fremont Culture, a people who lived in the area from around 300–1300 CE, after the Desert Archaic hunter-gatherers, who arrived around 10,000 BCE, but before the Diné, Hopi, Ute, Paiute, and other peoples who now live in the area. My favorite petroglyphs depicted a series of figures who were either bison gods or ultrajacked dudes with interesting hats, ascending skyward.

As I walked along the boardwalk, a park ranger approached me.

"Hi, how are you?" he said.

Well, I thought, *that's a flirt if I've ever heard one.* "I'm doing well," I said and waved my children's educational workbook in the air. "I'm doing my Junior Ranger thing." *Flirt ball's in your court.*

"Ma'am, would you be willing to complete a short survey about the park?"

The survey asked me boilerplate questions about my park experience. But as I neared the end of the questionnaire, the ranger pointed out the most important question: why did I think Capitol Reef was a national park? *Dude, you tell me,* I thought. In a state so beautiful, what makes one stretch of land worth protecting more than another? And, like, why *Capitol Reef*, a park no one has ever heard of? I wondered if the question had something to do with the recent reduction in public land protections; if Capitol Reef was worried about getting their story straight on why they deserved to be a national park in case the oil industry came knocking. "I'm going to put down a guess," I told the ranger, "but when I'm done, can you tell me the real answer?"

WHAT LAND GETS protected in America, and why? There's a lot of federally owned public land in the United States. "A lot" to the tune of roughly 640 million acres, which is about 28 percent of the total landmass of the country; put another way, it's 657 Delawares. If you're thinking: I didn't know so many Delawares' worth of acres were environmentally protected and open to outdoor enjoyment for my pleasure and that of my countrymen, you're right. Overwhelmingly, public land is not the same thing as protected land.

On almost all kinds of public land, even national parks, government regulations allow some use or extraction of resources. Which is not an inherently evil thing! After all, humans have needs and cannot eat beautiful vistas or live inside birdsong. And it's possible to extract resources from a landscape without devastating it, as many Indigenous cultures managed to more or less do for a long time before European colonizers arrived and were like, "We *must* cut down *all* the trees!" Resource extraction on public land would not be a crisis if it was done thoughtfully and responsibly, but . . . well, have you *met* the United States government?

Together, the US Forest Service (USFS) and the Bureau of Land Management (BLM) manage 438 million acres of land. When I was young and naive, with a heart full of love and a head full of Bambi, I assumed the USFS existed to protect forests. No. The Forest Service, which consists of 154 national forest units and twenty national grasslands, exists to a large extent to manage logging. BLM land is similarly managed for resource extraction, in its case via drilling and mining and cattle grazing. "Wait, I agree that drilling and mining are serious, but cows are cute!" *You could not be more wrong about cows.* Cattle in the West erode the soil, pollute water with their poop, and help spread invasive grasses, which more easily catch fire—not something we need in an area that is already constantly, catastrophically aflame. One study in the *Journal of Arid Environments*, to quote Christopher Ketcham's book *This Land*, "found that grazing on public land near the White Sands Missile Range was more damaging to the long-term vegetative recovery of flora than the 1945 Trinity nuclear bomb blast." *Worse than a nuclear blast!* And yet I see no government spending on a United States National Cow Defense to shoot down any cows that are coming our way.

Outside of actual national parks, which generally ban resource extraction, most public land management has nothing to do with outdoorsmanship or preserving nature. It's about enriching private interests. And for the privilege of having our public lands devastated by those interests, the taxpayer is losing millions of dollars a year. Logging and grazing are heavily subsidized, despite the fact that, according to Ketcham, logging on public lands accounts for "less than 4 percent of all wood products sold in the United States." And as David Gessner writes in *Leave It As It Is*, "[l]ess than 1 percent of US beef production comes from Western public lands." These subsidies amount to socialism for the already rich, often the very same people who claim to hate socialism. And as we all know, the goal of socialism is communism, quote, Vladimir Lenin.

Agitation to make federal lands more available for capitalist exploitation continues today. The fact that, as the West burns and global temperatures rise, there are interests trying to drill more, to open more fragile ecosystems to grazing—it's almost farcical. Maybe these people have accepted that the end is coming, and they just want to have the nicest possible car for the apocalypse. But for the rest of us, the fight to protect more land, and to defend the land that has already been protected, continues.

So—in the middle of public land that was much less protected and where every rock looked like it should be famous but would probably end up being mined for uranium or trampled by cattle—why did Capitol Reef deserve to be a national park? "Are you guys asking this because you're afraid of Trump revoking national monuments?" I asked the ranger.

Not exactly. He told me that park people were scared by what was happening to Bears Ears and Grand Staircase–Escalante, but that Capitol Reef wasn't under any real threat. They just wanted to know if they were doing a good job communicating why it was made a national park.

Well, if you haven't figured it out yet, the Junior Ranger program did genuinely teach me a lot.

"Is it because of the Waterpocket Fold?" I asked, referring to a 100-mile wrinkle in the Earth's crust that is the defining geologic feature of Capitol Reef.

YES, BITCH. IT WAS.

"Yes," said the ranger, affectless.

I didn't particularly care about the Waterpocket Fold (I'm not a geologist) but Capitol Reef was so outrageously beautiful, its canyons and deserts and its fertile valley so surprising, that I was just thrilled it was protected. The reason didn't matter. It felt like a miracle either way.

AS I REJOINED the massive line to get my Junior Ranger badge, I pulled out my phone to partake in one of my favorite hobbies: obsessively trying to connect to Wi-Fi. I wanted to let Aunt Chris and Uncle John know I hadn't perished on the way to Capitol Reef, but if I wanted to get a message out of this park, I was going to have to tie a note to a raven and hope it knew where Cortez, Colorado was and understood the word "KOA." Equally concerning was that my plan to save a Google Maps route to the campground where I was sleeping that night had predictably failed. I knew how to find the general area from reading a map (flex), but to get to the exact campground I was going to need GPS at some point.

The man at the information desk flipped through my book, checking my answers and asking questions to test me, as the less laid-back rangers sometimes do. And then he threw something at me that hadn't been covered by the study materials. "What," he asked, "is the ultimate journey of a rock?"

I had no idea what he meant, but the question was hilarious and, maybe, perfect. People say "cellar door" is the most beautiful phrase in the English language, but it's only because no one has asked those people "What is the ultimate journey of a rock?"

"Uhh," I said, "the ocean?"

"Correct."

Maybe I *was* a geologist after all.

ON THE STATE highway out of Capitol Reef, I assumed my phone would connect to cell service as I drove into a town big enough to sustain a Subway and a Days Inn, but no such luck. It was the first time on my trip that my phone became, for an entire day, a worthless brick, if bricks could function as cameras and iPods but not as phones or internet browsers. And yet I couldn't stop playing with my brick. This, despite the fact that one of the great freedoms of nature is supposed to be that you get off your phone. It's the entire reason they invented nature in the first place. To quote Henry David Thoreau, "You're in the great outdoors; don't complain about the lack of Wi-Fi, you Millennial bitch!"

Seemingly everyone in the United States these days is trying to look at screens less; a new app or book to this end is released every week. I too want to look at screens less. A few years ago I deleted Facebook because I wished to live deliberately. But I have not done great at weaning myself off social media. When I visited Yellowstone in 2016, I had no cell service, and my mom literally thought I had died because I didn't tweet for twenty-four hours straight. I agree that I am squandering my one and only lifetime refreshing apps, but I can't stop refreshing apps, at least not until I see something that makes me feel bad enough to put my phone down. I have what scientists call bad brain.

On this trip I was doing an okay job of not knowing what Donald Trump was up to at every minute of every day; I was doing a less okay job of not looking at my phone twenty times an hour. Now, at last, I properly had no cell service, and I was experiencing it not as liberating but as annoying.

And while I totally agree that yes, I should not be looking at my devices so much, the society I was living in was structured around looking at my devices. My writing took place on my computer; the job I had just left had taken place on two different computers; many of the leisure options available to me took place on a screen of some kind. I didn't invent this arrangement; it was the culture. That the culture was so obsessed with making people feel bad about looking at their screens didn't seem like any kind of solution. If the idea was to allow people to live their actual lives, to *be here now*, as they say, an actual solution might be to provide more *here*'s. A solution might be to protect more public land across the country that people could actually visit and less land for corporations to drill on at a loss to the taxpayer. Just a thought!

7

Wedgie Test

BRYCE CANYON DOESN'T LOOK LIKE IT BELONGS ON planet Earth; it looks like a set created for a sci-fi movie with a massive budget and a production designer on psychedelics. This is because of the hoodoos, spires left standing from walls of rock that have otherwise been eroded. They're named "hoodoos" because they seem like the result of goblin magic. As the Paiute story goes, the hoodoos in Bryce are the petrified Legend People, who were turned to stone by Coyote for being bad (relatable). Hoodoos are deranged, and there are more of them in Bryce Canyon National Park than anywhere else in the world. In 2019 it was the twelfth most popular national park, with over 2.5 million visitors. Sixty percent of those came to the park between June and September. Smack dab among those, in mid-June, was me.

I pulled into the massive visitor center parking lot and found only one single, solitary space open, a parallel parking spot probably meant for an RV but also perfect for a Prius driven by a woman who has, on multiple occasions, had male strangers on the sidewalk offer to parallel park her car for her. (It might seem like this calls for righteous feminist indignation, but actually my parking was truly that bad.) I worried about leaving my iPad in the car in view of so many people, so, as an antitheft measure, I covered it with a copy of *Against Our Will: Men, Women, and Rape.* Inside I stood in the bloated line at the information desk for at least ten minutes before a ranger kindly handed me my Junior Ranger book and advised me to start hiking soon, so I could be off the trail before the afternoon thunderstorms hit.

Bryce is a long, thin park, with one main 18-mile road running through it. Most activity is found in the Bryce Amphitheater, home of the famous hoodoos, which is accessed along the first few miles of road. I decided to head to the farthest viewpoint in the amphitheater, Bryce Point, and from there begin my hike. I zoomed the Prius up to the trailhead, turned into the parking lot, and . . . there was not even one space available. I was trapped in a line of cars crawling through, waiting for a miracle to happen and someone to leave. But no miracle happened, and I started to fill with a mixture of parking-lot anxiety and the angry annoyance that comes from too many people having the same idea as you but fifteen minutes earlier. Despairing, I pulled out of the lot, drove down the narrow, winding park road until I found a place to make a U-turn, and headed back up for a second round of torture. This time God took pity on me, and a space was open. Exhaustively grateful for my good luck, I pulled in and resolved never to leave.

What is with all these people going to national parks?

The freedom to go smell a rock, to, as Whitman said, lean and loaf at your ease observing a spear of summer grass, is a cherished American pastime. People come to parks seeking what Thoreau called "absolute freedom and wildness, as contrasted with a freedom and culture merely civil." They come to nature to dip out of civilization, however temporarily. In fact, some of the most famous nature narratives in this country begin with the protagonist dramatically cutting ties to society—though, I have to say, if (like Chris McCandless) your conception of freedom involves physically destroying all your cash, you are a moron. What many guys don't know is that you are allowed to go on a hike without first burning your Social Security card.

There's something about nature that makes many of us feel more alive—maybe because by entering nature we make our lives marginally more difficult, less convenient, less mediated by technology. Maybe being outside is life itself, and everything else we do—working our jobs and living in the cities where those jobs are—is a sacrifice of the time we could be actually living, a sacrifice we make to pay our way in society. Karl Marx divided time into the realm of necessity and the realm of freedom, and nature is squarely in the second category. What makes our lives meaningful is that we eventually die; maybe what makes our time in nature meaningful is that eventually we have to go back to the office.

Being at Bryce didn't feel like being in the office, but it didn't feel quite as separate from society and therefore as rejuvenating as I would have hoped, because all of society appeared to be here as well and attempting to grab the same parking spot. I wished it was less crowded, not only for logistical reasons but also so I might have a better chance of seeing animals or soaking in some undisturbed vibes—but I knew that everyone else here wished the same thing, and all of us wanting it was doing nothing to help matters. I threw a PB&J in my bag and joined the waves of people walking toward the trailhead.

From the moment I hit the trail, the view was enough to make my brain short-circuit. There were more hoodoos than my eyes knew what to do with. And the colors! These were Kraft Mac & Cheese–ass colors, something you'd swear was made of processed chemicals if you weren't seeing it on the side of a canyon. For almost a full minute I was able to hike while thinking my deep thoughts about the similarities and differences between macaroni and rock formations, until I found my path blocked by a photo opportunity. A photogenic couple (hiss) was trying to take a selfie, and a man on the trail offered to take their photo for them. I waited patiently as he did, then tried to sneak by to get on with my life. Not so fast. "Do you want me to take *your* photo here?" he asked.

"I'm good, thanks."

But he insisted. "I've learned taking photos of strangers on the trail is good karma." So I posed and did that thing I'm socialized to do as a woman: I started asking the man questions about himself. He was a business professor at a college near where I grew up and was spending the summer visiting national parks. He told me that he was making a documentary about it and was hoping to sell the documentary to Netflix for ten thousand dollars.

"Is there an angle, or is it just like, 'Here's my trip?'" I asked.

"There's no angle." But he—Professor Josh, let's call him—explained that Netflix was chock-full of "here's my trip" documentaries, that he watched them to fall asleep. "Although most involve a cute girl," he admitted. "If I had a wife or a girlfriend with me, it would probably make my doc more sellable." He stopped dead in his tracks, pulled out a selfie stick, and started filming a confessional video.

We hiked on together for miles, talking about our lives, our trips, and how our friends predicted we would die over the summer. "Everyone told me I'd be eaten by a bear," Josh said. "No one told me I'd be murdered." We discussed the works of Bill Bryson and whether or not men can talk about their emotions (they find it extremely difficult, Josh said). He told me about the friends he'd made at Capitol Reef and then serendipitously run into again at Bryce.

Eventually we reached the end of the trail and hopped on a shuttle that looped around the various parking lots. Josh's stop was first, and he offered to drive me back to my car so I could skip all the stops in between. A stranger was inviting me to get in his vehicle and be taken to a second location, after very recently saying "murdered" out loud to me. I responded instinctively: "Sure! Thanks!" But then I realized he was parked across from the visitor center, so I decided to poke around there first to work on my Junior Ranger booklet.

After thirty minutes spent reading every informational placard inside, then a shuttle ride back to my car, and then a leisurely drive up and down the main park road spent mostly looking for elusive open parking spots, I was still not done with the booklet. With multiple activities left to complete, I set off on a loop trail. This shorter, very accessible hike was packed with visitors. A few seconds in I passed a woman vaping on the side of the trail; fifteen minutes later I walked by a hot lady perched sexily on a fragile hoodoo as her boyfriend took her photo; after that I heard a teen boy near me say, in a tone making clear that he was trying to stir shit, "So, Mom, what do you think of ecofascism?"

The final activity I had any chance of completing tasked me with interviewing "someone visiting the park today" about what personal significance national parks have to them. It's easy to imagine what the creators of the *Bryce Canyon National Park Junior Ranger Field Book* had in mind when coming up with this activity: a heartwarming scene of a small child interviewing their parent, who would speak in gentle, loving tones about the importance of nature and the environment. Unfortunately I was not a small child but a small adult. I didn't have anyone to interview, and I was already far above my daily quota of making meaningful conversation with strangers. (This is a national park, not Hinge; I can't explain more than once a day where I grew up and what I do for a living.) So I fudged the "visiting the park today" element and called someone duty bound to pick up the phone, due to the sheer number of times he has called me solely because he was driving and "was bored": my dad.

I read to him from the interview script: what was the first national park he ever visited and when? He told me about driving through the Badlands in 1967, when he was eight years old. He remembered the park as being in the middle of nowhere and "very hilly," and he remembered thinking that "cowboys probably rode there."

"Okay. 'Of all the national parks you've visited, which was the most special to you' and why?"

"Glacier, because we had our family vacation there. Yosemite, for scenery."

That he had an answer ready to go—that he had options—spoke to how popular trips to the national parks were, not only the way I and other solo travelers were doing it, but in different ways from different generations, too. And how lucky

I was that that was true! Those trips were (in a phrase I like to use with people when they forget literally anything that they have ever done with me) "my cherished memories!"

I asked my dad what national parks meant to him, and he thought for a few seconds. "They're America's way of giving back to its citizens."

I DROVE BACK to the visitor center thinking about Professor Josh filming confessional videos for his travel documentary, about the woman posing alluringly and precariously on a hoodoo for content, and about my trip.

For years I had fantasized about driving around the country, about doing something fun for once in my sad life, and now that I was doing it and that other people were DMing me saying my trip was significant and exciting, it did feel that way. It no longer felt like a long time since I had been free, as I had so often felt at my job, while listening to a song about how it had been a long time since the singer was free. But was what I was doing actually "free" in any meaningful way? To go on vacation? When droves of other people are basically going on the exact same vacation as you? I was beginning to suspect that our culture values stories of people going rogue in well-trodden ways that don't really challenge authority.

I might have felt like the Great American Road Trip was some pinnacle of the quest for authenticity, but if thousands or millions had the same idea, how authentic could that quest be? Why had I quit the best day job I could ever imagine to spend my time circling parking lots? At Bryce I felt less like I was doing something interesting or important or in any way original and more like I was doing something the system had funneled me into. As I waited in another line to turn in my

Junior Ranger book, I couldn't imagine a way to live authentically and close to nature without dramatically changing my entire life. And I had already dramatically changed my entire life just to get in this line.

It would only get worse: the park I was heading to the next morning was the most visited of any on my itinerary and the trendiest park in America: Zion National Park.

AS I DROVE closer to Zion, the terrain around me got more mountainous, the trees taller. By the time I reached the park boundary, mesas surrounded me on each side. The road twisted and turned through the landscape until traffic slowed as we approached a mountainside: this was the Zion–Mount Carmel Tunnel. Built in the late 1920s for the exact purpose I was using it—to allow people to drive from Bryce Canyon to Zion—the tunnel is over a mile long and has gallery windows blasted out along the way to let light in. You aren't allowed to stop and take photos in these open gallery windows, both because it's extremely stupid to park your car in a tunnel and because in 1958 a woman standing in a window for a photo op fell to her death into the canyon below. Dying for a photo: *not* invented by Millennials, actually!

I emerged from the tunnel into Zion Canyon's towering red cliffs and valley floor spotted with green. It was impossible to focus on the road. My eyes popped out of my head and my tongue rolled out of my mouth and I drove that way, like a horny cartoon character, until I reached the visitor center.

I parked my car, left my possessions to melt in the relentless sun, and joined a long line for the chance to pester a park ranger. When my turn came, I asked about hiking the Narrows, which everyone on my phone and also my own real-life father had recommended. Sadly, the answer was "You can't": the Narrows were closed due to high water levels and risk of flooding. (As of 2017, when *Death in Zion National Park* was published, fifteen people had died in the Narrows when caught in flash floods. These floods can send a twelve-foot-high wall of water through the slot canyon, washing away hikers who have no way of scaling the smooth canyon walls to escape. The lucky few who survived flash floods in the Narrows were trapped on high ledges for days before rescuers found them, and I simply did not have time for that: by the time I was saved, my entire Prius would have presumably melted.)

Next I asked the ranger about camping—back in Denver I'd managed to grab a Zion campsite reservation for the following evening, but the day I arrived at the park was fully booked. "There's some BLM land with dispersed camping about forty-five minutes from here," he told me, giving me directions. Overstaying my welcome, I asked for Angels Landing tips, a Junior Ranger book, and some recommendations of the ranger's favorite trails. Then I set off to do the exact hikes he told me to.

IT'S HARD TO convey just how many people there were at Zion, except by saying that it was during my first hike there that I invented the Wedgie Test, a metric I have used countless times since. The test works like this: first, I get a wedgie. Second, I look around to see if there is another person either walking toward me or walking behind me. If there is, then I am unable to pick my wedgie, and the trail has thus failed the Wedgie Test. (What does *not* require any follow-up questions is why I was so frequently getting wedgies.) At no point during my time in Zion did any trail pass the Wedgie Test for even one moment. I was in some of the most breathtaking nature in the country, and I was never alone in it.

This does not mean the park wasn't beautiful. The canyons flipped my brain upside down; prickly pear cactus bloomed; the Virgin River flowed through the valley; a mule deer undeterred by the heavy foot traffic chomped leaves beside the trail. I picked up any trash I saw, an activity I found gross, but did because it was a requirement for my coveted badge. After hiking multiple trails to different waterfalls, I made my way to a ranger program, another requirement. This talk, the shortest one that best fit my schedule, would be on . . . bighorn sheep. Sure! Why not?

The entire audience was young children trying to get their badges, and those children's parents. The bighorn sheep fans, aka the bighorn sheeple, aka the hornies, were apparently not in town. As we sat waiting for the program to begin, the ranger, a young woman named Hayley, told us about working at the park. "A lot of visitors tell us they feel like it's Disneyland, in terms of crowding," she said. In the past five years Zion had become overrun to an extent that was endangering the plants, animals, and petroglyphs—and according to Ranger Hayley this exponential increase in visitors was due entirely to social media.

By then it was time for the program to begin, and Ranger Hayley told us all about bighorn sheep. Both the males and the females can have horns, it turns out. Feminism has gone too far!

When I got back to the visitor center, it was the end of the day and there was mercifully no line. As I approached the desks, two male rangers finished helping people at the same time, and both gestured for me to approach.

"You have to pick one of us," said the ranger on the left, flirtily.

"Which one of you is better?" I responded. (I am good at flirting.)

"I'm taller," said the one on the right.

"It's true," the other ranger conceded. "He is taller." The one on the right stood up, towering over everyone and everything. I had no choice! It's science! I walked to Tall Ranger and told him, unable to make it into a flirt despite my great powers, that I had completed my children's booklet and was here to claim my baby badge.

He flipped through my book until he got to a page that asks the prospective Junior Ranger to explain why it's important to protect petroglyphs and pictographs. It's kind of a heavy question for a child to answer! Three lines were provided for a response, and presumably the book's authors were looking for six-year-olds to respond along the lines of "Hurting the rock art is rude," but I was a twenty-eight-year-old woman who felt like I should probably do a bit better. So I had written a jeremiad about settler colonialism and the US government's history of white supremacy, about how the least we can do is not deface the cultural artifacts of the people this land was violently stolen from. Tall Ranger pointed at my screed. "Can you explain this?"

I stumbled on my words, trying to figure out how to stand firm in what I believe in without getting into a public argument with a conventionally hot white dude, a genre of person that, in my experience, does not always have my favorite politics in the world. But Tall Ranger quickly stopped me to say he agreed. This was something he had been thinking about too. Before coming to Zion he had worked at Klondike Gold Rush

National Park in Alaska, a park which my friend Rebecca once described to me as "an entire national park dedicated to genocidal white idiots who died in the snow." Tall Ranger found the messaging there about Indigenous people and the violence perpetrated against them incomplete and uncomfortable. "And at Zion we don't even tell visitors where the petroglyphs are anymore, because people weren't respecting them."

Tall Ranger and I chatted about his job and the NPS until I realized no one else was around and lights were being shut off: the information desk was literally closed. I asked for his email so we could continue the conversation and sheepishly left. For all the time I had spent in parks, all the people I had seen and all the information desks where I had stood across from a Park Service employee, this was the first time I had talked to someone at all critical of the NPS, who saw a lot of ways it could be better, while also clearly loving the parks. It was just one ten-minute conversation, but it was invigorating.

THOUGH I HAD originally planned to free-camp for most of my road trip, this would be my first night doing so. The dispersed camping suggested by the ranger from that morning was primitive: just rutted dirt roads with pullouts in the desert, not a water spigot or a trash can or even a pit toilet to be found. When I found an unoccupied campsite, I opened the car door to scope out a spot for my tent, noticed that the ground was crawling with beetles, and closed the door. *Sleeping in the car it is!*

Though I would have to wake before four a.m. to make it back to Zion for the first shuttle to Angels Landing, the sun had not yet set and I wasn't ready to fall asleep in the sweltering car. My energizing conversation with the tall, thoughtful, intense ranger had underlined for me the reality that on this trip I was sometimes with friends or, every once in a while, having a meaningful conversation with a complete stranger, but most of the time I was (even if surrounded by masses of other visitors) completely alone. Maybe as a concept, my solo trip was feminist and strong and free. As an experience, sitting alone in a hot car in the Utah desert, surrounded by bugs, with no Wi-Fi—it felt lonely, and slightly boring.

But while I had no internet, I somehow did have service bars, and so I did the only thing I could do at that point on my phone, other than set alarms or divide random numbers by other random numbers: I used it as a phone, to call my entire family. I told them about the previous day, when I had agreed to get into Professor Josh's car so that I could save a few minutes versus taking the shuttle.

"*That's* how you're going to get murdered," my mom, stepdad, and little brother said to me in unison.

"A car is a serious trap," said TB.

I told them about Tall, Slightly Disgruntled Ranger, and TB muttered under his breath, "He's probably a serial killer" at the exact same moment I noted that for the entire time Tall Ranger and I talked, he never once blinked. Tom whooped. "Did I call it or what!"

AT FOUR-FIFTEEN THE next "morning" (still night in my opinion, but okay) I drove forty-five minutes back to Zion in the pitch black to catch the first shuttle to Angels Landing. It was so dark I could see every star in the universe, but so early that I didn't want to. The mood on the six a.m. shuttle was "begrudgingly conscious," the fluorescent lights compassionately off and the passengers silent, in tacit agreement that it was too early in the morning for small talk. Then the lights were turned on. The woman next to me and I both recoiled viscerally, like vampires stepping into the sun. We recognized each other as kindred spirits and fell into chatting. Her name was Wren, and she was a yoga instructor and art teacher who lived on the East Coast with her boyfriend, Dev, a doctor, who was sitting across the shuttle aisle looking about as happy to be awake as Wren and I were. She had a barbed sense of humor; I immediately liked her.

The shuttle spat us out at a place called the Grotto, and as we crossed the street Wren introduced me to Dev. Together we walked to the trailhead, and I realized with horror that we were about to hike together. This may be a normal thing for "physically fit" people, but, while I consider myself in good enough shape for my lifestyle, my lifestyle does not involve regularly doing a 5.4 mile hike with 1,488 feet elevation gain. To make matters worse, the trail to Angels Landing starts out immediately going uphill in a series of switchbacks, which are then followed by a series of *worse* switchbacks. For ten or fifteen minutes I was able to keep up with my new, fit, healthy, hot friends while interspersing our conversation with heavier and heavier breathing, but eventually I had to admit defeat. "You guys go ahead," I told them. "I need to slather myself with sunscreen anyway."

I did, then began my slow ascent while thinking about the trail and all it signified. It was the trail that everyone I knew who had visited Zion told me I *had* to do; it was also, as Tall Ranger later pointed out to me via email, the encapsulation of everything that is wrong with Zion. It's a pretty strenuous trail, and not the best suited for everyone, but it's the one that everyone attempts anyway. It's extremely popular and crowded, and for that reason it's dangerous: more than a dozen people have died hiking it. I knew that waking up pre-dawn to be the first on the trail wouldn't mean the trail would pass the Wedgie Test. It just meant that my hike would be a little less likely to end in me falling off the side of a cliff.

By this point I had finished the first set of switchbacks and made it to the most unremittingly difficult part of the trail, a series of steep, short switchbacks called Walter's Wiggles. (These were much more cardiovascularly taxing and much less mischievous than Blythe's Wiggles, which is what I call it when I have two glasses of prosecco.) I stopped to catch my breath probably eighteen times on my way up the Wiggles, but when I got to the top I had basically climbed as high as the trail would take me. I had reached Scout Lookout, a place where the trail widens. I spotted Wren and Dev resting there, and together we set off on the final bit leading to Angels Land-ing. This section is where the majority of deadly accidents oc-cur. At one point, the sandstone fin you're hiking on is less than six feet wide, with thousand-foot drops on each side. It was eight a.m. and we were having a near-death experience: these are the thrills America's national parks have to offer.

And then we were there. The millions of people who told me about it were not wrong: Angels Landing was stunning. We stood above all of Zion Canyon, jutting out with 270 de-grees of views, as the sun cast dramatic shadows on the red, brown, and pink cliff walls and on the Virgin River cutting through the valley floor. The name "Angels Landing" comes from a remark allegedly made by a hiker in 1916, who said that only an angel could land there. (Though you would think it would be called Angel's Landing—a landing for an angel—and not Angels Landing, a thing happening in the continual present. If angels were in fact trying to land there that morning, I can tell you: there was no space for them.)

On our way up to Angels Landing, as the first shuttle load of people to ascend that morning, traffic on the sandstone fin had been one way. But as Wren, Dev, and I descended, we ran into scores of people anxious to use the narrow trail to make their way in the opposite direction. What had felt exciting but doable on the way up now made us nervous. After a particularly stressful incident when a kid ran past, forcing all of us within inches of the cliff edge, we passed Professor Josh on the sandstone fin. "Hi!" I said, excited.

"Hi," he said, stressed out about the sheer drops to his left and right.

Not only was everyone doing the same general vacation, it seemed: everyone was doing the exact same vacation, the same parks in the same order. I remembered how thrilled Professor Josh had been to run into friends he'd made at Capitol Reef a couple days later in a park a little bit further west; now here was our own identical reunion. My happiness at "coincidentally" seeing him in such an "unlikely" place—over a thousand feet in the air—was only slightly dampened by the realization of how much of a cliché I was.

After my morning at Angels Landing, I swung by Walmart to buy ingredients for Wren, who had invited me over to her and Dev's campsite for dinner. In the pasta aisle I found a man staring intently at a can of sauce. He was wearing baggy shorts, his blond dreads were pulled back by a rubber band, and on his feet were an absolutely trashed pair of Crocs. *Oh my God.*

"Excuse me," I said to him. "Were you at Capitol Reef National Park like three days ago? I think I was standing behind you in line."

"That was totally me!" he said. We were both now at the stage of our identical vacation where we talked to unshowered strangers, no questions asked. He told me that he and his brother were on a grand cross-country road trip to national parks. From Zion they were heading to the Grand Canyon, which cheered me to hear, because I wasn't, and could feel slightly original for one more day.

Crocs Guy and Professor Josh and Wren and Dev and I, and all the other people on similar trips, wanted to use our vacation time going somewhere that was widely known to be beautiful. So instead of chancing it by visiting a random corner of public land, we went to a national park, a Congressionally designated beautiful area. (Though, why we trust Congress on this when I wouldn't trust Congress to tell me the time of day, I'm not exactly sure.) We tourists wanted to spend our few days at these parks wisely, so we did the hikes and the activities we had seen other people post about doing. And then we would likely post about it ourselves, inspiring yet more people to do the exact same thing.

WHILE WREN PREPPED chili, we talked about life and nature and art as I stood too close to the fire and watched an ember burn a hole through my shirt. I taught Dev and Wren about cultural touchstones they had somehow never heard of, like Slenderman (icon) and the Babadook (gay icon), and handed Wren a green pepper, a wooden spoon, and a six-pack I bought at Walmart. The pepper and spoon she placed on the picnic table, but the beer needed to be kept cool. "Follow me," Wren said, and we walked from the site to the nearby Virgin River. Wren took out a few beers and twisted them down into the sand in the shallows of the frigid water. "That should do it," she said. *This is the real America*, I thought. *This is what our Founders envisioned.* Chilling beers in the ice-cold waters of a river that carved one of the most gorgeous canyons in the country: I could barely stand how immaculate the vibes were.

In the years before my trip, when I formed the idea of driving around the country and daydreamed about hiking in national parks and thought about what it all meant, I had ideas of things I might get out of such a trip. None of those were "new ways to look cool while storing alcohol," and neither were any of them "acquiring homies." Put another way: I wasn't here to make friends. But out in the real world, missing my life back home and surrounded by funny, open, kind people who also cared about the parks, it turns out that maybe I *was*. Lucky me.

8

Where Do They Put the Bison at Night?

THIRTY-FIVE NATIONAL PARKS AND MONUMENTS AL-
ready existed by the time somebody had the idea that
there should be an agency to wrangle these darn places. In
1916 Congress passed the Organic Act, creating the National
Park Service. The fundamental purpose of the NPS, the Organic Act states, is "to conserve the scenery and the natural
and historic objects and the wild life therein and to provide
for the enjoyment of the same in such manner and by such
means as will leave them unimpaired for the enjoyment of
future generations." Conserving the scenery *and* providing
for enjoyment of the same—no problem! It's like being in the
room with Hannah Montana and Miley at the same time—I
see no conflict here!

The battle between developing the parks for tourists and
preserving them for plants, animals, the good of the ecosystem, and the existential future of humanity, was not much of

a battle at all: from the jump, the men in charge favored tourism. As Mark David Spence notes in his book *Dispossessing the Wilderness*, just two years into the NPS's existence, Secretary of the Interior Franklin Lane wrote a letter to Stephen Mather, the first director of the National Park Service, encouraging Mather "to develop the parks as a new 'national playground system' that should be made accessible to the public 'by any means practicable.'" Those means, Spence writes, included "the construction of roads, trails, and buildings, and active cooperation with tourist bureaus, chambers of commerce, and automobile associations." They also included cutting down trees that blocked any sick views and killing any bears or wolves or mountain lions that might reduce the population of less threatening, more tourist-friendly animals like mountain sheep or deer (the biggest change I see between a hundred years ago and today is that back then, apparently, deer were still thrilling).

In 1956, forty years after its establishment, the National Park Service checked back in with itself and its mandate. How was it doing at the conservation and also the providing for enjoyment? The answer was a resounding "We need *more* development, actually! Give us all the roads! We stan a parking lot!" Cars were a thing now, the Interstate Highway System had been created, more Americans had disposable income, and as a result park visitor numbers had more than tripled since the beginning of World War II.

To better equip the parks to handle huge numbers of tourists, the head of the National Park Service proposed a ten-year development project called Mission 66. The project was approved by Congress, and the NPS got to work updating campgrounds, utilities, and roads, and creating a new type of amenity altogether: the park visitor center. One of the visitor centers built as part of Mission 66 was in the park I was driving to now: Great Basin National Park, in remote Nevada. As wary as I am of development, I am obviously a big fan of visitor centers and was eager to be inside yet another one.

WELCOME TO NEVADA, a highway sign declared, with another sign under it which reminded, PACIFIC TIME ZONE. The Great Basin Visitor Center was located outside the park, in a town that consisted of not much more than a handful of houses: Baker, Nevada, population 68. (The entire population of Baker could come to one of my parties, and I would still be like, *why is there no one at this party?*) Inside the drearily lit visitor center were a desk, a rack of cotton T-shirts, a spinny metal thing with postcards for sale, and that was basically it. It was, by far, the most dismal visitor center I had yet encountered. The ranger sitting at the desk, valiantly maintaining his will to live despite having to work here all day, handed me a Junior Ranger book and told me I'd have to attend a ranger program to get my badge. "The easiest option is probably going on a cave tour."

Cave??? I had no idea that Great Basin National Park entailed a cave. I had no idea what Great Basin entailed at all, except maybe . . . a big ole basin, of some kind?

As it turns out, the eponymous basin refers to a watershed. While most of the precipitation that falls in North America flows to either the Atlantic Ocean, the Pacific Ocean, or the Arctic Ocean—Canada, ever heard of her?—there is a large area of the American West that is surrounded by mountains to such an extent that water cannot find a way to an ocean. Instead, this water drains into the Great Salt Lake or simply sinks into the desert, having completely abandoned all its coastal ambitions (it's giving: me in my thirties). This area, which stretches over parts of Nevada, Utah, Idaho, Wyoming, Oregon, California, and Baja California, is called the Great Basin.

But circling back, yes, this specific area of the Great Basin had caves, too—forty of them, in fact, though only one was open for tours—and they were the original reason the land was protected. I got back into my car and drove into the park, through the desert but toward snow-capped mountains, at the foot of which sat the Lehman Cave Visitor Center, built in 1963.

Inside, a ranger—Ranger Green, according to his nametag—handed me my tour ticket. "Do you have anything on you that's recently been in another cave?" He was asking, I knew, because of white-nose syndrome, a fatal bat disease that was slowly spreading around the globe. ("Not relatable"—me in 2019.)

"Uh . . ." I stammered. He clearly was expecting a perfunctory *no*. "Other than myself?"

He looked at me like I was crazy. "Yeah, unless you haven't showered?"

"No, no, I've showered. Um. Also my phone? Is that okay?" It wasn't. He handed me a Clorox wipe to clean my phone. "And my shirt?"

"You . . . haven't changed clothes since the last time you were in a cave?"

"No, I have, I just haven't done laundry."

"We would appreciate it if you would put on a different shirt before you enter the cave."

I went out to the Prius and dug a different shirt out of my duffel bag. For a moment I tried to figure out how to change without anyone seeing my perfect body but then realized that, in stark contrast to the massively overcrowded park where I had woken up that morning, Great Basin was basically empty. I changed shirts in the parking lot.

IT DOESN'T MATTER how many caves you see on vacation: they never get old. Lehman Cave, named for—this will shock you—some random white guy from the 1800s, is more than two miles long, making it the longest cave in Nevada. Our very serious and very twenty-two-year-old ranger tour guide led us into the cave through a man-made tunnel that seemed exactly like tunnel that would lead us into a secret crypt under the Vatican in a Dan Brown novel. We walked under the cave's natural entrance, observing a moment of silence both to honor the cave's importance to the Indigenous cultures that had lived nearby for thousands of years, and to avoid waking up the bats who had only recently rediscovered the entrance, which had been at least partially artificially sealed for over a century. (This was just one of many ways tourism had massively messed up the cave; much of the Park Service's work now was to repair damage done by earlier tourists and to mitigate the lesser damage we, the current tourists, were unavoidably also doing.)

BACK ABOVEGROUND, I wound my way up the park's Wheeler Peak Scenic Drive. That I had woken up that morning at a national park so hot that all my belongings melted, and was now within miles of snow, delighted me. As I gained elevation, the sagebrush around me turned to juniper, then fir, then aspen—which at the time I thought was birch but was, in fact, not birch, though birch should possibly sue it for copyright infringement.

Added to the list of things I didn't know about Great Basin

National Park when I showed up there was that the park has a number of bristlecone pines. These trees look squat and warped ("squat and warped," my Hinge bio); they grow so slowly that some years they don't even add a new ring to their trunk. But this also means that the wood of the Great Basin bristlecone pine is very dense, which protects the tree from fungi, insects, and rot. And so bristlecone pines live, in their warped and weird-looking way, for thousands of years: they're the oldest nonclonal species on planet Earth. There's a bristlecone in California that is, as I write, 5,075 years old. This tree is roughly as old as the concept of writing. This tree was roughly as old as I looked after driving directly into the sun for two weeks.

I drove the Prius as far as I could up Wheeler Peak until the road was closed due to snow, stepped out of the car on a June day and, looking out over Nevada, breathed in the winter air.

ON MY WAY down the mountain I stopped into the Lehman Cave Visitor Center one last time to get my Junior Ranger badge. The same ranger who'd told me to change my dirty-ass shirt a few hours earlier now flipped through my book, mocking my stick-figure drawings and my illegible handwriting. One of the activities was, in honor of the bristlecone pines, about determining the age of a tree. It presented a drawing of a wood slab and asked if I could find a ring from the year I was born. "No," I had written, "I'm old as hell."

"How old are you?" Ranger Green asked.

"Twenty-eight."

"Ah. That's the peak," he said, flatly. "It's all downhill from there."

"Oh, come on, I don't think that's true."

"No, I'm thirty," he responded. "I know."

I slept that night in Salt Lake City, and began a cursed portion of my trip called The Loop. I arrived in SLC on a Thursday night; I needed to be in Denver on Tuesday to pick up my friend Emmy, who was joining me for about a week. So instead of heading north to Glacier, the next national park on my Junior Ranger list, I'd be heading back to Denver and cutting through Utah again. But first I was stopping at Yellowstone to visit my childhood friend Greg. We'd traveled to the park together a few years earlier, and he loved it so much that he had been working there every summer since. I left Salt Lake at 7:30 in the morning so that Greg and I could set out back-country camping that afternoon, by far the most rugged thing I would do on my trip, or, come to think of it, my entire life thus far.

I hit park-bound traffic outside the entrance in West Yellowstone, Montana. I inched past motels and gift shops and a combination gas station/Subway before finally entering the park, where I inched through a forest along the Madison River. "Forest?" you might think. "I thought Yellowstone was all geysers!" And it's true—Yellowstone *is* a lot of geysers. In fact, with five hundred of them, Yellowstone National Park has more than half the geysers in the entire world. The park contains more than ten thousand hydrothermal features like hot springs and boiling pools, all of which exist because Yellowstone sits on top of an active volcano, which I will never mention again in this book because thinking about it for even one minute gives me clinical anxiety, and I do not find it constructive!

But Yellowstone is a huge park, larger than Rhode Island and Delaware combined. My drive through it, roughly forty miles from the entrance to the Canyon Visitor Center, took me mostly through forest, which covers 80 percent of the park, occasionally opening up into grassland. In the distance, I could see mountains. Between the landscape and, again, *more than half the geysers on our entire freaking planet*, I could see why Yellowstone was made the first national park, all the way back in 1872.

I had time to look around, as traffic was moving more and more slowly. The arrival time on my GPS had been gradually ticking up all morning, and now it jumped by an entire hour. My heart rate spiked as the cars in front of me stopped moving altogether. I threw my car in park. I was stuck in a buffalo jam.

A buffalo jam is, as you may have guessed, *not* when a bunch of buffalo rip some hot licks on the saxophone but instead a traffic jam caused by buffalo. There are two versions of this. The first is when, like the feral horse at Theodore Roosevelt National Park, buffalo decide to walk in the road as if they are a car. While this is annoying for the drivers stuck behind them, it's also kind of funny and charming and at the end of the day it's unavoidable, because much like how corporations are legally people, buffalo are legally cars. The second version of a buffalo jam is when one idiot decides to park in the road to take a photo of a buffalo and it causes me to sit in standstill traffic for, and I wish I was exaggerating, *three hours*.

There was nothing to do but unfold my legs on the dash, dip some Tostitos in hummus, read an entire profile of Elizabeth Warren in *The New Yorker*, and stew. All these thousands of people were idling in the road, spewing exhaust into the atmosphere, because someone just *had* to take a photo of this specific bison. As happened far too often while I was behind the wheel of a three-thousand-pound vehicle: I was pissed. This is how disconnected people are from nature, I thought:

they travel across the world and create a massive traffic jam to get a photo of an animal that, as they will soon learn, can be seen in huge numbers all over the park.

The thing about nature in America is that so often so much of it is squeezed into one space that it goes from unthinkably rare and special to totally overdone within the space of an hour. The first time you see a bison, you think it's majestic. You take a million photos, whispering "Who is she . . . ?" Then, in the next fifteen minutes, you see approximately five hundred more bison. By the end of the day you have seen sixteen million bison. "I get it, a bison," you say, a bison stepping on your head because you've gotten too close to it for a selfie.

This traffic jam spoke to the "provide for enjoyment" versus "preserve nature" paradox. The road through Yellowstone had allowed all of us to see bison, maybe for the first time in our lives; it had also allowed us to cut through pristine ecosystems, to sit idling on pavement doing little except turning fossil fuels into car exhaust. The mere existence of a road does more damage to an ecosystem than you might think: a one-lane, unpaved road will divert rainfall, leading to heavier runoff and erosion. Roads endanger animals, in very visible ways when they end up dead on the shoulder and in less visible ways when their habitat becomes fragmented. (Many animals are rightly scared of roads and some species will never cross them, unlike my mom, who loves to declare, "I grew up jaywalking!") Most insidiously, roads encourage more development: they serve as a foot in the door toward no longer regarding a natural area as "pristine."

The National Park Service's commitment to making parks appealing to visitors was why Yellowstone had gift stores selling cheap shirts and mouse pads and "Advice from a Geyser" signs (VENT WHEN YOU NEED TO) and other future trash. Until the past few decades it meant that park officials killed predator mammals but at the same time maintained open-pit dump sites with nearby bleachers to attract bears, so that tourists could photograph the bears that did remain. Having Bears Eat Literal Garbage: America's Best Idea.

The Park Service does prevent the absolute worst-case tourism scenario: Niagara Falls, the world's tackiest waterfall. Long before Yellowstone became the first national park, Niagara Falls was known as a tourist destination, and private interests bought the land with the best views and access points. Instead of the falls being preserved as a national marvel, they were essentially privatized as developers built stores and restaurants along the rim. I only know this secondhand because when my family went on vacation to Niagara Falls, I said, "It's gonna be a no from me, dawg." (I said it was because I couldn't get the time off from my job slinging bras at Victoria's Secret, but really it was because I have a terminal case of snob's disease.) In Yellowstone, thank God, you don't have to look at a McDonald's sign while seeing Old Faithful erupt; instead, the McDonald's is just outside the park boundary. But the parks still encourage millions of people to visit every year. And among those millions, adding to the car exhaust and the need for roads and parking spots and trash cans, was little old me. Was I doing something morally indefensible by adding my body to the mob of visitors?

In a very real sense, the parks need the mass tourism they attract. The revenue from entrance fees, recreation fees, and fees paid by the concessionaires who sell food and souvenirs, amounts to a healthy portion of the parks' operating budget. And this budget is woefully inadequate: as of 2021, the park system had $18 billion in deferred maintenance. Though increased tourism means increased revenue from visitor fees, it also means increased maintenance and increased damage to ecosystems.

Crucially, it wasn't like Yellowstone or any of the parks were protected solely to preserve the wilderness, with tourism thrown into the mix late in the game as a way to fund the preservation projects. Often these places were protected for the express purpose of becoming tourist destinations. The 1872 establishment of Yellowstone National Park had a lot to do with the fact that in the second half of the 1800s, as the Industrial Revolution ripped through American society, a new urban middle class emerged with both leisure time and disposable income. All they needed was a place to spend both. But before Yellowstone could be protected as a tourist destination, its proponents had to make clear that it wasn't useful for any other economic purpose. A report by Congress during the approval process for Yellowstone notes that the place was not amenable to agriculture, was too cold for livestock, and seemed unlikely to contain any precious minerals available for mining. Thus, protecting the sublime landscape wouldn't cost the nation anything.

The fact that revenue from tourism is at the center of so much of the discussion of preservation in America cheapens my experience of going to nature. There is more worth to a wilderness than as a site for recreation. Animals and plants have a right to exist that is separate from their direct economic benefit to humans, separate even from the pleasure they can provide to a human who travels long distances to look at them. I think most people genuinely agree that bears and bison and trees and even geysers have value outside capitalist metrics.

But I also think most people feel uncomfortable expressing this, because it makes them sound like snowflake cucks who aren't living in the real world.

But if capitalism is currently synonymous with the "real world," it's not because capitalism is the only system that could ever exist. It's the system we have because we made the choice to allow a select few to become immorally rich at the cost of most of the world's people, and animals, and ecosystems. We can make the choice to have a different system. Using the logic of capitalism to argue for small concessions against the worst impulses of capitalism may sometimes work, but conceding to the system cuts us off from the better parts of our soul. But this is just the kind of stuff you think about when you're in traffic for three hours for no reason!!!

BY THE TIME I found Greg outside the Canyon Village General Store, I was hours late. We wouldn't be able to go back-country camping after all. Greg was kind about it, but I was massively bummed and even more massively annoyed that I wouldn't escape the capitalism-forward parts of Yellowstone. "Everyone in this park needs to be arrested," I told Greg.

"Let's go hiking," he countered. Greg lent me a coat and took me on a quick tour of the Employees Only areas of Canyon Village.

What a casual visitor may not realize is that the vast majority of people employed at a national park, especially at a very popular park like Yellowstone, are employed not by the National Park Service but by the company that runs the restaurants and gift stores. At the time I visited, Yellowstone concessioners employed 3,200 people, whereas the National Park Service employed fewer than four hundred. The largest national park concessioner, Xanterra, is controlled by Philip Anschutz, a billionaire whose father was an oil tycoon. Strolling around the concessioner employee dorms, talking to people who shall for legal reasons remain nameless (Greg said, for legal reasons, nothing), I heard it alleged that Xanterra's working conditions are exploitative, that the pay is low, and that the employees refer to the company as "Xanterrible" or "Xanterrorists." (I was later reminded of this when I learned that one-sixth of all known suicides that have happened at Yosemite National Park were by employees of the park's various concessioners. No employees of the National Park System have committed suicide at Yosemite.)

But as shitty as Xanterrible was, working at Yellowstone could still be magical. Greg spent his weekends backcountry camping and his evenings soaking in a hot spring that happened to be the perfect bathing temperature, referred to as the Employee Hot Tub. "One time we were in there drinking Bud Light and listening to Lynyrd Skynyrd when a bald eagle flew by," he told me. This may not be John Muir's vision of America, but it seemed to me the kind of thing that made it worth moving across the country and having to deal with tourists asking you, as one asked Greg, "where they put the bison at night."

Greg and I drove to a trail, which took us along the rim of the Grand Canyon of the Yellowstone. Nobody talks about the Grand Canyon of the Yellowstone! This is probably because the country already has a Grand Canyon which, to be fair, absolutely slaps, and also because Yellowstone is thought of as a place with geysers which, again, rightly so. But Yellowstone also happens to have a river, the Yellowstone, which over the past 160,000 or so years cut its own canyon, the Grand Canyon of the Yellowstone, which would probably warrant its own national park even if it didn't happen to be surrounded by superheated stinky water. The canyon has two major waterfalls, creatively named the Upper and Lower Falls, the second of which drops 308 feet. Ospreys fly above the canyon, roosting on rock spires. We walked along the edge and I followed Greg's lead. It was, after all, his home.

9

Be Respectful for Fuck's Sake

FOR THE FIRST TIME ON MY ROAD TRIP I WAS IN THE PASsenger's seat, and it was divine. I could eat the second half of a massive breakfast burrito and not have to concurrently operate heavy machinery! I could read my little Simone de Beauvoir travelogue and still make forward progress! I could put my beautiful gams up on the dashboard to soak in the carcinogenic sun. This was living. I had picked up Emmy at the Denver airport the preceding afternoon for a vacation within a vacation. For the next handful of days we'd be hanging out with some friends in one location: Cisco, Utah, our friend Eileen's ghost town.

I can't say I'm some sort of interstate superfan—I'm not planning on showing up at HighwayCon cosplaying as a median anytime soon—but it's just facts that the stretch of I-70 between Denver and Utah is one of the best roads in the country. I had first driven this road west over the Rockies back in 2016 on a somewhat aimless trip around Colorado. The interstate climbs up mountains, then winds along the edge of the Colorado River at the bottom of steep valleys. I was driving alone at 80 miles per hour, and the fact that I had no one to share the beauty with drove me insaner than I already was, made me feel particularly lonely. Emmy and I had driven the same road in the opposite direction in 2018, and here we were, doing it again. "Isn't this road crazy?" I said.

"Dude," said Emmy. "I know."

We pulled off the highway in Fruita, Colorado for groceries, gas, and water. We were still forty-five minutes from Cisco, but here's the thing: Fruita is the closest town to Cisco, and Cisco has no running water. It obviously has no grocery store. It's the kind of place that really makes you think about your consumption, about every drop of water you use, because getting more is a pain in the ass. Emmy filled our grocery cart with food while I grabbed cases of LaCroix to give to Eileen, who, rumor has it, does not drink normal water. We made a final stop for iced coffee, the *real* "black gold" for Millennials, and set off for the ghost town. For almost an hour we drove through the desert, past hills and flats and distant cliffs in an array of beiges that would bring the likes of Nancy Meyers to stunned tears. And then we were in Cisco.

EVERYONE WAS BUILDING when we arrived. There were J., Eileen's girlfriend at the time, and Z., a friend from Milwaukee, sawing wood and swinging hammers. There was M., an older man living in the desert behind Cisco, contributing manual labor in exchange for using Eileen's Wi-Fi to write a novel about his years working at Yellowstone in the '80s, getting drunk and peeing into Old Faithful. There was Bart, Emmy's partner, who was helping Eileen build a camper on the back of an abandoned Ford pickup. He was tanned from the Utah sun and sweating into his teal Goodyear hat; Emmy, after not having seen him for a week (during which she started wearing a chain around her waist that everyone called her chastity belt), hugged him for a full minute. And looking like the coolest person in the universe in paint-scuffed pants, a tee with a Sharpie hanging from the collar, and a bold pair of glasses, was the reason for the season: Eileen.

Several years before, Eileen—who is originally from Milwaukee, Wisconsin, and who uses they/them pronouns—was working for the Chicago Park District and on the brink of turning thirty when they took a trip to Utah to see the Holy Ghost panel of pictographs in Canyonlands National Park. The person sitting next to Eileen on the plane struck up a conversation as they started to land, something Eileen appreciated: "She was queer possibly?" said Eileen about their seatmate. "But I don't want to talk to even a queer person on an airplane." The woman told Eileen that there was a ghost town they should check out on the way to Canyonlands. There are ghost towns all over the American West, but Eileen had never even thought to go to one. The only reason they remembered the name of the town—in fact the only reason they were now doing what they were doing instead of still living in Chicago—was because of the "Thong Song." So when they passed the Cisco exit on I-70, they pulled off to see it.

The town consisted of just a few blocks. Since its founding in the 1880s Cisco has been a stop for the railroad, a ranching town, an oil town, a uranium mining town—it burned through industries like a middle schooler burns through identities. At its most booming, around 250 people lived in Cisco. It had a hotel, a saloon, a gas station, restaurants. But eventually the train no longer needed to stop there, and then the interstate was built, bypassing the road that cut through town. Without the traffic the town began to die. The last permanent resident moved out decades before Eileen took their seatmate's advice and drove through to check it out.

By then the boomtown wasn't recognizable. The buildings were collapsed or collapsing or no longer there at all. Only one looked remotely habitable. "I thought it would be like a movie set with saloon doors and shit," Eileen told me, but the structures had never been as elegant as all that. But still, it was a ghost town! It was covered in trash or, depending on how you look at it, "interesting historical artifacts." Eileen reached out to the man who owned the plot of land where the sturdiest-looking building stood and did some math: if they bought the land and sublet their apartment in Chicago for the winter, they would actually be saving money. So they did.

ONCE EMMY AND Bart were done hugging and once all power tools were turned off and anything small enough to blow away was secured, Eileen and their superlatively enthusiastic dog, Rema, took Emmy and me around town. It had been six years since Eileen first sublet their Chicago apartment, and they had long since moved to Cisco full time. During those six years, Eileen had been rebuilding the town using mostly scavenged materials. First Eileen took us to their log cabin, the sturdyish-looking building that had inspired them to buy the property in the first place, so that Emmy and I could refrigerate some food and La Croix and one precious jug of cold brew. Since buying the cabin, Eileen had cleared it of rubbish and mouse poop, ripped the faux-wood and plaster walls down to the logs, then mortared the gaps.

Before buying Cisco Eileen had never built a house, had never worked in construction. (They had attended a year of art school, which is kind of similar, except instead of teaching you to build a place to live, they teach you to build things that are very *challenging* that no one will understand.) The most experience Eileen had in "constructing a ghost town out of a pile of garbage" was when, in their midtwenties, they had helped their mom demolish a completely gross kitchen. Eileen's mom was convinced that under her kitchen's linoleum was hardwood flooring, so together they pulled up the floor and scrubbed tar for days. Eventually Eileen realized there *was* no mythical hardwood at the end of this journey, just tar-covered plywood subfloor all the way down. Knowing their mom would have a mental breakdown if Eileen told her this without also bringing a solution, Eileen remembered that their mom had a plywood mural in the basement. Eileen suggested they cut the mural into wide strips and use *that* as a floor. With no other options, having ripped up her kitchen for no reason, Eileen's mom agreed. Later Eileen learned how to do drywall, insulation, and plumbing, until they were able to completely demo a ghost town—a ghost town where many of the floors now are made of cut-up strips of painted plywood. "It started with the floor," Eileen says. "And it's all because it was a disgusting kitchen."

We crossed the street and walked along the wooden walkway Eileen had built for the rainy season, when the dirt town became one big mud puddle. We passed a chicken coop made out of metal scraps and doors that had long ago fallen off of their buildings, and sunflowers blooming out of dry dirt. Emmy dropped her bags in an abandoned bus Eileen had cleaned out and turned into a bedroom. Since I'd last been in town Eileen's friend Nick had painted two murals on the bus:

on one side, a man herding sheep across the desert, and on the other, a gun fight featuring Eileen's actual gun. Last we circled back around to see the camper that Bart, Eileen, and company had been building.

From just after Eileen bought the town, when Nick had stayed in Cisco to watch it (town-sitting, I guess) while Eileen went back to Chicago to make some money before they moved full-time, Cisco had been a place conducive to art. Nick had some mural mock-ups he needed to get done and, as he reported to Eileen, he found Cisco was the perfect place to do them, because there was literally nothing else for him to do. It got Eileen thinking: they didn't want to be out in Cisco all alone, both for safety reasons and because life is just better when you're surrounded by creative people. "There's no meaning for me anyway in restoring old buildings and then just looking at them," Eileen told me. Instead, they wanted to invite painters and writers and filmmakers to come through, "to show how living in a place like that for a month would have an effect on someone, because it definitely had an effect on me." With the help of their sisters Renée and Margaret, Eileen was, in 2019, in the process of creating an artist residency in Cisco. The only problem was that the ghost town didn't actually have anywhere for an artist to *reside*.

So Bart had driven across the country to build a residence in the form of a wooden camper on the back of a turquoise pickup rusting away on Eileen's land. When Emmy and I showed up, he had built the main structure, an elegant wooden jewel box with a pointed arch roof and windows torn off an RV abandoned across town. Twenty feet away, Eileen had gutted and begun to restore an old Winnebago that would eventually be used as an artist studio. At the moment it held construction materials: random wood, boxes of nails, WD-40, and a loose copy of *I Must Be Living Twice* by Eileen Myles.

I looked around, wanting to help but terrified of accidentally nailing the wrong thing into the wrong other thing and irrevocably fucking up the creation of an artists' haven deep in the Utah desert. I looked at Bart and Eileen. "So, uh . . . what do you need me to do?"

"Ugh, it's too hot to work right now," Eileen replied, which is why I love them.

At a certain point in the day when it's summer and you're in the desert, it gets too hot and too windy to work, so like snakes that spend the afternoon under a rock, you take a break. The day Emmy and I arrived was Z.'s last day in Cisco, so a bunch of us decided to visit Arches National Park. Eileen stayed behind but suggested we skip the interstate and treat ourselves by driving there on Highway 128.

Listen: I know I've already described forty roads in and around Utah as the most beautiful road in the country, but Highway 128 from Cisco to Moab might really be it. For miles you cruise along the edge of the Colorado River with free-roaming cows hanging out on the side of the road as if speeding hunks of metal pose absolutely no risk to them. After about fifteen minutes, the river begins to weave through canyons of the red rock Utah is famous for. Far in the distance, poking above the red mesas, are the snowy La Sal Mountains. Many people drive about two miles per hour on this road, presumably because they're trying to take in the view and also because the edge is at times perilously close to the drop-off to the river, with no guardrail to save you from driving straight into the water because you were too preoccupied doing your best impression of Owen Wilson saying "wow." To cut down on "dragging vintage Volkswagens out of the Colorado" costs, there are pullouts along the way, and we stopped at one to take photos, Emmy on Bart's shoulders in front of the desert, and red cliffs, and mountains.

ARCHES NATIONAL PARK is exactly what it says on the box. It's named after the natural stone arches found all around the park; there are two thousand in Arches alone, making it the densest concentration of such formations on the planet. We took the main road far into the park, looking for somewhere to hike a little off the beaten path, somewhere Emmy and I hadn't seen on our own southwestern road trip the year before. The windows were down, our hair blowing in the warm wind, the desert desolate and open all around us. "I've always thought park rangers would make the perfect serial killers," Z. said. "They would know exactly where to hide the bodies." *Oh great!* I thought. *A whole category of people I forgot to be afraid would kill me!*

We applied our sunscreen at the Devil's Garden trailhead and took off. Staying on the trail is important no matter where you're hiking, but in Arches it's especially urgent because much of the ground is covered in cryptobiotic soil. (Cryptobiotic soil: "the only good crypto.") Also known as "living soil" or, in my opinion, "freaky dirt," this soil is what makes possible any of the plant life we see in the desert. Lichens and mosses and cyanobacteria combine to enrich the soil by fixing nitrogen. Living soil allows the desert to absorb rain and to, very simply, not blow away. It can take more than a hundred years to grow back after being damaged—you can still see places where pioneers' wagons rolled over it in the 1800s—which means that when you've got a bunch of hikers . . .

or more likely, cows. . . . . stomping all over the place, you've got a lot of soil that is in danger of blowing away. Perhaps you remember "the Dust Bowl?" Of "dirt catastrophically blowing all over the place" fame? Well, guess what: cows did the Dust Bowl. Anyway!

We turned onto a spur trail to see Pine Tree Arch. The arch was massive, looming above the sand and shrubs below. We turned around and hiked another spur to Tunnel Arch, set back from the trail in a light brown fin of rock stained with desert varnish. "These shouldn't be called *arches*," Bart said. "They should be called *crazy holes*."

"Yeah," I said. "Crazy Holes National Park."

MY SECOND DAY in Cisco began in the post office, where I was sleeping, combining my two passions of (a) receiving mail and (b) not being awake. Next to the post office was the outhouse: no running water means no flush toilets. Instead, with the help of a couple Mormon boys who passed through town on their mission, Eileen had dug a huge hole in the ground and built a double-seated toilet above it. (It's both "place to pee" and "art.")

Waste was in your face in Cisco. Unless Eileen had personally cleaned and rebuilt a building or a patch of land, that part of town was covered in trash. There were pipes, tarpaper, old cars. In the time they had lived there, Eileen had found a blonde wig, dirty magazines, gunpowder. I found, among the broken bottles and corroded metal strewn about, a floppy disk. If you are too young to know what that is, I invite you to watch the first *Mission: Impossible*, an entire film about Tom Cruise doing stunts for a floppy disk.

Out of this wasteland Eileen had built a functional, aesthetically considered town. But make something beautiful, and people with a smartphone will find it: Cisco had something of a tourist problem.

Cisco tourists are usually people who have read about the town on an internet list of cool places or seen one of the unauthorized YouTube videos that are always popping up. They park their car somewhere in Cisco and get out, walking all over Eileen's property and the property of Eileen's absentee neighbors, touching stuff and taking pictures. They climb under fences to do this. They do it despite the hand-painted signs Eileen has put up around town that say, TOURISTS PLEASE! PHOTOGRAPH FROM THE ROAD! and NO DRONES NO TRESPASSING! and, to get straight to the point, FUCK OFF. The tourists imagine that it is okay for them to do as they wish because they imagine they are among the few people in the world passing through this desolate spot, when in fact a couple who looked exactly like them was doing the same thing forty-five minutes ago, and in forty-five more minutes it will happen again with another couple who look exactly like them, but Swedish.

For a while Eileen tried to monetize this interest. They realized they needed a revenue stream to fund the project of rebuilding the town and the project of "Eileen eating food to continue being alive," so they rebuilt two collapsing shacks—an old home and the old post office—and listed them on Airbnb. The Airbnbs were a hit with tourists passing through the nearby, wildly popular town of Moab, especially tourists who wanted to save money and were looking for an adventure. But the county had recently been giving Eileen trouble about the Airbnbs because you need a permit, and to get a permit you need to be up to modern code, and when your restroom is a two-seater outhouse, "being up to modern code" is never going to happen.

Here's a confession. Emmy and I didn't meet Eileen in Milwaukee. We didn't get an invite to Cisco through a mutual friend. Emmy and I first encountered Cisco as pesky tourists. She had heard of the town through the Milwaukee grapevine, so we visited on our road trip the year before. We saw the abandoned RV Eileen had spray-painted to say TAKE NOTHING BUT PICTURES. BE RESPECTFUL FOR FUCK'S SAKE, and we took pictures of it. We were poking around town looking at what Eileen had built when all of a sudden they appeared, the coolest person I had ever seen, with a buzzcut and giant sunglasses and a gun on their hip. "Are you my Airbnb guests?" Eileen asked. We said no, and then Emmy mentioned Milwaukee and how she had heard of Eileen, and instead of telling us to get lost as they had every right to do, Eileen said, "It's too windy to work today, do you want to hang out? I have popsicles."

I was so grateful that Emmy and I had met Eileen, though the more I learned, the more mortified I was in hindsight at our behavior. All too often the people who feel entitled to Cisco cross over from annoying to dangerous. Random men DM creepy messages to Eileen all the time. Once, Eileen was working outside when two men in a parked truck started shooting in their direction. So it makes sense that Eileen carries a gun. It's a necessity, not a lifestyle statement, unless the statement is "I am going to be difficult to murder." Eventually, Eileen had gone around spray-painting SORRY PRIVATE HOUSE on abandoned buildings and boarding up any entrances. They told me: "I just want to know where all the hiding places are."

WE SPENT THE day working on the camper. Bart and Eileen cut wood and did serious-looking things. Emmy sanded the metal sheeting that was serving as the camper's roof. I asked

Bart for an unfuckupable task. "Can you measure the inside of the camper so we can cut insulation?" he asked me.

"You got it!" I spent forty-five minutes measuring and still, somehow, fucked it up. After that I focused on handing Emmy fresh sanding pads so she didn't have to get off her ladder.

Emmy made dinner that night for all of us, including R., a computer programmer who was a local (lived an hour away) and a friend of the town. We sat around catching up and laughing, talking about what we'd done that day and what needed to be done the next. As I ate out of the one bowl in Cisco, I told everyone about Professor Josh from Bryce and his documentary project, and how he thought it would be better with a girlfriend.

"Maybe he's just really lonely because he's traveling by himself and it's not as poetic as he thought it would be," Emmy said.

"What he's doing is kind of like Van Life," someone said, and then *everyone* had an opinion.

Van Life, or, more accurately, #VanLife, is a movement of people who leave behind straight life and the corporate world to live in their vehicles, often built-out vans, usually traveling and posting about it on social media. There are often cute dogs. There are often textiles in vaguely Native American prints. There are often hammocks, and twinkle lights, and conventionally attractive women in Birkenstocks. Van Lifers have managed to take something everyone would love to do—travel, live in beautiful places—and make it somehow extremely annoying. It's a wealth-washed version of a transient lifestyle other people live out of financial necessity (including many who live and work in Moab, which is in the middle of a housing crisis. Because Van Lifers clog the campsites around town, service workers who can't afford housing are forced to sleep in their vehicles farther and farther away.)

In some ways it echoes what Eileen was doing. Both involve a departure from urban living with a nine-to-five job. Van Lifers take aesthetically pleasing photos and videos for their blogs or YouTube channels or Instagrams; Eileen was making an aesthetically pleasing town. But a key difference, as I saw it, was that Van Lifers were living this alternative lifestyle in the pursuit of making their individual livings from it. They might not have traditional jobs, but being a Van Lifer is its own kind of grind and deeply capitalist. That they've so fully played themselves is, I think, why it's funny to us when travel influencers are exposed as having the same clouds in every photo, or when a profile about them details the tedious reality of making sure they always have a bag of Popchips in the shot. It's like: *you're trying to make us jealous of you, but you're as miserable as everyone on this cursed planet! Admit it!* And since they were always on the move, it seemed to me that the Van Lifers I knew of weren't building the kind of community that Eileen could, simply by staying in one place.

I didn't see myself as better than Van Lifers, really. I was driving around the country, hoping to get paid to write a book about it. Sure, I wasn't trying to become a travel influencer, but how much of that was down to the fact that I couldn't aestheticize my travel if my life depended on it, due to my inherent inability to understand shapes and colors? If I knew how to look cute in a photo in a national park instead of looking like I am covered in dirt and haven't showered in six days, I would do it. We all need money! If I could get sponsored by an iced-coffee company to drive around the country, I'd say yes. And even though I wasn't yet monetizing my travel for my own gain, in posting about it on Instagram I was monetizing it for Mark Zuckerberg's.

Eileen, on the other hand, was making no money from the tourists who poked through Cisco every day. Although they put out a donation box and set up a Patreon, they still had to get jobs as a landscaper and at a sawmill to afford to live. Eileen wasn't sponsored by snack brands or laxative tea companies, though to me it was obvious that LaCroix should sponsor them because, again, I do not think Eileen drinks normal water. Unlike the ubiquitous #VanLife accounts, all visiting the same places and taking the same photo, what Eileen was doing feels sui generis and as far outside the capitalist system as an artist can be while still living in the United States. No one was paying Eileen to make their art; they made it because they are an artist. And that's not romantic! Artists like having money to buy food as much as anyone else does.

WE SPENT THE evening sitting in chairs next to the camper, watching Bart spray-paint a cicada onto the camper's roof in the strong beam of a spotlight. "It's in honor of a cicada that landed on the camper one of the first days," he said, grabbing another can. Emmy and I finally grew too tired and were walking to our sleeping quarters when she grabbed my arm and pointed back toward Bart. "Look." Bats were dipping and swooping over the camper, eating the bugs that were drawn to Bart's spotlight. We stood and watched, then turned around and looked at the stars.

The stars in Cisco, forty-five minutes away from the nearest town whose electrical grid consists of more than a couple extension cords, were unbelievable. I think the stars are something you have to take for granted and then totally lose access to in order to appreciate. I grew up in a town of six thousand or so people. I didn't even realize it was possible *not* to see stars at night until I moved to New York City. Seeing the Milky Way in Utah while on vacation from New York is like drinking a cup of water after sleeping eight hours in a dry room—or to put it in terms a New Yorker would understand, like walking into an air-conditioned Gap store on a day where the temperature is 110 degrees and the city smells like the hot garbage it is. It's enough to make you wonder if you could completely restructure your life in order to see the stars more often.

I couldn't become a Van Lifer because I don't have it in me to hunt down and refurbish a vintage shaggin' wagon, to take artsy photos on 35mm and scan and upload them, to be my own hot girlfriend doing yoga on an oceanside cliff for thirst likes. But I could, maybe, move somewhere closer to nature. I had friends in Denver, didn't I? I even had a friend who had moved from the country's third-largest city to live in a Utah ghost town.

Though I wasn't explicitly shopping for a new home, leaving New York has never been far from my mind. I fantasized about living somewhere I could hike and forage and see the stars but also, somehow, be surrounded by friends and good restaurants. I clicked through Zillow listings in Moab and Missoula and Seattle, in every town in Vermont, and, mostly for climate change reasons, in Duluth. But I was suspicious of how many of my peers seemed to be having the same idea, moving en masse to the West and Southwest, buying vintage trucks and Yeti coolers and then, having completely lost the plot, buying baseball hats that said "Yeti," too. Even those friends who stayed in New York seemed to be taking the Metro North to the same cute upstate towns and hiking the same trails and posing at the same overlooks in the same Parks Project fleeces. What seems to me like my generation's craving to experience the nature we still have and to escape the capitalist system that does its best to oppress us, is being aestheticized and sold right back to us. The novelist and essayist Jess Row writes about experiencing the same thing in the 1990s: "My imagination, which I thought of entirely in idealistic, ecological, aesthetic terms, was literally being monetized under my feet."

I had been on the road for three weeks. I had seen beautiful places that I'd always wanted to see; I'd hiked up cliffs and walked in desert streams and seen all of America spread out below me from the top of a very tall South Dakota hill. I felt free in a way I couldn't remember ever feeling. But the more I thought about it, the more I ran into people who had done the same things I had done or were currently doing those things, park for park, I realized I was following grooves set out for me by our culture. When I thought about leaving New York, I was thinking along similar grooves. Was I free, really, or was I performing what our culture presents as freedom? Was anything I was doing even slightly meaningful?

On the other hand, did I really need to reinvent vacation?

MY FOURTH DAY in Cisco was my last. After a day spent digging a trench to run an extension cord out to the residency space, during which M. found the first scorpion I had ever seen, we got as cleaned up as you can in a town without showers and piled into cars for a trip into Moab. We crammed into a booth at the restaurant where J. worked, then wandered down the main street to grab ice cream, trying to stretch out the evening. I was sad to leave, but Bart's work on the camper was almost done and it was time for me to acquire more Junior Ranger badges.

By a long shot, this had been the best part of my trip so far. I was with friends, laughing and telling stories and getting to experience things together. I was staying in one place and helping, in my own not-very-good-at-construction way, to build something, instead of showing up somewhere, getting a badge, and rolling out—basically taking a survey course of America. What was most special was seeing what Eileen was doing and feeling like a small part of the Cisco cast of characters.

Eileen always intended for other people to come to Cisco, for friends and family to visit. "No one wanted to hang out with me until I started this thing," they once jokingly told me. "[In Chicago] I was surrounded by people and didn't have that many friends . . . but then I go to a ghost town." Cisco itself drew people too, not because it had spectacular views or amenities but for the opposite reason: it was a place ravaged by industry and left for dead but which was being reborn. It was a race against time, Eileen says: "I'm watching the Southwest dry up and burn down and blow away." But as great as the buildings and campers and composting outhouses are, the Cisco community is the greatest thing Eileen has built. To me Cisco looked like the best way I'd yet seen to be as free as you could, to live somewhere where every view was gorgeous, but also to have that thing humans need on a biological level: the company of friends.

And here I was, about to leave my friends in pursuit of plastic badges.

The West Coast

10

Heroic Nature Adventurer

From the ghost town I meandered up to Glacier National Park by way of Mystic Hot Springs and Spiral Jetty and Craters of the Moon. I took two full days to get to Glacier and spent a grand total of maybe five hours in the park. It had been a week since I had last showered, so I went crazy and spent a night in a hotel in Spokane, Washington. After showering a week's worth of grease and desert dust and random sticks out of my hair and after ordering Chinese food, I sprawled on my room's king-sized bed, trying to make a very important decision. Doing a trip like mine really puts into perspective the things that are important to you, and I was deeply feeling that what is important to me is the golden age of television. It had been a month since I had properly watched TV, and I was ready to die. A certain type of person loves to sound enlightened by saying, "I don't even *own* a TV!" These people are idiots. I too am an idiot, but I love TV, and this, I think, is true enlightenment.

I considered my options before throwing on the first episode of season two of *Fleabag*. Needless to say, I watched the second episode immediately after, then the third, until I had watched the entire season in one sitting. A month too late, I entered the zeitgeist of being incredibly horny for Hot Priest. Had I known before pressing play just *how* horny the season would be, I don't know that my sex-deprived self would have been brave enough to watch it. Then, recharged by a night of the junk-food comforts I missed from home, I headed back into the wild.

North Cascades is another of the national parks barely anyone has heard of. The year before my trip, 30,085 people visited the park. For comparison, in 2018 more than twenty thousand people visited the Metropolitan Museum of Art in New York City on an average *day*. If you think that's just because it's easier to get to the Met, you've never had to walk the fifteen minutes from the 6 train.

The landscape outside Spokane was generic. Boring. Shitty? Over a handful of hours I drove through the barren, semi-arid scenery between the Cascades to the west and the Rockies to the east, occasionally passing a small town. But slowly the world I was driving through transformed. Nearing North Cascades, the road cut between the steepest mountains I had encountered thus far on my trip. You know when a kid draws a mountain, and it's essentially a V flipped upside down with some snow on top? That's what these mountains looked like. After weeks of sweating in the blazing heat, helplessly watching my Oreos melt, I was thrilled to have reached cooler temperatures. I drove through pine forests and past icy blue lakes. At a certain point I passed from the eastern to the western side of the mountains and entered a temperate rainforest. The forest was ancient, and lush, and enchanting, but I sped through it to get to the park's visitor center before it closed.

AN HOUR OR so later—after getting my Junior Ranger booklet from a visitor center with more taxidermied bears than I'd ever seen, after using their Wi-Fi to check every single app on my phone, and after scoping out my hike-in campsite, so far up a trail that the picnic table had decayed and they'd just left it there—I set off to hike. I decided on a trail called Thunder Knob simply because that's what I call my dick.

The trailhead was unassuming, just a brown sign on a thin wooden post announcing THUNDER KNOB TRAIL, with an arrow pointing the way. *Oh hell yeah*, I thought, taking a photo to put on Instagram later. Figuring out where exactly the trail was, was less easy. The arrow pointed toward an area strewn randomly with rock and puddles and running water and woody debris—this was Colonial Creek. Any surface that was not actively a creek seemed to have been an active creek mere days before. I crossed the water to the other bank, where the trail became more defined, and walked through hemlock and cedar and Douglas fir, the air wet and a little chilly. Every once in a while I came upon something that commanded my attention, like a fallen tree blocking the path or a glimpse of mountains through the forest. But mostly the trees obscured everything but the trail right in front of me, and there was no vista or obstacle to focus on. All my attention turned to putting one foot in front of the other.

This is what I like about hiking. There's very little else, at least that I've found, that forces you so entirely to live in the moment. What else are you going to do? You're taking just about the slowest way to get somewhere. The entire point of it is to pay attention to the world around you. In an age when I can fly around the world, when I can borrow my stepdad's Prius and drive around the whole country so quickly that I somehow feel like I'm actually seeing none of it, hiking forces me to slow down. It allows me to really notice the world around me, to understand the distance I'm traveling on a body-deep level, to feel the air of where I'm at—and, if I'm lucky and I try hard enough to manifest them, to see the snakes of where I'm at, too.

The trail climbed upward until the forest broke open and I reached the summit of the knob. A bench faced out toward the vista. Nestled in the valley was Diablo Lake, turquoise from the finely ground rock in the glacial melt, picked up as the glaciers did their imperceptible work of shaving down mountains. Before me, steep slopes were covered in emerald green pine, the peaks obscured by clouds. I wished I could somehow live there in North Cascades National Park while also pursuing my dream of writing and directing movies about every crush I've ever had.

FROM THE MOMENT I woke up the next morning, I felt, for once in my poser life, legit. I had fallen asleep to the sound of rain, and my cheapie Walmart pup tent had made it through the night: I woke up dry. I broke down camp, hiked the few minutes back to the Prius in several trips, then popped into the campground restroom to brush my teeth. A squat rectangular mirror hung on the bathroom wall: my hair was wild with two days of tangles and grease. I stared at my reflection and admitted: I was a total Pacific Northwest babe.

I was vibing as I rolled into the park's visitor center to claim my Junior Ranger badge. On duty was Ranger Gwen, who laughed as she checked the answers in my booklet. "If you could see one animal found in North Cascades National Park during your visit," the book asked, "which would it be?" *Wolverine.* "Why did you choose this animal?" *I live for drama.* Another activity asked me in what ways I was similar to a mountain goat. After some thought I had written "I'm an herbivore."

"Heck yeah!" Ranger Gwen said. "High five!"

Gwen gave me my badge and I stepped back outside into the glorious morning. I was hot, I was an herbivore, I was on the trip of a lifetime, I had found maybe the most beautiful corner of America, I was having a great day, and nobody could take that away from me. I sat on a bench and pulled out my phone to post my North Cascades photos to Instagram. I edited my photos, wrote my little "Thunder Knob is what I call my dick" caption, and watched as the loading bar edged toward 100 percent. Around 70 percent, it stalled. I stared at my screen for a full minute of my life that I will never again get to experience: an activity that might well be described as my main hobby. *Must be the Wi-Fi!* I decided and got into the Prius to drive to Seattle.

I drove west until I reached Interstate 5. To my south was Seattle; to my north, Vancouver, Canada, and Bellingham, Washington, where my great-great-grandfather may have started a second family after my great-great-grandmother developed postpartum depression and he threw her into a mental institution, shipped their kids back to Ireland, and moved to the Evergreen State. (But that's a story for another book, where I track down his second family and annoy them as an excuse to hang out in the Pacific Northwest.) This was it, a point of no return: the rest of my trip lay south from here. My heart twinged, but I turned left. And then, almost immediately, I pulled off the interstate to get coffee and to write out THUNDER KNOB IS WHAT I CALL MY DICK repeatedly, as it continued to fail to upload. I sipped my Starbucks and watched the photos refuse to post again and again. Only after one thousand attempts did it occur to me that the problem might not be my phone service. Maybe Instagram was just being buggy that day. Why was I letting this app drive me insane?

Someone once said that every trip is really three trips: the trip you take when you're planning it, the trip itself, and the trip as you remember it. The trick is to experience each while it's happening, which, as anyone who has ever tried to "live in the moment" knows, is difficult. When we take photos, we might be living in all three at once: we might photograph something in a particular way because we saw a photo someone else took in the same way, and maybe that photo is what brought us here in the first place. And we're also taking a photo to help us remember. As the memories of our experiences fade, our photos will more and more constitute our trip as we remember it.

But also, taking photos gives us a way to live in the present of a trip, especially if you're not sure how to actually *experience* things. Taking pictures forces you to stop and look. Like my Junior Ranger badges, it's a form of vacation homework, a task to focus your subjectivity. Photography allows you to feel like you gave a view, a location, a special place its proper due, that you took it all in. When I stood on top of a mountain or gazed at an overflowing creek or found my path blocked by a cool log, stopping to take a photo made me feel like I took the extra moment to truly appreciate it.

At every national park I visited, I did three things I hoped would add up to a feeling that that park had revealed itself to me: I got a Junior Ranger badge, I went on a hike, and I posted some photos to Instagram. Posting pictures meant I was always looking very intently at the views and at small, photogenic details—a daisy floating in a trailside puddle—(kill me)—but I started to get freaked out when I realized I was seeing the views through my phone instead of with my actual eyeballs. I was beginning to have what Susan Sontag calls in *On Photography* "that mentality which looks at the world as a set of potential photographs."

The compulsion to take a good photo becomes not just questionable but physically destructive when we all try to get photos of the same exact parts of nature. It's not great when a horde of hot young people all stomp to the same vistas for content because, much like the moose on Isle Royale, their stomping can wreak havoc on the environment. You'll remember the year that the desert outside Los Angeles experienced a superbloom, and then all the influencers swarmed to take their photos, and trampled the flowers. In this case, the federal government is not legally allowed to introduce wolves to bring down the influencer population jk jk jk.

So why do it? Why spend so much energy on getting these photos? On Insta we're performing for each other, sure. Trying to prove to strangers and friends that we're living our best lives is one of the three main uses of Instagram. (The others are "looking at photos of my friends having fun" and "selling bras.") But I think we're performing for ourselves too. I can't be the only person who has ever looked at my own Instagram to see if I am happy.

I think all this annoyance and anger with Instagram and with travel photography might come from recognizing how much our selfhood has become enmeshed with the version of our life we present on social media. We recognize the inse-curity we feel about it and we judge other people for too obvi-ously feeling the same way. I put my phone down, trying not to feel too embarrassed by my obsessive Instagram behavior but eager not to further cheapen the experience I'd had at North Cascades. In about an hour I would stop for lunch in Seattle; maybe there I could be fully present for once in my life.

I PARKED MY car in front of a *Bon Appétit*—recommended ice cream spot in Capitol Hill and took a walk around the neigh-borhood, imagining living in Seattle. Would my life involve weekend trips to North Cascades and magazine-endorsed food at every meal and sidewalks full of people who looked like members of the touring band for Fleet Foxes?

Before I could search any open houses on Zillow or scroll Am*zon job listings, it was time for me to climb back into my gorgeous metal prison, Miss Prius. I set my GPS for Cougar Rock Campground in Mount Rainier National Park, two hours away. And then, ready to be let down once again by an app that no one had actually *asked* me to use, I opened Instagram. I se-lected my little photos and clicked the caption box. "Instagram being buggy has forced me to type this five hundred times but i stand by it," I wrote. "Thunder Knob is what i call my dick." The uploading progress bar scooted across the screen and dis-appeared. My dumb post had finally loaded. The likes rolled in, and then a comment: "100% almost commented 'thunder knob? That's what I call MY DICK' before I read your caption."

It was late by the time I made it to Mount Rainier's Nis-qually Entrance, a giant gateway arch that answers the ques-tion, "What if a chuppah was made out of old-growth forest?" The entrance booths were unstaffed, so I grabbed a park map and newspaper and drove the last, leisurely stretch to my campground on the winding park road through dense, green pines. I set up my tent with the last of the sunlight and read the park literature until I fell asleep. When I woke up, it was July 4th. I had been on the road for exactly one month.

SINCE TIME IMMEMORIAL the Indigenous people who lived around Mount Rainier—the Cowlitz, Muckleshoot, Nisqually, Puyallup, Squaxin Island, Yakama, and Coast Salish people among them—considered the volcano sacred, refusing to climb onto its glaciers. As someone who hates being cold and isn't particularly fond of the idea of falling to my death down an icy crevasse, this makes a lot of sense to me. But then white people came around and decided they wanted to get on top of Rainier.

In 1870 a mountaineer named P. B. Van Trump (a name better suited to an overpriced, horrible sandwich at a novelty sandwich shop) and his friend General Hazard Stevens (surely, somewhere, the name of a swamp rock band) decided to summit the volcano. Van Trump and Stevens, or Hazzy Steves, as I like to call him, hired a Klickitat guide named Sluiskin to help them climb the huge white cone. Sluiskin got them up most of the way, but refused to climb to the summit. He tried to convince Hazzy and Van Trump not to proceed to the peak either, telling them that the volcano's crater was guarded by an angry spirit and held a lake of fire. This is as good a description of a volcano as I've ever heard, but because many men seem to share the hobby of "not listening," Hazzy and Van Trump summitted anyway. Theirs was the first known successful trip to the summit.

Nowadays around five thousand climbers each year make

it to the top of Mount Rainier. But it's not guaranteed: about half who start the journey don't make it, and since Hazzy and Van Trump's ascent, around 125 people have died climbing at Mount Rainier.

THE RANGER WORKING the desk at the visitor center that morning was a pale, redheaded woman in her late twenties. She explained what I would need to do to get my Junior Ranger badge and asked, "I'm gonna assume you're older than twelve?"

"Yes, barely."

She laughed a genuine laugh, and I missed riffing with my friends so much that I almost asked her to marry me.

I plopped into a nearby armchair and started working through the packet. There was a crossword, one clue asking for the name of the "Indian guide for General Hazard Stevens and P. B. Van Trump, the first successful climbers of Mount Rainier, in 1870." *How is it that they were the first?* I wondered. *Is the drive to climb tall, dangerous mountains for no reason somehow related to our capitalist, colonialist patriarchy?* The danger and the hubris of it appealed so little to me that I began to find thinking about mountain climbing actively annoying.

There's a way of interacting with nature that follows what the artist Mierle Laderman Ukeles calls the Death Instinct. She defines this as "separation, individuality, Avant-Garde par excellence; to follow one's own path to death—do your own thing, dynamic change." These are not bad things! Separation, individuality, dynamic change: sounded very much to me like deciding to go on a cross-country road trip all alone. (It sounded, too, very American, and as it was the Fourth of July I was certainly thinking about what that meant.)

The "follow one's own path to death" part interests me.

So many people's enjoyment of the outdoors hinges on the element of danger. There are many things I enjoy doing, that I did on this trip, precisely because they are dangerous. Being close to a bison. Changing lanes while driving in Denver. Hiking Angels Landing. So rarely, when you play the "Would I Die If I Fell Right Now?" game, can you honestly answer "yes." Humans have loved pushing themselves to the brink of existence since, presumably, the invention of existential malaise, circa Eve talking to a weird snake and eating a suspicious food she had not yet seen anyone eat and survive. It's why people have died trying to get photos since cameras were invented, because photos on the edge of something dangerous are just better. One of my How People Die in National Parks books scolds the reader: "It won't matter how many 'likes' you get on your video if you don't survive to post it." My honest response to that bit of sanctimony is: if I die taking a selfie on a cliff, you *have* to post that content to my account. Think of the engagement rates!

And yet, I find a lot of the Heroic Nature Adventurer stuff people try to do—summiting Mount Rainier, free soloing El Capitan, and so on—irritating. It sometimes feels like men need to assert their dominance over nature to imbue their lives with meaning. Rich white men who have no problems climb mountains to see what having problems feels like. There's something about it that just seems so pointless to me. We already have the technology to get on top of any tall thing: it's called helicopters. What could be more following-your-own-path-to-death than summiting a mountain that people routinely die trying to summit? Just as every billionaire is a policy failure, I see every person of any gender identity on top of a truly dangerous mountain as a failure of toxic masculinity. Another way of phrasing it comes from the writer Terry Tempest Williams: there is a love of nature that is predicated on arrogance, and there is a love of nature that is predicated on humility. It seems especially stupid to try to assert your masculinity by dominating nature in the age we're living through, when it's becoming clear that any control humans felt we had over nature is completely illusory. Nature's back with a vengeance, and it's handing us our ass.

But our culture tells stories about white boys and men going to nature to measure themselves against it: Huck Finn, the works of Jack London, *The Snow Leopard*, and every book, feature film, and documentary TV show my dad is constantly watching about people climbing Everest—a supply so steady that I almost wonder if these Everest movies do not actually already exist and if my dad is somehow manifesting them with his mind. It makes sense that men want to go to the woods to humiliate all these mountains: it's what, they are taught, makes them men. But the forests and vistas and wildflowers I had already seen in the park were so lovely that it frustrated me to think about people who valued Rainier only as an obstacle to overcome.

Let me say that I understand why people try to summit mountains. Climbing peaks is another way of organizing one's nature experience—it's just a more uncomfortable, much more expensive Junior Ranger badge. And I find myself suspicious of my instinct to judge people for putting themselves in a position where they may fall to their deaths or die of exposure. Isn't my whole thing that you shouldn't listen to people who say you're going to die doing something?

But let me note this as well: everyone told me I would die on my trip. Most of them probably meant that I would get murdered, but in fact men are more likely to get victimized in public, and by strangers. If I didn't get murdered, people thought I would most likely die from accidental injury or death in a park—while hiking a trail on the edge of a cliff or trying to get a sick photo while dangling off the top of a waterfall or trying to pet a bear because I just felt "drawn to its energy." But, as it turns out, that's all extremely male shit, too. According to the deeply researched and comprehensive book *Off the Wall: Death in Yosemite*, "Males comprised 88 percent of injury victims." Of the people who have died while rock climbing in Yosemite, 94 percent were men. The statistics are similar for scrambling deaths. Men make up 78 percent of people who have died falling off waterfalls in the park and 82 percent of all drowning deaths. This trend holds true for all the parks I have researched. The authors of *Off the Wall*—one a search-and-rescue leader, the other a former national park ranger—call this "semi-vertical terrain testosterone poisoning."

I DECIDED TO hike to a couple different waterfalls in Mount Rainier National Park and see how many I could not fall off. The first was Narada Falls, a quarter-mile jaunt from a roadside parking lot: essentially you crossed a stone bridge, walked down a set of dirt-and-log stairs, took your photos, and walked up the stairs again. On my way up I passed a woman doing the quarter-mile walk down the staircase in a front-buckle backpack with hiking poles in each hand: she may not have been a Heroic Nature Adventurer, but she at least had the fun of wearing the outfit. My second hike, to Comet Falls, was much longer and mostly uphill, and probably because of that it passed the Wedgie Test. Stopping every once in a while to take note of something I needed to observe for my Junior

Ranger book, I realized that my whole Junior Ranger bit was like when you mention one time that you like frogs, and then for the next thirty Christmases your family gives you only frog-related presents—except that I did this to myself. I was giving myself the frogs.

Nearing Comet Falls, I caught up to a family hiking together. Among them was a young woman wearing the exact same green American Eagle flannel as I was. Both of us wore black T-shirts and black leggings, carried an orange backpack, and had our brown hair tied into a braid. It was like the part of a horror movie where an alien kills you and takes over your life: we were exact twins, except she was hotter. My shyness and deep New York City training to leave strangers alone kept me from saying anything, until finally my human need to talk to other people and the sheer coincidence of it all won out.

"We're wearing the same shirt!" I said, and she was delighted. We got her step-grandma to take our photo in front of the falls.

"Are you by any chance a Gemini?" asked my twin, a Gemini. I'm not—Gemini are my enemies, usually—but wouldn't it have been cool if I were?

I happily chatted with my twin and her family by the river's edge and then for most of the hike down to the trailhead. Our outfits had been an excuse to say hi, but now I was just meeting and connecting with some people I'd likely never see again. For fifteen minutes, bizarro Blythe's family became my bizarro family, too.

MOST PEOPLE WHO try to summit Mount Rainier don't die. They work hard to learn about the mountain, they prepare themselves physically and mentally, they know to be wary of the mercurial weather, they practice crevasse rescue. But when things go very wrong for climbers seeking individual glory, it's the community of rangers, search-and-rescue leaders, and volunteers that saves them. Even when some humans put themselves in patently dangerous situations, their fellow humans have their backs. If things go sideways, we don't just look at nature as an avenging angel who gave those climbers or hikers of selfie-takers what was coming to them; we go out and try our best to bring them home safe. It was a fact that made me love humans.

I fell asleep on July 4th in the passenger seat of the Prius while, thousands of feet above me, people climbed toward the summit.

11

Living the Life of a Normal Human

HEAR YOU'RE EXPERTS ON FREE-CAMPING!" I SAID TO TWO
men waiting in line at the Olympic National Park Visitor
Center. I smiled wide and turned on all the flirt I had left in
me after a month on the road. "Or are soon to be, at least."

The visitor center in Port Angeles was slammed by the
time I got there, and the ranger in her sixties who was working the desk didn't want to answer my questions; she clearly
just wanted to go on lunch break. I know this because when I
got to the front of the line she said, "I will help you, but I was
supposed to go on lunch break." She told me that all the park's
first-come-first-served campsites were likely already claimed
but that two men had just asked her about dispersed camping. She didn't want to repeat the information, so she pointed
them out to me and suggested I talk to them.

The men were less informed than advertised. "Oh, uh,
we're going to ask the backcountry ranger if there's anywhere

they prefer we go for dispersed camping," one said. I looked at the backcountry line they were in and wondered if I should join, or if I should just browse the visitor center's postcards until the guys had their answer so they could share it with me.

"But there's a whole national forest to the west of the park," the other man added.

Problem solved! If what I had previously heard was true, I could sleep anywhere in a national forest, so there was no need to wait in line to figure out if the rangers had a preferred spot for me. "I'll just sleep there somewhere," I told the guys. "I'm so small, how will they ever find me?" The men did not find this charming, maybe because instead of "cute and bub-bly" I was "random and covered in 3.5 days of sweat."

With several hours before sunset, I figured I'd go on a few hikes before venturing into the Olympic National Forest. But every other person in the Pacific Northwest apparently had the same idea. I stewed as I struggled to find any trailhead with parking and then stewed as I waited in a long line for the pit toilet. I stewed as I hiked, never losing sight of someone in front of or behind me. My family had visited Olympic in 2004, and I didn't remember the trails being so busy when I was a kid. But maybe other people just bothered me less back then. The range of humans who had all decided to drive to a remote corner of Washington and hike this specific trail as-tounded me: I passed an older woman talking to her friend about a new law restricting abortions and how troubling she found this conservative trend. A minute later I passed a white male teen explaining that he and all his friends have the same gun. When I stopped for photos, a group caught up to me, a family of mother, father and small son. The little boy said to his mom, "You know why I need you more than I need Daddy? Daddy doesn't really know how to cook, but you know how to drive Daddy's car."

I realized that my annoyance wasn't really about the other people on the trail. After a month of waiting in long lines at visitor centers, of driving hours and hours between parks I'd only stay a night at, of feeling like I was spending approximately the same amount of time trying to find parking spots as I was spending hiking, I was experiencing burnout. Burnout from being on vacation for too long, can you imagine the gall! But it was true. I was frustrated by how crowded everything was, by how little time I was really getting to explore any of the gorgeous places I was visiting. How often did you get a chance to take a trip like this? And here I was, completely biffing it, wasting my Great American Road Trip, spending none of my time giving myself over to beauty and all of my time driving, or, sometimes, as a little treat, getting gas. I missed my friends and "missed my life," even though I knew that I was, by dint of continuing to breathe, living my one and only life at this very moment.

And I missed being able to shower whenever I felt like it! On that trail at Olympic it hadn't been that long, only four days, and the longest I'd gone on the whole trip was a little over a week. I've probably hooked up with men in Brooklyn who were on a similar shower schedule, despite living in a home with a bathroom. But it made me feel unattractive, dissociated from the self I identified with. If I were really surrendering myself to being on the road, wouldn't I be cooler about being grimy? And *also*, every time I showered, I shaved my legs. Was I a bad feminist? Who was I doing this for? Why did I quit my job? What was wrong with me?

I was jolted from my spiraling when I reached the Sol Duc Falls. They were arresting, magical, they reminded me it was all going to be okay, that I was a speck in this beautiful mystery we call the universe. Just kidding: they were overrun with people. People sat on the banks, people stood around taking photos, people climbed onto the falls to play. But the falls were still beautiful. I was on the Olympic Peninsula now, the wettest part of the state, of the entire contiguous United States, in fact, as you might remember from the *Twilight* novels. The air was so humid it was basically also water. The Sol Duc River cuts through old-growth forest, everything lush and green and fern-y, the trees humongous and covered with moss and psychotically big mushrooms. Here at the falls the river tumbled sideways off a ledge, pouring in three distinct cascades. If there weren't so many people here, or maybe if I were thirteen again, I would have played in the falls, too.

I had one more place I wanted to see before the sun set. I parked my car at the Rialto Beach parking lot, across the Quillayute River from La Push, the beach where Edward Cullen is famously not allowed. I walked onto the rocky beach past driftwood tree trunks and stopped to roll up my leggings. July 4th had marked one month on the road; on July 5th I made it to the Pacific Ocean. I had driven as far as I could without driving off the continent. I walked straight into the ocean; something in me felt reset.

Maybe I'm a cliché idiot. Maybe I'm too steeped in a culture that equates water with rebirth. Maybe I've been Christ-pilled and can't see this act as anything but a baptism. But I know that when I pulled up at the beach, I was feeling stressed and bummed out, tired of the Sisyphean task of always having to park my car, tired of all the other people, tired of being so, so, so horny. After dipping my feet in the salt water, after smelling the air, after picking my way around sea stacks, after peeking at urchins in tidepools (there were no sea stars—a random man on the beach told me they had been knocked out by sea star wasting disease), after getting my whole ass hit by a wave multiple times, I felt happy. Staring out at the ocean, the enormity of my trip became visible: I had really crossed the entire country.

As I walked back to my car, my phone started blasting a tinny version of One Direction's "No Control"—I had service, apparently, because this was my ringtone. The caller ID said Buddy Young Catholics. This was a man named Buddy (not his real name) who was in a band called the Young Catholics (not his band's real name, but also, not a bad name for a band).

If there is a clinical depression version of a "meet cute," that is how Buddy and I met. We met at [redacted for his privacy]; I was about a week into having an IUD, was less than twenty-four hours post my first real breakup, and on top of everything was wearing socks that said I LOVE MEAT AND CHEESE despite the fact that I actually eat neither of those things.

"Hello," he said (flirty).

"Hello," I said. "I cried in a closet for three hours this morning."

This did not dissuade him, and he asked me on a date soon after. We got drinks, he explained to me why he thinks it's important to separate art from artist in the case of Woody Allen movies, he drove me home, we kissed in his car and then in my apartment, but we didn't have sex. I didn't reach out to him again after that; I was going through a hard time with all my new hormones and my meat socks and my decision to quit my job. He didn't reach out to me either. Until I was standing on the edge of the Pacific Ocean.

"Buddy Young Catholics, hello!" I said, cutely, answering the phone. I definitely knew his last name, or at least I learned it when I added him to the list of people I've kissed, which I keep not because I have kissed a million people or am gross but because I have a horrible memory. But I refused to change his name in my phone, on principle.

"What?" Buddy said. "I can't hear you. Do you have bad service?"

I walked away from the ocean and perched atop a drift-wood log to see if that would help. "BUDDY, HELLO!" I said. "Can you hear me?" I had been separated from my life in New York for a month, and I wasn't going to let a lack of cell coverage stop me from reconnecting with even the most random slice of that life.

He could hear me. He had seen my Instagram stories from Olympic and was in Port Angeles that night, playing a show or something. Did I want to hang out? Port Angeles was where the park's visitor center was, all the way across the Olympic Peninsula from where I sat looking out at the ocean; getting back there would involve an hour and a half of driving.

I told Buddy that tonight was no good but that I'd be in Portland, where he had grown up, a couple days later. We made plans to see each other.

JUST BEFORE SUNSET I piled back into the Prius and set a course to a primitive campground in the Olympic National Forest. Almost as soon as I entered the national forest, the road turned to gravel, then rutted gravel, then rutted gravel climbing steeply up the side of a mountain. I didn't want to drive around in the dark on bad roads searching for a campground that might be full anyway, so when I saw a large turnout, I parked the Prius in it. The mosquitoes flying around in the 99 percent humidity air were so large and so numerous that I didn't even think about getting out of the car to pee; I just climbed into the passenger seat, read a little of Simone de Beauvoir's *America Day by Day*, and went to sleep.

In the morning I woke early and drove toward Olympic's Kalaloch Ranger Station to get my Junior Ranger badge. I pulled over on the side of the road at the "Welcome to Forks" sign so that I could take a selfie to prove I had visited the place where the *Twilight* novels, formative texts for me, the topic of multiple papers I wrote in college, were set. I had hoped to pee at the town visitor center, but when I found it closed I decided to brush my teeth in the parking lot anyway. As I pulled out my toothbrush, a massive pickup truck pulled into the empty lot and parked one spot away from me.

A man wearing camo and wraparound sunglasses got out of the truck and discovered, as I had, that the visitor center wasn't open. I was creeped out that he had parked so close to me, creeped out that we were all alone, creeped out that he had all the trappings of a red-blooded American male, not that there was necessarily anything wrong with that (lol jk), just that it was all extremely on the nose. I kept him in my peripheral vision as I continued brushing my teeth, quickly now. *Huh,* I thought, *am I about to get killed at eight in the morning? Before I even had time to put on a bra?* The man walked toward me; I avoided making eye contact as he got in his car.

And then. "Hey," he said.

Oh God. I turned around to see him leaning out the window of his truck, expression inscrutable under his Oakleys. *This is not going to be good.*

"Your tire is kinda flat."

It took me a second to process that I was not being harassed, but when I turned around to look at the Prius, he was right: my rear right-side tire was kinda flat. "Thank you!" I told him, for alerting me, but also, secretly, for not stabbing me.

The high from not getting murdered lasted as long as it took for the man to pull out of the parking lot, at which point I realized: shit, I have a kinda-flat tire, and no idea how to deal with it, early on a Saturday morning, in a small town. I had passed a cardboard cutout of Edward Cullen on my way through Forks; I definitely hadn't passed a tire repair store. I texted a photo of the tire to TB, who told me I should drive back into Forks, add air to the tire at a gas station, and then if the air kept leaking I should get the tire patched the next time I was in a proper town. "But you're going to need a tire gauge," he said. "They should sell them at the gas station."

"I don't even know what a tire gauge *looks like*!" I wailed.

"Good luck!" TB responded cheerily.

I drove back into Forks and pulled into the Shell, one of two dueling gas stations situated across the street from each other. A young man was working the cash register. I smiled as I approached him. "Do you sell tire gauges?"

"Uhh . . . no."

I took a deep breath, got back in the Prius, and drove across the street to the Mobil. There, the attendant was a middle-aged woman. "Good morning," I said. "You wouldn't happen to sell tire gauges, would you?"

"We used to," she said. "But then we stopped." I chuckled darkly.

Back in the Prius I contemplated my future, stuck in Forks, Washington, unable to ever fix my tire and thus unable to leave, forced to move here, becoming whatever Bella would have become if she hadn't met a creepy vampire who had amassed intergenerational wealth without the having-to-die part. Then I remembered that I had driven past a True Value two blocks back. I pulled up their number on Google Maps, and a man's voice greeted me.

"Hi," I said, "I'm just checking to see that you're open and that you sell tire gauges?"

"We are and we do!" he assured me.

Flooded with relief, I drove over, worried my tire was about to explode or my rims were about to break or some terrifying third option (I don't understand cars). When I walked into the store, I saw an older gentleman shelving items. "I just called about tire gauges," I said.

"Oh, hello!" He led me to the correct aisle while asking exactly what kind of gauge I was looking for.

"Let's just assume I'm an idiot," I said. "Which one would you recommend?"

He would never assume I was an idiot, he said, but he found and handed me the most basic, $3 gauge. He asked me about my trip as he walked me back to the cash registers. I told him about missing showers and missing my friends in NYC, and he told me that he had lived most of his life in upstate New York. Somehow this small moment of connection made me feel a little more able to deal with my massive emergency (slightly flat tire).

Back at the Mobil I parked by the air machine and went inside to get quarters. TB coached me through checking the sticker inside the driver's door which listed the optimum tire pressures, and I uncapped the flat tire's air valve and put some quarters into the air machine. I connected the air hose to the tire and watched as the tire . . . slowly deflated. *Is this supposed to be happening?* I wondered. The tire kept deflating. This was not supposed to be happening. Just as the air I had paid for ran out, I noticed a handle on the air hose that I was possibly supposed to be pushing down. I now had no quarters and a completely flat tire.

There are people who build entire personalities around "knowing about cars." When women, especially, know about cars, it's considered sexy. But guess what! I don't know about cars and I don't want to. I don't care about them. Knowing how to fix a car holds no moral or cultural value for me; this is why God invented paying someone else to know something for you. But don't listen to me: that opinion is what led me to nearly cry in a Mobil parking lot in Forks, Washington.

I got more quarters, put them in the air machine, and tried again. This time it worked. I checked the tire with my shiny new gauge and then, high on knowledge, checked the pressure in all the tires. No longer near tears, I went into the Mobil one last time and bought a celebratory 54-cent cup of ice to pour my cold brew into.

This trip was forcing me to learn more about cars than I ever wanted to know—which is to say, anything—but that morning, in a small way, I was forced to take care of myself. I now owned a tire gauge, and I knew how to use it. I saved myself on the Olympic Peninsula—I was my own Edward Cullen. (Or, Edward Cullen if he was having a mental breakdown every step of the way, and also begging his stepdad for help over the phone.) I was furious to have a new skill, but hey: I still had a new skill. It felt like the most tangible personal growth my trip had yet given me. I poured my coffee into my ice and got the hell out of Forks.

THE RANGER WHO checked me into my campground at Oregon's Nehalem Bay State Park that night was gorgeous. He was tan and fit with perfect hair, like he wasn't a ranger at all but a movie star cast to play the ranger in a studio film where everyone needs to be attractive.

"How long are you going to be staying?" the ranger asked.

"Just tonight," I said.

"Only one night?! What, you don't like our park?" he said, smiling.

"Yeah, I hate your park." We both laughed. During my time on the road I hadn't been totally estranged from the kind of life I lead back home: there had been days when I hung out with friends and a couple evenings when I holed up with my computer to write. But not once had I been able to express the side of me best described as "human woman who enjoys kissing human men," and the longer I went, the more I felt that lack. I was so horny I needed to be arrested.

A line started to build up behind me. "You should go to Olympic National Park next," the ranger told me.

"I was just there this morning!"

"Oh yeah, I see your . . ." he reached out and touched the Junior Ranger pin I had grabbed on my way out of Forks and pinned to the chest of my flannel shirt.

At this point I was basically batting my eyelashes. I laughed. "Mm-hmm, I work there."

I needed to let the man do his job, so I took my campsite registration and left. The state park was right on the Pacific, but more importantly, it had showers. I brushed out the knots in my hair and stood in the hot water, worrying about the Prius, and thinking about how I'd soon be in Portland.

IN NEHALEM THE town I poked around a few antique stores and then called TB to have a talk about the Prius. If I was going to keep this thing running for long enough to get me down the West Coast, east along the southern border, and from there who knows where, I was actually going to need to know how to take care of it. TB talked me through opening the hood and checking the oil and stayed on the phone while I expertly checked the tire pressure with my gauge. Then I brought up another car problem that had been bugging me since the night before. "So I noticed a couple little bugs crawling around the front of the car," I said. "Do you remember that episode of *Car Talk* where there were baby spiders living in the dashboard?"

"There aren't bugs living in the dashboard," he said.

Eventually I thanked TB for his help, hung up, and plotted my next moves. Before heading into Portland, I decided, I would swing down the coast and see Twin Rocks. These were, as advertised, a pair of rocks standing 100 feet high, just offshore. The Oregon coast is famous for sea stacks like these: the preceding day I had stopped at Haystack Rock, a 235-foot-tall stack featured in *The Goonies*, which, for all its charms, is still 50 percent fewer giant rocks than Twin Rocks. My Google Maps route to Twin Rocks sent me down a rough dirt road. *I should drive slow because I don't want to bottom out the car,* I thought.

I slowed down to 6 miles per hour. I immediately bottomed out the car.

I pulled into a small, three-space lot for Twin Rocks and

called TB while crouching next to the Prius, trying to get my whole head underneath it to see what damage I had wrought. "TOM!" I panicked, "THE CAR IS LEAKING!"

"It's probably just the AC," he assured me calmly. "Nothing important is under a Prius."

"*Probably* just the AC?!?" I was halfway across the country and my only way home was a car that was breaking down in front of my eyes (it was probably just the AC). But there was nothing I could do there, next to the ocean. I pushed my stress down deep into my body, where it would eventually emerge as either a cold sore or a sensation that my hands were on fire, I got into the car, and I kept driving.

BY THE TIME I got to Portland I was starving. I looked through the places I had starred on Google Maps, based on an email from a friend about food to eat and things to do in Portland, then hurried to Lan Su Chinese Garden, so hungry I was beginning to vaporize. I fed the parking meter and then, rounding the corner to the entrance, saw a line of people at a ticket booth under a sign that listed admission fees, around twelve dollars for adults. *A twelve-dollar cover for a restaurant? At lunchtime??* I took a second look at the building, which appeared to take up the entire block, and realized: *oh my God. This isn't a restaurant. This is an actual Chinese garden.* Though I was famished to the point of nausea, I walked up and bought a ticket. I had already paid for parking and I was already there, and I didn't want to turn around and eat some random sandwich because I was the woman too stupid to realize that Lan Su Chinese Garden was a garden.

Through the front gate I entered an entirely different city, different century, different plane of vibes altogether. There were serene courtyards with magnolia and bamboo, the land-scaping carefully planned to seem almost wild, stones covering the ground in mosaic patterns. There was a pond filled with koi fish and lily pads crossed by bridges and covered walkways drooping with ornate woodwork. Reading my visitor pam-phlet as I wandered around, I learned that Lan Su was mod-eled after a typical courtyard in a wealthy family's home in sixteenth-century China. I ducked into a room that displayed carved gingko panels. One was engraved with lines from the poet Wen Zhengming, my pamphlet told me: "Most cherished in this mundane world is a place without traffic; Truly in the midst of the city there can be mountain and forest." If this was relevant to the journey I was currently taking, it didn't occur to me. I was too focused on how badly I wanted food.

Had there been, before my road trip, a version of me that liked culture? That valued the intellect? What was book? Museum: never heard of it? In my life back home I was defined by my mind, but over the past month of hiking and existing in nature I'd been defined by my body. Being a body made everything feel more urgent, but it also made me feel a lot less refined, like someone had taken a cheese grater to my person-ality and shredded it off like dead foot skin.

For example: by the time I got to Portland I had begun to worry every day about whether the sun was giving me wrin-kles, and about whether I was gaining weight or losing weight or neither. Who cares?! Literally I knew that it did not matter to me. I looked like what I looked like, and I felt strong, and also, when my hair was washed, I felt hot. (After my trip peo-ple kept telling me I looked refreshed, looked happy, looked like I had "cultivated a healthier relationship with the world." When people tell women they look "tired" we know it is code for "you look like shit," so when people said the opposite to me, with looks of amazement on their faces, I knew it was code for "hubba hubba.")

Still, this was the longest I'd gone without weighing myself since I was fifteen, and I reverted to the training I had received as a teen girl, to constantly worry about the shape and weight of my body. Over the course of my twenties, I had figured out how to feed myself—when I was in a city. On the road I had no clue. I ate regionally spicy Tostitos dipped in hummus, not because hummus tasted so much better than guacamole or salsa but because I felt that you could keep hummus in a 100-degree car and it wouldn't go bad—which, I should say for legal reasons, is probably not actually true. I ate apples and clementines, the cores and rinds of which I threw out the window, thinking *it's organic!* until I learned you are definitely not supposed to do that. I ate a wide assortment of Starbucks snacks because my family loves to give me Starbucks cards for Christmas even though I haven't regularly gone there in a decade, so I had an insane amount of money in my Starbucks app. At one point I had more money in my Starbucks app than I did in my 401(k). So whenever I stopped at a Starbucks to pee, I treated it like a grocery store. None of these things, you'll notice, are truly meals. On my snack-based diet I knew I was continuing to live, but I couldn't parse what exactly was happening with my body.

A month on the road had distilled me to the physical embodiment of myself, with the Prius as an auxiliary, and now both were falling apart. When I visited a city, I didn't crave a trip to the art museum or tickets to a play as I once would have; I just wanted to eat food that wasn't raw, wet bagels.

I looked at the map on my pamphlet to see which part of

the garden they suggested I visit next and realized—God is good—there was a tea house. The tea house served snacks. I rushed over and ordered vegetable dumplings and steamed buns and rice noodles, everything on the menu that looked vegan, and became a solid body again.

A FEW HOURS later, after I had bounced around some book-shops and witch stores, Buddy drove his parents' SUV down to the doughnut place where I was holed up. He parked nearby and I watched him as he walked back to greet me: he was tall, with dark hair and a face that made women ask around if he was single. In the grand tradition of twentysomethings with no better idea, we decided to get a drink.

The pub he brought me to was just as charming as every-thing else I'd encountered in Portland. It was dimly lit with dark wood everything and with a framed photo of Princess Di next to a framed painting of an old-timey man in a massive hat choking a goose. I hadn't been much in the practice of in-teracting with humans over the past weeks, but conversation flowed as we caught up. Buddy and I talked about music and art and the city and about every single person we knew in common (generously, two) and then began the long walk back to where we were parked.

It had been more than a month since I'd had sex. Despite what you may assume about a woman who wrote a book called *How to Date Men When You Hate Men*, this was the longest I'd gone in years. Buddy and I might not have had a romantic spark between us, and we might have been hanging out only because of the sheer randomness that we were both in Port-land, but I was mostly a physical body now, and that physical body had become the emoji of the little red guy panting with a drop of sweat on his brow: irredeemably horny. We got to my car, and when Buddy kissed me, I kissed him back. It felt so good to be kissed; I felt like a woman with a full life again.

After a few moments Buddy stood up (he was at least a foot taller than me—making tall men uncomfortably stoop to kiss me is my feminist praxis) and tried to get in my car, to kiss with more privacy.

"No!" I almost yelled. "It smells *horrible*."

"I'm sure it smells fine."

"No," I said gravely.

"Well, can you at least drive me to my car, then, so we can kiss there?" he asked. I cringed, thinking about the Prius's distinct odor of "an everything bagel that just did a high-intensity interval workout."

"Do I have to?" Buddy just stood looking at me, unblinking. "Okay! Fine!" I moved everything off the passenger seat, rolled down the windows, and invited him in. "Don't smell anything! Try not to breathe."

His parents' SUV was not far away, and I parallel parked (brag) across the street from it. "I'm staying at my parents' house," he said. "So . . ."

I nodded. "How big is your back seat?" I hadn't driven across a continent to not make out with someone in their parents' car! I had never made out in a car before, due to losing my virginity at age fifty and not even kissing anyone until my last weekend at college. What was my trip about if not trying new things?

We were on a side street, and other than one person walking from their car into a nearby house, it looked fairly safe from observation by random passersby. We walked to the SUV and Buddy opened the hatchback. We climbed into the rear, where the seats were folded down. For me, a five-foot-two woman who had been sleeping in a Prius passenger seat on a regular basis, this felt luxurious. For him, a tall man living the life of a normal human, it was a squeeze. Someone was walking out of the nearby house toward their car, so we lay down out of sight and got back to kissing.

I don't know how long we fooled around back there—half an hour? forty-five minutes? Someone had his hands on me. I had my fingers in someone's hair. Time became liquid. Only when another person walked into or out of the nearby house did I feel pulled even slightly out of my body, back into the world outside the car. And then Buddy leaned back and looked at me. It was night and we were on a side street, but I could still see him clearly in the light from the streetlamps and the glow from the houses. He spoke quietly: "Do you want to . . ."

Did I want to? I thought about it for a moment, as another person seemed to enter the house thirty feet away. "Um, I think there's a dinner party going on next door?" For all the sinful things Buddy and I had been doing, we had managed up to this point to stay mostly clothed. "I don't want to get caught."

"Okay," he said. He moved his body so that it was diagonal across the trunk, getting maximum stretch. "But I don't know how long I can do this for. It's hurting my neck." I murmured sympathetically—*sounds like a personal problem*—and got back to kissing. And then I thought: I've been on this road trip for approximately six years and I may be on it for the rest of my natural life. I've flirted with every living person I've seen since Utah, and my sexual energy has been so strong that 80 percent of those people then followed me on social media. I may never have this chance again. What the hell.

"You know what, yes. Let me get condoms from the Prius. But you have to drive me somewhere more secluded."

He drove us around pointing out possible locations, all of which were directly next to a house on a street with at least one person walking around. Did he *want* people to see his butt? "No," I said. "*Secluded*." He grew up here. Shouldn't he know the spots? After a few minutes he drove up next to a large, tree-lined yard with an ornate building set back from the street, a campus of some kind.

"How's here?"

There was no one around. It seemed like the place. I looked at the institution's sign and made my peace with God. And then I had sex in a car parked outside a seminary.

12

No Offense to Clouds

KNOWING WHAT WE KNEW ABOUT MEN AND ALSO KNOW-ing about the sheer number of TV shows in existence that could be watched instead, *why* did people have sex in 2019? It certainly wasn't to have kids—maybe one or two couples across the country had sex for that reason, but, while I don't like to yuck anyone's yum, I really wasn't interested in that particular kink. I guess some people were having sex to express their love for each other: sounds great, congratulations. For me, that night, I just wanted to feel good. I wanted to feel like my body was attractive and capable of pleasure instead of "molecularly 70 percent human and 30 percent Tostitos Hint of Lime" and capable of "having the worst farmer's tan of my life, but on my legs." And it worked: as Buddy drove me back to my car, I felt a little like my New York self. I had had fun; I was glad I did it.

And then Buddy told me not to post online that I had

finally had sex, because people would figure out that it was with him.

Oh right! I remembered. *Men can make me feel BAD!* So far the only people I had interacted with on my trip were total strangers or my very favorite people in the world, friends and family I specifically drove across the country to see. Tonight I was reintroduced to the genre of "people who have had their tongues inside your mouth, but consider it a human rights violation to be asked to consider your feelings." It was easy for me to be horny when it had been a month since I'd dealt with the small humiliations that come with being a straight woman. Innocuous as it was, Buddy's comment deflated me, and plus I was so tired, and kind of needed to pee, and still had an hour's drive to Mount Hood National Forest, where I had only a vague idea of where I might be able to sleep. I told Buddy I wouldn't post about having sex, said goodbye, got right back in my car, and drove.

MY DRIVE THE next day took me hundreds of miles south to Crater Lake National Park. Along the way I stopped for coffee and realized all the ice in my cooler had melted, waterlogging my groceries past the point of edibility. Once in the park, I sped to the campground, and after waiting in line to reserve a site, was told the couple in front of me had claimed the last one. I realized the Prius's tank was low, so I waited in a long line to pay for overpriced gas, thinking about every bad thing that had ever happened to me in my life, in order, as everyone else filled their cars.

In a now very familiar event, the parking lot at the visitor center I drove to next was completely full. Slightly down the road I parked outside the backcountry permit office, which didn't seem like something I was allowed to do, but by that point I absolutely did not care. I needed to change my shirt; I opened a side door and made only a half-assed effort to shield my body from the office windows. So what if an employee of the Department of the Interior should see my boobs? Good for them! Ask not what your country can do for you.

I got my Junior Ranger book, and as I sat doing it I realized I could complete it in full before ever going on a hike. So I sat and did my homework. One exercise asked me to name another national park and what makes that park special; remembering my previous homework, I wrote "Capitol Reef" and "Waterpocket Fold." Then I got to a page that mentioned that swimming was allowed in Crater Lake. *Huh,* I thought. *For real?*

I couldn't very well turn in my book at the same visitor center where I had just requested it a half hour earlier, so I drove up to the Rim Village Visitor Center instead. There I stood at an overlook, finally able to properly fulfill my biological destiny: looking at a big lake. Crater Lake looks like something on a 1970s postcard. I had driven three and a half hours through large expanses of basically nothing to get here; it seemed too random to exist in the year 2019 and not just in some musical where once every 100 years a group of rangers teach tourists about the true meaning of volcanic craters.

The lake is five to six miles across with an island in the middle, and is a rich cobalt blue. The reason Crater Lake is so blue is that it is deep—it's the deepest lake in the United States—and pristine. It's one of the purest lakes in the world, with visibility of more than 100 feet deep. This is because the lake is fed only by rain and snow; it sits in a massive crater caused by a volcanic eruption 7,700 years ago. It was unlike any other lake I had ever seen, and I couldn't believe I was allowed to put my body inside of it.

The only safe trail from rim to shore was the Cleetwood Cove Trail: a mile long, views of the lake all the way down, gorgeous the entire time. A half hour earlier I had no clue that swimming was even an option, so I had no idea what to expect when I reached the lake. As it turned out, about a dozen people were swimming off a rocky shoreline. And a few were jumping off a twenty-foot cliff into the water. Well, shit. I tucked my backpack out of the way and joined the line to jump.

When my turn came, I peered down from the edge. Twenty feet seemed a whole lot higher from up here. I couldn't really see the bottom—there's a rock ledge about ninety feet below the surface, I'd later learn, then the bottom quickly drops to twelve hundred feet. (At its deepest, Crater Lake is nearly two thousand feet deep.) There was no one behind me waiting to jump, so I stood there in physical coward mode.

"Just jump!" a little kid sitting nearby encouraged me. "I've done it three times already."

He had a point. I took a deep breath, and jumped.

Crater Lake was *cold*. Jumping off the cliff was a thrill, but hitting the water was an entirely different kind of intense. I plunged into the nearly freezing lake—a park ranger would later tell me the temperature was around 41 degrees—suddenly aware of every part of my body as the warmth leached out of it. It was nothing like I'd expected; I felt fully alive. I popped back up to the surface and tried to say, "Holy shit!" but found that my blood was now ice and I could no longer form words.

I was euphoric. I was also, I suspected, experiencing shock. I couldn't speak and could barely swim, could barely keep my head above water, and most importantly could barely get out of the way so someone could jump in after me. (We all die eventually, but God forbid I'm rude while doing it.) Shivering, smiling as hugely as I could given my constricted blood vessels, I scooted toward the rock cliff, hugging close to it as I made my way toward shore. Eventually I reached the land, where people who had watched my jump congratulated me.

Face covered in snot, I managed to weakly say, "Holy shit!" The wet food, the lost campsite, the overpriced gas, the leaky tire, the man who had sex with me and then told me not to talk about it—none of them mattered to me now. I felt right, and purposeful, that I was where I should be, doing what I should be doing.

AMERICANS HAVE BEEN going to nature to feel alive since the Industrial Revolution, when a middle class arose that could afford to travel, and at the same time the world became less personal and more complex. Workers became small parts of a larger system, no longer making something from start to finish, and as people became estranged from their labor, they also became estranged from their sense of purpose and from their humanity. In modern parlance: the Industrial Revolution created the culture of wanting to "touch grass." Yosemite, Yellowstone, and other sublime natural places gave the new middle class a place to go and to experience an intensity that they perhaps no longer felt in their quotidian life.

An idea of wilderness-as-church was laid out by the transcendentalists, who wrote about a Godlike unblemished nature, where one could retreat and learn. John Muir did perhaps more than anyone else in American culture to equate the divine with the wild, writing about "our holy Yosemite," about mountains as altars, and saying about the Sierra Nevada,

"No description of Heaven that I have ever heard or read of seems half so fine." He has a point: if I'm choosing between heaven as a bunch of clouds where everyone who has ever lived is milling around making small talk in robes, or heaven as hiking in the mountains for all eternity, I'm choosing the Sierra Nevada (no offense to clouds).

Today the idea that God is in nature is so embedded in our culture that you don't even need to believe in God to feel that it is true. It's been more than half my life since I regularly went to church, but I do find a peace and a sense of sanity that feels soul-deep when I interact with the natural world. The wild helps me connect to what is bigger than myself, which for me is the delicate, interwoven relationships between every living thing on our planet. I don't believe in heaven, but I believe that after we die, if we're lucky and our family remembers our request not to be embalmed or cremated but instead to be thrown raw into a shallow grave (*as I previously mentioned*) (please do not forget, cc: my loved ones), our body continues on through those interwoven relationships, feeding a worm or a mushroom or a tree or a vulture if you're metal enough. That sounds like heaven to me.

That's what it felt like to jump in Crater Lake.

EVERYTHING AFTERWARD WAS like floating. I drove to a waterfall, hiked a trail covered with snow in July, slept for free next to a gushing river. In the morning I decided the time had come to get my tire fixed, and after buying groceries and giving myself a Clearasil wipe shower in a Starbucks parking lot, I did just that. Tires fully functional, I set my course for something I had always wanted to see: the redwoods. Soon enough I had crossed into Northern California and arrived at the Jedediah

Smith Campground in Jedediah Smith Redwoods State Park, part of Redwood National and State Parks. If this park name sounds byzantine, let me explain.

The depletion of old-growth redwoods took place extremely quickly. Before the gold rush in the mid-1800s, California had an estimated two million acres of coast redwoods. But by 1918 so much of the old-growth forest had been logged that the Save the Redwoods League was established to try to protect some of those trees before it was too late. The league had some success, and in the 1920s California created three state parks to protect significant redwood groves. But outside the parks redwood logging only sped up, as the invention of chainsaws and bulldozers made it easier to fell the massive trees and as the post–World War II building boom created a need for more lumber. All the while the federal government did nothing to protect the redwoods—so private citizens began to buy up forest land as if they were lumber companies, then held onto the land until the government took steps to protect it. Among those citizens was Laurence Rockefeller.

The Rockefellers, in fact, had a hand in the creation or expansion of many national parks: Acadia, Great Smoky Mountains, Shenandoah, Grand Canyon, Yellowstone, Grand Teton, Yosemite, and Crater Lake too. When I first learned about this I thought: *wow, how generous!* But then it struck me how messed up it is that so much land was stolen, then privatized, and that a few people amassed so much capital that they could afford to buy land and "give" it back. Billionaires only exist because of the exploitation of land, anyway, so what if they just . . . didn't do that in the first place? What if the top 100 landowners in America *didn't* control an area as large as Florida? What if . . . no one . . . was allowed to own land? Private property as a sacred thing didn't even exist until sixteenth-century England, when the aristocracy started enclosing the commons that peasants relied on to graze their animals, to collect water and fuel, and to forage. Enclosure so impoverished farmers that they were forced to travel to North America looking for opportunity; when they got here, they squatted on Indigenous people's land until they decided they owned it.

All of which is to say: the fate of the natural world shouldn't rely on billionaires waking up on the right side of the bed. But what do I know! I'll never be rich enough to own land.

In 1962, Rachel Carson published *Silent Spring*, and society started to care more about conservation; in 1968, Redwood National Park was created. Since 1994, the National Park Service and the California State Parks system have co-managed their redwoods parks. But after all that, only 4 to 5 percent of the old-growth redwoods remain. Just how small and parceled up our nation's protected land is became even more evident to me as I drove between parks, passing chain stores and development along the way.

THE RANGER WORKING at the Hiouchi Visitor Center was a woman around my age but very neatly put together, whereas I was the kind of dirty that comes from hiking, jumping in a lake, having sex in a car, sleeping in a messier car, and using only face wipes to clean your body. I was scared of what this lady would think of someone her own age asking for a Junior Ranger book.

As it turned out, she didn't care. She answered thoughtfully when I asked her for hiking recommendations, and when I asked what had brought her to the National Park Service, she told me about her time in the Navy before becoming a ranger.

When someone got in line behind me, I excused myself and started working on my booklet to kill time until the campground opened. One of the activities was about tidepools. *Are you freaking kidding me?* I thought. *This park has giant trees AND tide pools?!* What more could a person want in this lifetime?

I walked back over to my Navy friend and sheepishly asked her if she had any tidepool recommendations. "Actually," she said, "Let me give you directions to my secret spot. I've never seen a single other person on this beach." She pulled out a pen and paper, and in her careful handwriting wrote down how to get there. "And you'll need this," she said, handing me a tide chart. "Go at low tide so everything will be visible."

Feeling like a marine biologist or a secret agent or maybe both, I left to hike through the redwoods.

AND SO TO the tallest trees in the world. I crossed the Smith River on a small footbridge, crossed its tributary Mill Creek, and within minutes was in the Stout Grove. This land was donated by a lumberman's widow in 1929 and has never been logged. I stepped into forty-four acres of old-growth redwoods and was overwhelmed. Many of the trees in Stout Grove are three hundred feet tall, taller than my body was designed to comprehend. Fallen redwoods, covered in ferns and moss and salal, had trunks easily three or four times taller than me.

The tallest coast redwoods can grow to nearly 380 feet, as tall as a thirty-five-story building, two and a half times taller than the midtown office building where I had spent most of my time over the past several years. Which is crazy because—I can't emphasize this enough—*they're trees.* And because the climate is so favorable and their bark so resistant to insects and fire, coast redwoods can live more than two thousand years, making them nearly as old as I am. I wandered around in the drizzling rain, not alone in the grove but nearly feeling that way, since sounds were dampened by the carpet of redwood duff and wood sorrel on the forest floor. As I walked between the trees, tears welled up in my eyes. What else could I do but cry a little? These trees were huge!

I spent the next few hours hiking a trail that hugged the clear waters of Mill Creek on its way through the forest. The Navy ranger told me this trail wasn't overly popular, and she was right: as soon as I left Stout Grove, I didn't see a single other person. Here too I was walking among old-growth redwoods, though the forest was thicker here with maples and other normal-sized trees I couldn't name. A banana slug crossed my path, and I crouched down to take a good look, though I didn't know yet that you can kiss it, to make your lips tingle. (Even later I would find out the NPS prefers you *don't* kiss them or any other slightly toxic animal, which I learned from a *New York Times* article with the headline "National Park Service Asks Visitors to Please Stop Licking Toads.") No matter how it happened, I was so grateful that this forest had been protected. It was a piece of an intact ecosystem, and being there somehow made me feel intact too. On my way back to the campground I patted one huge redwood, and said "Good job, bud."

I DROVE INTO Crescent City the next morning to kill time at Starbucks until low tide. I had become a person who "kills time until low tide!" It seemed like a profound shift. What would I do next? Get rid of my GPS and navigate using the direction of tree branches and the angle of the sun? Eat only freshly foraged berries? Talk to possums?

I waited as long as I could and then drove to the ranger's secret tidepool spot. Like a spy, I parked at an unassuming picnic area and, clutching her directions, set off toward the Pacific. Soon I was on a trail hugging the coast, luxuriant in plant life: green grasses under my feet, and just off the trail ferns and shrubs and some of the biggest mushrooms I had ever seen. After a classified amount of time, I followed a small path cutting down to the shore and emerged on the rocky beach of a small cove. It was a perfect place, though I'm biased: the ocean will always be especially magical to people like me who grew up surrounded by corn.

As soon as I looked into the first tidepool, I lost track of time. The tidepools were full of life. Almost immediately I saw a sea star and gasped in delight. While the sea star population up in Washington had seen heavy mortality from sea star wasting disease, the ones here in California weren't hit as bad. I saw at least a dozen that morning, purple and brown and bright orange. They shared the tidepools with lime green sea anemones or clung to wave-bashed rocks next to sheets of mussels, which would quickly take over the coastline if sea stars weren't there to eat them. I picked my way over rocks and along the water line, trying to see everything in my private tidal cathedral, or at least as much as I could without getting hit by a sneaker wave and dragged out to sea. I felt completely removed from the world where I had been less than an hour earlier. The little cove felt like pure nature, a retreat.

But thinking about nature this way, as a sublime and untouched Eden, can work against the interests of nature. If only the most heart-stopping parts of the natural world—waterfalls, mountains, canyons, dramatic coasts—can stir us to profound spiritual transformation, what's the point in protecting a prairie? A bog? That's why there were no national parks where I grew up: I spent the first eighteen years of my life surrounded by prairies and bogs (and, if you biked three miles into town, CVSs). But those places are just as natural as this coastal rainforest was. More urgently, if we think of nature as only completely untouched parcels of paradise, it means that when land is compromised in any way it's deemed no longer worthy of protection. Businesses and ranchers sometimes play directly into this, letting cattle graze or cutting a road to weaken a place's claim to preservation. Should we throw up our hands and give in? Should we admit that every place on earth has already been affected by climate change, so we might as well just turn it all into condos from which we will watch the apocalypse?

This argument—that only untouched, Edenic wilderness deserves protection—becomes even more obviously illogical when you consider that, as Mark David Spence writes in *Dispossessing the Wilderness*, "uninhabited wilderness had to be created before it could be preserved." That is to say, the only reason we have huge national parks where no one hunts or forages or lives is because the United States government violently removed the Indigenous people who were using those lands to hunt and forage and live. Soon after, without the stewardship of Indigenous people, entire ecosystems changed.

I'm suspicious of the compulsion to find purity, anyway. The search for it is about trying to feel in control in a world where you can never be in full control, really. The parks I saw weren't pure—they had gift shops and roads crawling with massive RVs, were bordered by hotels and gas stations and chain restaurants. I might have found it tacky, but it didn't make me want to throw in the towel in search of a purer wilderness out there somewhere. I had driven all over the country: it was becoming clear there wasn't some massive, pure wilderness in the continental United States, or I would have run into it by now.

If we can find spiritual meaning in nature only in places like the secret tidepool spot—a place completely unlike anywhere I have ever lived—does that mean we're cut off from finding similar meaning in our day-to-day lives? I'm not here to argue that watching pigeons try to kill or fuck each other (maybe both?) on my fire escape could match the wonder of peering into tidepools at sea urchins and limpets and honest-to-God real-life starfish. But I'm a couple subway rides away from my own ocean, a few minutes' walk from two parks, and surrounded by street trees I spent years never giving a second thought. We're all surrounded by nature, even if we've been taught not to see it as such. If we don't start to value nature closer to home, there will be no one to protect it.

It was time for me to go, or I'd never make it to the next national park before its visitor center closed. It was almost low tide now, and as I climbed back up to the coastal trail I passed a family heading down to the shore. My cathedral wasn't so secret after all.

13

Against Stripping Yosemite for Parts

THE PARK I WAS HEADING TO NEXT OWED ITS EXISTENCE in a small way to one amateur photographer. In 1914 Benjamin Franklin "Frank" Loomis was a lumberman/entrepreneur/Aries living near the recently declared Lassen Peak National Monument. Lassen Peak is the southernmost active volcano in the Cascades Range, but when Theodore Roosevelt gave it national monument status in 1907, Lassen was considered inactive. After all, it had been dormant for twenty-seven thousand years.

On May 30, 1914, it began to erupt. A few days into the eruption Frank Loomis took a series of six dramatic photos of Lassen Peak spewing an immense cloud of ash. These photos were picked up by news organizations, sparking national interest in the event. The volcano kept erupting, and Loomis kept taking photos and guiding dignitaries and scientists who visited, and soon people in America were like, "This shit is metal as hell. We should make a national park about it." In

1916, at which point the volcano had been erupting for two years—this is a thing volcanoes do, I guess—they did make a national park about it.

Loomis maintained a connection with the park for the rest of his life; I probably would have too, if I lived ten miles from a volcano that randomly erupted, and then the photos I took of it went viral. Frank and his wife, Estella, bought forty acres near the park on which they built a museum to house Frank's photos of the eruption. Crucially, this was a private museum built by two people to honor some photos one of them took thirteen years before. But the photos really were that important, and when the Loomises donated their land to the National Park Service, the park kept the museum going.

LASSEN VOLCANIC NATIONAL Park was one of the parks I'd never heard of before planning my trip. I wasn't happy to tear myself away from my sea star babies to drive to it. On one hand, sure: Lassen and Mount Saint Helens are the only two volcanoes in the lower forty-eight states that erupted in the 1900s. On the other hand, in a state already bursting with national parks, Lassen seemed to me a little like a park made to celebrate something that happened 100 years ago and probably wasn't going to happen again for another 26,900.

I was on a tight schedule now. I had a nearly five-hour drive to get to the Loomis Museum before five p.m. to get my Junior Ranger booklet, and when I hit the road after seeing the tidepools, it was eleven thirty. I'd be cutting it close. After that my schedule didn't get any better. It was Wednesday, and I needed to be in Los Angeles the next Tuesday. In the interim I had to squeeze in Lassen; a visit to my best friend, Todd, in

San Francisco; Yosemite; Sequoia and Kings Canyon; Pinnacles; Big Sur; and a night in San Luis Obispo. I wasn't going to have a moment to breathe. Here I was doing my part to subvert canonical travel narratives by making sure vacation was *not* relaxing and was instead *incredibly stressful*. It felt like I was behind on all my deadlines, but in this case my deadlines were "having fun" and "experiencing the great outdoors."

I hit construction on a winding switchback road and knew it was over for me; I watched my arrival time at the Loomis Museum inch later and later until it passed five p.m. Once I had no chance of making it, I could just enjoy my drive. I stopped getting annoyed at every driver I perceived as worse at driving than I was, which is to say, every driver. When I arrived at Lassen Volcanic National Park, I set up my little pup tent at a campsite and went for a leisurely mile-and-a-half stroll around nearby Manzanita Lake. From the far shore I looked at Lassen Peak cresting above a line of pine trees, its mirror image reflected in the water. *It really just looks like a mediocre mountain,* I thought. *It doesn't look like a volcano at all.* But that's the thing about volcanoes. That's how they get you.

INSIDE THE LOOMIS Museum the next morning, I got my Junior Ranger booklet and looked around. It housed much more than the photos now: there were geology exhibits, woven baskets, a huge topographical relief map. Then I set off on the thirty-mile scenic drive through the park.

I had no idea as I drove—stopping occasionally to take in a view, to touch a wall of snow still fifteen feet tall in the middle of July, to smell the sulfur of boiling pools and hydrothermal features—that two years later half the park would burn in the Dixie Fire. Much of what I saw from the road would be unaffected by the burn, but the fire was by far the largest the park has ever experienced, impacting just over 73,000 of the park's 106,452 acres. The next largest, 2012's Reading Fire, burned 16,993 acres in the park. Before that, only a few fires had impacted more than 1,000 acres.

But all this was in the future. As I took the last turn into the park's visitor center, Lassen seemed to me like a beautiful if not particularly famous park where something destructive had occurred a long time ago and likely wouldn't for another long while. And then, far too quickly, I left the park.

A FEW HOURS on the Interstate brought me to the San Francisco suburb where my best friend, Todd, was living at home for a few months as he studied for the Bar. We hadn't seen each other for a while, but Todd was one of those people you could pick right up with even if you hadn't hung out in a year, even if you had written in your book that Todd never returns texts. I walked up the steps of the Burlingame library just as Todd was walking out to meet me. Seeing Todd was better than seeing some old volcano, by far.

We holed up in the library, where I returned emails as he studied trust law. Then over dinner and after some more studying at his house I told Todd about my trip thus far, the highs of Cisco and the redwoods and the lows of feeling rushed and missing my life. "I'm kind of tired of being on the road," I told him.

"Well, thank God your trip is almost over!" he replied, deadpan.

We didn't do anything particularly San Francisco-y, just sat in a room working next to each other and watching a couple episodes of *I Think You Should Leave*. I still had weeks and weeks of driving ahead of me, but for eighteen hours it felt like I was back inside my life. In the morning we got breakfast near the library, where Todd was dutifully spending eight hours a day studying, and I, bad influence that I was, I forced him to hang out with me until my parking meter expired. It was painful to leave: I saw Todd so rarely and wished I could spend more time with him, and I felt dumb for getting myself across the country to his house, but giving myself only eighteen hours there. But it was time for me to head to Yosemite so I could free-solo El Cap.

Free Solo, an Academy Award–winning documentary about two people who do not seem like they should be dating, one of whom successfully climbs the three-thousand-foot sheer rock face of El Capitan in Yosemite National Park with no ropes, had come out the year before my trip. I'd been to Yosemite as a kid and had a great time, but now my main association with the park was this insanely stressful movie. I joked about it all the time. "I'm going to Yosemite to free-solo El Cap!" I told one friend.

He replied, "Is there a Junior Ranger badge for doing that?"

People have been making art about Yosemite for a long time before *Free Solo*. It's another park that (much more than Lassen) owes its existence partly to photographers and painters and writers. Artists like Thomas Hill and Albert Bierstadt traveled to Yosemite Valley before it was a national park, and their paintings helped inspire public feeling that the valley should be protected. When the shipping magnate Captain Israel Ward Raymond wrote to California senator John Conness, telling him he should get Congress to protect Yosemite, he included with his letter a bunch of photographs. John Muir and his exposés were also instrumental in the efforts to protect the valley.

Many parks share a backstory involving artists of one kind or another. Muir's writings also contributed to the establishment of Sequoia National Park and Grand Canyon National Park. At Isle Royale I noticed a trail marker dedicated to a writer and editor named Albert Stoll Jr., "whose untiring efforts made possible the preservation of Isle Royale as a National Park." The author Ernest Oberholtzer was an advocate for what is now Voyageurs. In Utah, Frederick S. Dellenbaugh painted Zion Canyon in 1903, exhibited his paintings at the 1904 St. Louis World's Fair, and wrote about the canyon in a 1904 issue of *Scribner's*, all of which influenced President Taft to protect the area as Mukuntuweap National Monument. I could go on! As I traveled through the parks, I was blown away by how many had origin stories which involved journalists or painters or photographers pointing out that, oh, maybe this place *shouldn't* be stripped for parts.

This seemed to me one of the main reasons to write about natural places: to aid in any way the effort to preserve them. In this nightmare world we live in, it can be hard to feel good about being a comedy writer: who exactly am I helping here? One plausible mission of writing, I began to think, is to remind people that nature is good before we convert it all into single-use iced coffee cups. Writing is one of the three marketable skills I have, along with "professional-grade internet stalking" and "watching teenagers take practice SAT tests." I want to use it to give back to nature by noticing and appreciating the world, especially as biodiversity is in rapid decline. And maybe by noticing I might inspire others to notice, too.

In this exact moment, though, I was not doing much noticing. I was mainly driving as fast as I could to get to Yosemite and get my Junior Ranger booklet at one visitor center, pound it out, and turn it in at another visitor center before closing time. I had given myself a goal, and I was going to achieve that goal even when it became a huge pain in the ass and honestly not even fun: this was vacation in America.

I was becoming frustrated by my self-imposed inability to stay anywhere and dig in deep, to learn about the intricacies of each park's unique web of plants and animals and climate and humans. From the very beginning, when I had decided to make a day trip to Isle Royale instead of finding a way to lug all my gear to the island for an extended stay, I had put myself on a fast pace. Due to a commitment I had in Los Angeles, my pace in California had only gotten faster. Because I felt like I didn't have enough time in any park, all my time spent driving became more and more annoying, totally dead time made frustrating by the fact that *I had done this to myself* and even more frustrating by the actions of everyone else on the road. This annoyance turned into road . . . let's call it "anger." It's not true road *rage*, I think, unless you threaten to kill the other person and they hear you. I became more and more stressed as I hit traffic, took a wrong turn, and stopped to pee at Starbucks, where the overworked staff took half an hour to make an iced latte I had ordered only out of bathroom etiquette obligation. There was no part of me that wanted to quit my trip—and even if I wanted to I'd have to keep driving back across the country, to return TB's car—but I looked forward to the rest of the trip after LA, when I hoped I would be able to slow down.

Finally I made it to Yosemite's Wawona Visitor Center. Instead of the usual National Park Service Rustic style, sometimes called "parkitecture," this visitor center was a wood building in an older style, complete with flourishes on the eaves. A sign on the building identified it as HILL'S STUDIO; inside were reproductions of the paintings of Thomas Hill, the artist who helped bring the area to prominence. As relevant as they were to my emerging consciousness of the role of the artist in conservation, I ignored the paintings and beelined to the ranger working the combination information desk and cash register. "Hi!" I said brightly, long past any compunction about asking for my kiddie book. "Can I get a Junior Ranger packet from you, please?"

"Sure," the ranger said, pointing at a shelf in the gift store behind me. "That will be $3.50."

I didn't have time to worry about what it said about the United States if our National Park Junior Ranger programs were no longer free; I wanted to give the twelve things I was already worrying about my full focus. So I paid my *nearly four dollars* and headed outside to work.

I finished the book in twenty-five minutes because I have a degree from Harvard. For a second I considered turning around and asking the ranger who had just sold me the book to trade it in for a badge, but what I was doing—acquiring badges as an end in itself without properly experiencing nature first—was patently embarrassing, and the shame of revealing that to the ranger was too great. I plugged the next closest visitor center into Google Maps. It would take one hour to get here. If I sped (and I was temperamentally incapable of doing anything else) I'd probably make it with fifteen minutes to spare before closing time. I threw the Prius in drive and tore out of the parking lot like Vin Diesel attempting to drive fast enough to save the world in any *Fast & Furious* movie after the fourth one. Game on.

I zoomed north on Wawona Road at a thrilling 40 miles per hour. I took blind curves without slowing down, watching as my ETA ticked earlier a minute at a time. *She's doing it!* I thought. I passed a sign that said SPEEDING KILLS BEARS and made a mental note not to kill any bears. I caught up to a car that was driving the speed limit without a care in the world and felt my heart rate accelerate in inverse proportion to the Prius. When the road came to a rare straightaway, I pulled into the oncoming lane and passed. Nothing would stop me from achieving my arbitrary, frustrating goal.

A tunnel took me through the mountains and when I emerged as if from a womb, all of Yosemite Valley spread out before me, the iconic vista you see on postcards—the one where you can practically hear angels singing, the one that makes you stop and give thanks that such a place exists on this planet. The drivers ahead of me pulled into a roadside parking lot to stop and really savor being here in this place in front of El Capitan and Half Dome; I saw them pull over and thought *sweet, adios* and drove even faster.

I parked my car with fourteen minutes to spare, absolutely triumphant. But then I looked around: the visitor center was nowhere to be seen. As it turns out, there wasn't a lot adjacent to that building. Rather, this giant lot provided parking for the entire valley; from here visitors could get around on a shuttle bus. This was environmentally savvy but meant that to get to the visitor center in the now thirteen minutes before it closed, my quickest option would be, according to my GPS, walking fifteen minutes. The adrenaline from my hour of driving curdled into hot annoyance with myself and my entire trip.

I called my mom, the only person who will put up with me complaining about facing the consequences of my own actions. "I don't know what to do!" I said. "I'm sleeping outside Sequoia National Park tonight. That's three hours away. To get this badge tomorrow is going to take six hours of driving round trip! And then I won't have enough time in the next park!"

"Well, sweetie," my mom said, more soothingly than I deserved. "What if you just don't get a Junior Ranger badge from Yosemite?"

"If I don't get a Junior Ranger badge from Yosemite, then why am I doing any of this at all?"

Mom clocked that I wasn't open to logical solutions and was just looking to wallow. "Look at it this way, at least you have your health."

"I don't care about my health!" I wailed. (Note to karma: I do care about my health.)

"At least your father and I are alive."

I knew I was being a huge baby if the only thing that could make me feel better about showing up at a visitor center after it closed was that I hadn't yet experienced the trauma of a parent dying. I thanked my mom for listening to me, told her I loved her and was happy she wasn't dead, and hopped off the phone. It was time to figure out what my trip was, if not a scheme to embezzle children's badges from the US government.

Why am I doing this? is a question endemic to solo travel, when you don't have another person there to validate your choices simply by going along with the plan. After a while you begin to wonder if what you're doing is justified. The more I thought about the history of the parks, about the ramifications of putting boundaries around which nature is and is not protected, about the fossil fuels I was burning to get everywhere, about the impact I and the hordes of other travelers were having on these areas, and, very acutely how much I missed my friends, the more I wondered if what I was doing made any sense at all. I had quit my job. The entire world was open to me. I had saved enough money to not work for the summer. Why had I decided to take a tour of America's most scenic crowded parking lots?

There are a lot of reasons I went on this trip. I wanted to feel like I wasn't wasting my time on this planet. I wanted to see the beautiful places I'd heard about. I wanted to interrogate narratives I grew up enamored of. The badges weren't a reason for the trip at all; they were just something to give it structure— the trip's skeleton, not its soul.

It wasn't until months after I got home that I was able to admit the biggest reason I went on my trip: I just wanted to have fun. And at this moment in that particular parking lot, it was hard to see how, exactly, what I was doing was fun.

WHEN I THOUGHT I could *The Fate of the Furious* my way to the visitor center with enough time to get my badge, I had planned to tell the rangers that I hadn't yet completed the requirement to attend a ranger- or naturalist-led activity but to promise that I would. Now I decided to attend one anyway. Maybe I'd drive back tomorrow, or maybe I'd mail my book to Todd and have him turn it in for me on an upcoming visit. To that end I drove over to the Majestic Yosemite Hotel, where such a program was about to start.

At the hotel I couldn't catch a break. Signs posted warned me not to leave anything edible in my Prius because bears at Yosemite *did* associate cars with food, they *would* break into your car to eat your Doritos, they *were* smarter than you, and if you put your Doritos in your trunk, they would simply rip open your car door and demolish your back seat. If you wanted to leave even one crumb, even one minty-smelling toothpaste tube in your car, that was on you and Yosemite would refuse to cover any damages. My options were lugging my entire cooler around with me on the naturalist walk or leaving the Prius open to disarticulation via *Ursus americanus*.

I decided to risk it. Inside the hotel I dropped my expensive new Bryce Canyon water bottle, denting the shit out of it. *This is more stressful than* Free Solo*!* I would have texted anyone if I'd had enough service. I made my way through the hotel decorated with stained glass and tapestries and more sofas in one room than I would be able to afford in my lifetime, and found a group gathering outside for the naturalist program.

For an hour the naturalist, a young woman named Brooke, led us around Yosemite Valley, showing us how to notice things, how to find delight in small corners of the natural world. We looked at flowers and trees, talked about butterflies and about the history of the place where we stood. Brooke was soft-spoken and so evidently enamored with the things she showed us that the walk was a balm for the tantrum I was having. I couldn't stay annoyed, especially when I got to talking with an older woman on the tour. When she found out I was from Wisconsin, she told me she had a relative who had died in Sheboygan, drunk in a snowbank "like the good Irishman he was."

Brooke was talking to us about the overcrowded forests in Yosemite—there were more trees per acre now than when Indigenous people set controlled fires, especially since even natural fires had been suppressed between the 1850s and 1970s, and it was damaging the health of the ecosystem—when a man on the tour pointed toward something maybe twenty yards away in the underbrush. "Look!" he said. We looked. "It's a bear!"

It really was. I was looking at, for the first time on my trip, a bear, or at least the butt of one. At this point my annoyance-to-feeling-rejuvenated-by-nature cycle was moving way too fast for my liking, but what can I say: seeing that bear's beautiful ass was the fun I had been looking for. "Looks like a baby," Brooke said. "This time of year they like to eat berries." We ooh-ed and ahh-ed while dragging ass out of the trees because where there's a baby bear, there's a protective mama close by.

At the conclusion of the program I walked up to Brooke to thank her and ask her to sign my Junior Ranger book. "I got down here too late to turn it in, so I'm driving back tomorrow," I told her as she signed.

"Oh, don't do that," she said. "Give me your address. I'll turn it in for you." Between the bear butt, my IUD, how tall the trees were, and how absolutely floored I was by Brooke's kindness, I almost cried.

"What's your Venmo? Let me pay for shipping at least."

She wouldn't hear of it.

I didn't know if I'd be able to write a book that would encourage anyone to care about the environment. I didn't know if, weighed against every reason I had discovered that what I was doing was problematic, my trip was at all justified. But meeting someone like Brooke—hoping I could be kind like she was and that my delight in nature, like hers, could be so expansive as to spread to those I talked to—made everything feel worth it. I hoped to spend the rest of the trip, no matter how rushed, looking at nature the way I did on that unhurried walk through one small corner of Yosemite Valley.

14

The National Parks Suck Ass

THERE COMES A TIME ON EVERY VACATION WHEN YOU completely lose touch with the days of the week. And why not? "Days" may not be a societal construct—I'll admit that the sun does appear and disappear on a pretty consistent basis—but "weeks" seem pretty random. Every seven times the sun comes up, that's supposed to mean something to me? Why seven? Is it because of the dwarves? And each of the seven days has a different name and theme? I'm supposed to eat tacos on Tuesday for some reason? Once a week, a cat somewhere looks up from eating its lasagna to complain about the fact that it's "Monday"? I can't see any particular reason why we've all agreed to devote our lives to enriching billionaires five days out of every seven, as long as we get to spend two days straight going to the farmers' market. Which is all to say: I've never been that good at telling a Wednesday from a Thursday to begin with, so by this point on my trip it was completely hopeless. When I arrived at the visitor center at Sequoia and Kings Canyon National Parks, I was confused why there was a long line at 9:36 in the morning until I remembered I was in the country's most populous state, it was summer, and—*oh*—it was Saturday.

Sequoia and Kings Canyon protect, as you might guess, giant sequoia trees, which are the largest trees by volume: in other words, the world's swolest trees. Roughly one-third of the world's naturally occurring thicc boi sequoias grow in these two national parks. Although technically they're two separate parks, Sequoia and Kings Canyon have been jointly administered since 1943, so they're not fooling anyone. They're like those hip couples who have been together for thirty years and have kids together but who aren't legally married. Cool! You're proving a point, I guess, for sure!

Junior Ranger book in hand, I planned my route for the day. The swolest tree in the world as well as a big rock the ranger said was worth seeing were both to the south, in Sequoia, so I settled back into my beloved Prius to drive to them. The drive didn't last long. I was barely into the park when I hit a roadblock: rangers were directing all cars to pull into the Wuksachi Lodge parking lot, leave their cars, and get on a shuttle.

I'm a huge fan of public transportation. I've seen those infographics that show how many vehicles it takes to move a thousand people, and it's like 625 cars with five acres of parking on each end, or one subway. Making public transportation more widespread, more convenient, and more easily accessible does seem like one of the things we can do that might actually have an impact on climate change. But I won't claim that when I saw the rangers telling us to ditch our cars, I started applauding and cheering and getting my fellow tourists to chant "PUB-lic TRANS-port, *clap clap, clap clap clap*."

I parked my car dutifully, glanced at the chaotic throng standing in the hot sun waiting for a shuttle, and thought, *Oh God, this is probably going to be a nightmare.* After a long wait, a short shuttle bus pulled up, and all hell broke loose. I saw families about to murder other families for seats. It was like gang warfare, it was like a state of nature, it was like the scene where Billy Zane does reprehensible things to get on a lifeboat in *Titanic*.

I made it on, and after a short ride we transferred to another shuttle, packing in bodies in defiance of the laws of physics. Finally we were allowed to pour out of the shuttle, gasping for air, at the trailhead for the General Sherman Tree. Along with about thirty other women, I headed to the bathroom before beginning my hike. Granted, I didn't particularly *have* to pee, but I have midwestern mom's disease: those women who tell their kids to try to pee "just in case" every time they leave the house—that's me. I pee before I leave the house even if I just peed fifteen minutes earlier. I pee so often that my friends ask me in hushed tones if everything is okay *medically*, and I tell them I'm fine. It's just that if I think there's any chance I'm going to need to pee later and it might be even the slightest hassle, I pee now. But peeing at the General Sherman shuttle stop was its own hassle: the facilities were covered in damp toilet paper and mystery liquids forming puddles so large they deserved to be named on a map. It seemed that Sequoia National Park was dealing with more visitors than it could handle. I went ghost mode in the restroom (left my physical body, tried not to touch anything) and then hiked into the large trees.

Standing in front of the General Sherman Tree, all I could do was stare at it, my gaze traveling slowly upward like the camera filming a hot woman in any movie directed by any man. I let my small body feel its relation to the massive thing I was looking at. It was 275 feet tall, with a trunk diameter of thirty-six feet, about as wide as the street I lived on including the cars parked on both sides. There are trees that are taller than the General Sherman and trees that are wider but none that are larger by volume, which they figured out by putting it in a bathtub and seeing how much water it displaced. It seemed so unlikely that we'd get to live in a world where plants could be this big, but we do, and here I was standing among them. The air around me felt special, sparkly, and I could see why a utopian socialist commune had been founded here in the 1880s and renamed the tree the Karl Marx Tree.

Back on the shuttle I dissociated until the bus spat me out at the park museum, where I found another atrocity-level bathroom and a ranger who could give me my Junior Ranger badge. The ranger checked over my work, which included a supplementary bingo game with things I had spotted in the park: a pinecone, a giant sequoia, a wildflower, a park ranger, a bug, that kind of stuff. "What was your favorite thing you spotted?" the ranger asked me.

"Oh, I love the giant sequoias," I said.

"Oh," he said, hurt.

"Was I supposed to say something else?" I racked my brain. The sequoias were the whole point of the park, weren't they? Maybe there was some sick bug I had missed?

"We like it when people say their favorite thing was the park rangers," he answered. I assured him I loved him, too, very much.

MORO ROCK, WHERE I headed next, is a big old granite dome that looms over the park at 6,725 feet above sea level. The park road takes visitors up most of that height, but the trail to ascend the last bit is all climb, over 350 steps. I passed people who were standing aside panting, because while I was not in professional athlete shape by any stretch of the imagination, I am famously not a "management consultant," "investment banker," or "Kylie Jenner," and therefore cannot afford to live in a building with an elevator. Climbing 350 steps was basically what I needed to do anytime I came home. The only time I stopped was when Yaedra, the blond woman hiking in front of me, kept blocking the entire trail with a pose that she forced her boyfriend to photograph. (I learned her name when her boyfriend suggested she let the dozen people queued up behind her pass, and she responded by yelling at him for taking "just one photo" when clearly she needed options.)

None of it mattered when I reached the top. Everywhere I looked there were mountains. I walked out to one end of the narrow, handrail-enclosed viewing area: to my west was wilderness and the snow-capped peaks of the Great Western Divide. To my east, the mountains sloped down until they opened up into the San Joaquin Valley. I took some photos, and when I turned around there was a line of people waiting to do the same. I had become the Yaedra.

Near Moro Rock was an oddity I wanted to see: the Tunnel Log, a tree you could drive through. Unlike those famous old-timey images of cars driving through standing sequoias via tunnels that maimed and eventually killed the trees they were cut through, this tunnel was cut through a sequoia that fell onto a newly constructed road. The log was too big to move easily, so the Park Service just cut a truck-sized hole out of it. When I got there, a man was taking a photo of his family, standing inside the log. I told him I'd take a photo with him

in it, and he asked if he could take one of me in return. "Sure!"
I said and kneeled down in the tunnel, my hands together in
prayer.

"Are you sure you don't want to stand normally?" he asked.

I got happily lost on my way back to the park museum,
pausing often to consult my trail map against the scant signage I
passed. Around the third or fourth time I stopped dead in my
tracks to figure out where the heck I was, a lone man walked
by me. I said hi. He said hi. And then I noticed he was carrying a sequoia pinecone.

All five weeks of my Junior Ranger training flashed before my eyes. Though there are exceptions—some parks allow
limited berry foraging, and usufruct rights were guaranteed
to Indigenous nations in treaties—a general rule of thumb is
that you are not allowed to remove anything from a national
park. This was especially important for sequoia pinecones,
because sequoia seeds have such an uphill battle to germinate
at all, requiring the cones to drop their seeds, the seeds to
not get eaten, the young trees to get the perfect amount of
shade . . . basically this tree needed all the help it could get.
One guy stealing one pinecone probably wouldn't matter, but
more than 1.2 million people visit Sequoia and Kings Canyon National Parks every year, and it's easy to see how quickly
things could get dire. I weighed all the Junior Ranger oaths I
had taken, in which I swore to share what I had learned with
others, against picking a fight with a jacked man with no one
around in shouting distance.

"Have a good one!" I said and let him pass.

THE EXTENT OF my failure as a protector of nature went
beyond failing to stop one guy from stealing one pinecone.

Given the obvious downsides to over-visitation, I began to worry that not only was I doing something bad by adding my body to the mass of tourists, but perhaps I was doing something worse by writing about the national parks. Maybe it's human nature to want to experience breathtaking natural beauty, throw your toilet paper on the floor, stop too often for pictures on the trail, and steal a pinecone. Maybe that's in our DNA! But did I really need to add to the problem by putting out a book about how much I loved my own journey to these places? This was the flip side of my thinking at Yosemite about how artists could inspire people to protect nature: artists could also inspire more industrial tourism, more visitation by people who didn't care about fossil fuels or climate change. Was my moral duty as an environmentally minded America instead to write a book about how the national parks suck ass?

Writing about places inspires people to go there. This is not some unintended side effect: it has been a primary aim of travel writing throughout United States history. When the US government wanted to encourage Anglo settlers to journey westward as part of the campaign of Native dispossession, it sent John C. Frémont on "mapping" expeditions and had him write about his adventures. Before Frémont, only about a hundred people had traveled the Oregon Trail. After his *Report On an Exploration of the Country Lying Between the Missouri River and the Rocky Mountains* was published, thousands did so over the following few years. Jealousy is real, and it works!

It used to baffle me when people I knew who rode the rails—hopped freight trains to travel around the country—wouldn't talk openly about it. *What's with all the secrecy?* I thought. As a writer, I had come to believe that experiences congealed when you talked about them, either with friends or in writing. To tell stories, you have to think about the significance of things that happen to you and their causal relationships, so that by recounting the events of your life to someone else, you reveal those events' meanings.

But now that secrecy felt less rude, less like in middle school when the skater boys told me I couldn't "really" be a fan of Nirvana based on my general appearance and personality. I was beginning to see people's reticence to talk about their experience of nature and travel as an admission that so little in our world can be ethically scaled up. If you talk about riding the rails, pretty soon a bunch of Kerouac wannabes start freight hopping, which leads to more policing, which leads to no one being able to do it. If everyone tries to go to Walden to live a quiet, deliberate life, pretty soon you've got the bustling Walden metropolitan area.

THE NEXT DAY I drove westward out of the Sierra Nevada to Pinnacles National Park, blindly doing whatever my GPS told me to do, realizing that if a serial killer hacked my Google Maps to send me straight to their murder hole, I would follow it there without a moment's pause. Pinnacles has been a national park only since 2013, and I hadn't heard much about it. I was interested to learn exactly what it was, but even more interested in checking it off my Junior Ranger list and making it to LA in time.

I did wish I had more time to give the park its proper due, but immediately on stepping out of my car at the visitor center, I realized those dreams would have to wait: in punishing contrast to the mountain temperatures I had woken up to at Sequoia and Kings Canyon, the air at Pinnacles felt like the heat of a thousand hair straighteners being applied directly to my body. According to the Prius's dashboard thermometer, it was 110 degrees. When I asked a ranger what she'd recommend I do at Pinnacles that day, she answered, more or less, "Don't die." If my heat-stroked ass really wanted to hike, I shouldn't do it for more than an hour.

I completed my Junior Ranger book in my hot car in the parking lot. (Please do not break the window, she has water and is listening to her favorite music.) An activity about "sky predators" taught me that owls are the only nocturnal raptors. Another asked me to name a place near my home that should be a national park. I named Devil's Lake, but: should it be, really? Probably not. We have to draw the line somewhere.

At a trailhead I threw on a lightweight, long-sleeve shirt, covered every exposed centimeter of my flesh in sunscreen, grabbed multiple water bottles, and set out for my short hike to Bear Gulch Reservoir. I hiked up rocks, around rocks, through little tunnels made by rocks. *Oh. . . . . okay. . . . . I thought. Pinnacles is just rocks. . . . .* I made it back to the Prius without becoming lunch for sky predators and headed north, driving around the mountains in a long horseshoe that would bring me to Big Sur.

I JUMPED ON the Pacific Coast Highway and followed it south, a sheer drop to the ocean on my right. This road was its own great American road trip, and I had long dreamed of driving it. I caught the PCH north of Monterey, and for the next hour each time I saw a bridge I thought: *Oh my God, it's the bridge from* Big Little Lies! (I had to have been right at least once.)

The ravages of the aesthetic crowd were evident at my campground in Pfeiffer Big Sur State Park, where posted signs begged people to stop stealing succulents. I decided to take a hike up a mountain at dusk and passed a couple who were waving small, leaf-covered twigs around their faces. "It's Australian bug spray," they explained, in an Australian accent so it wasn't offensive. Up on the ridge I watched the sun set over the ocean and understood why this place was so famous for its beauty. I turned around and, hoisted by my own petard, hiked back down the mountain in the dark. Owls hooted in the forest around me. *Ah yes,* I thought. *The only nocturnal raptors.* Using my iPhone flashlight to light my way I made it back, and in the dark near the parking lot I ran into the Australians again. "Oh! Lovely!" they said. "You lived!"

I spent most of the next week in Los Angeles seeing friends, eating restaurant-prepared chana masala, accidentally scratching an Audi, and taking meetings. Again and again I found that people who were supposed to be talking to me about my career goals were, without fail, much more interested in hearing about the places I'd seen over the last month and a half. Their enthusiasm for what I was doing reminded me of how much I'd fantasized about this trip back when I was the one in an office where I was supposed to be Googling someone else's career.

After the week in LA I planned to sleep in the Angeles National Forest and make my way to the next park. My friend Jose, at whose apartment I was crashing, listening to Taylor Swift and bossing around his smart home ("Siri, turn on lamp one"), immediately vetoed this idea. Apparently MS-13 had been committing murders and dumping bodies in the very national forest where I planned to free-camp. To my knowledge I hadn't recently done anything to cross MS-13, but better safe than sorry. So it was in the comfort of the West Hollywood apartment Jose shared with his angelic husband, Patrick, and his adorable adopted daughter, me, that I woke up on a Saturday morning to drive west for a day trip to Channel Islands National Park.

Before my ferry to the islands left, I popped into the mainland visitor center to get my Junior Ranger booklet. I would return from the islands after the center closed, so I asked the rangers if they'd just give me my badge now and trust that I'd do the work to earn it. Sure, they told me, they were easy. "But there's also a ranger on the island who has badges," one added. "Ranger Lucas. Big mustache. You'll see him as soon as you get off the boat."

I told them I'd wait to get one from him and ran back to catch my ferry, the *Island Adventure*.

Channel Islands National Park is made up of five islands and the water surrounding them. As so often happens on islands, evolution got freaky-deaky here, and over time animals evolved into species completely distinct from those found on the mainland. Almost 150 species are endemic to the Channel Islands, which is one of the main reasons the park exists. I would be spending the day on Santa Cruz Island, the largest island at more than twenty miles long and up to six miles wide, nearly three times the size of Manhattan—meaning it could conceivably sustain up to three M&M stores.

We pulled into Scorpion Cove, a small rocky beach with cliffs on each side, and queued to disembark. Next to me was a woman about my age. "Are you traveling alone?" she asked. I told her I was. "Me too!" she said. "I always wanted to go out here but I could never get any friends to go with me. And then I thought, I can just go alone! You know? Traveling alone as a woman feels so powerful because . . ." But before I could have her write my book for me, I spotted a ranger with a big mustache.

"Sorry, I have to talk to that guy," I told her and beelined it to Ranger Lucas. "I've been told you have the capability to give me a Junior Ranger badge when the time is right," I said to him.

"Yep," he said, not thrilled.

"Perfect! Can I interview you right now too?" I asked, not because I wanted to write a book about the parks and this would be good research but because one page of the workbook required me to interview a ranger.

"Sure," he answered, even less thrilled.

I asked him the listed questions, then told him I'd leave him to his duties. "How will I find you when I want to turn in my Junior Ranger booklet?"

"I'll be around."

FOR THE NEXT six hours I hiked. After spending the past weeks rushing my way down the West Coast, I finally felt able to relax in a park. After all, I was on an island. There was no visitor center. Unlike many people on the ferry, I hadn't brought my bathing suit or rented snorkels or kayaks. And the one ranger I could find didn't want to talk to me. Literally all that was left to do was find a trail and follow it.

And so I did! I walked past historic farming equipment and ranch buildings left over from a nearly ecologically disastrous period in the 1800s. I spotted an island fox, a distinct species of fox that exists nowhere on earth but the Channel Islands. I walked through an oak woodland valley and then up a large hill until I reached a cliff where the island met the ocean. After an overcast morning, the sky had opened up, and the water in its brilliant blues and teals looked like paradise against the dramatic cliffs. The inlet I was looking at was called [checks park brochure] "Potato Harbor." Not all names can be winners! I followed the cliff line around the island and five miles later was back where I started, at Scorpion Cove.

I dipped my feet in the ocean, watching families snorkel and considering what to do. Only a couple hours had passed since I had arrived; half the day still lay ahead. I studied the hiking map and set off into the island's interior on the Scorpion Canyon Loop Trail, a path apparently so rarely used that it soon was completely overgrown with scrub. I bushwhacked my way into the canyon. A machete would have come in handy, if cutting these plants hadn't been a federal crime. It was, after I made my peace with the ticks that were surely crawling onto me at every moment, thrilling.

AS MY TRIP went along, feeling uncomplicatedly thrilled in a national park was a rarer and rarer occurrence for me. Thinking about industrial tourism in nature had left me feeling morally bankrupt. I felt, as I so often felt in twenty-first-century America, like I was constantly causing harm and could perhaps lessen that harm but never stop causing harm altogether. If humans were always hurting the natural places they visited, spoiling the unspoiled wild, then logically humans shouldn't be visiting these places at all. When, in my weakness for mountain air and waterfalls and weird-looking animals, I visited anyway, I was doing something irredeemable.

This line of reasoning is as useless as it is misanthropic. Humans have existed in nature for hundreds of thousands of years and have impacted their environments for just as long. The idea that the purest state of nature is the complete absence of humans is a fiction created to serve the purposes of settler colonialism. Humans have done a lot of damage to nature, but acting like we can only do harm is an oversimplification that lets us avoid grappling with the issue. Saying, "We're the bad guys and we should stop being bad, but it's our nature to be bad so we'll probably keep on being bad" creates a system in which we exchange feeling nebulous guilt for getting to continue doing whatever the heck we want. The one does not balance out the other, no matter how guilty you feel. Even if you cry on the phone to your lover for the entire week you spend reading *The Uninhabitable Earth*, like I did, you're still not *actually* doing anything to create the habitable earth.

But humans aren't solely agents of destruction! If we were, the answer would be no one visiting nature, all of us living in cities like Blade Runners (I have never seen *Blade Runner*), wistfully looking off toward the distant mountains where the Avatars live (I have never seen *Avatar*). Or maybe the answer would be the extinction of humans as a species. I don't love this idea either! I'm a human, and I'm obsessed with being alive. And though I've experienced my share of negative feelings about other humans and things they did, I've also loved a lot of other humans. My crushes! My parents! My siblings! The friends who felt like siblings—are you kidding me?! If I said that the solution to all our environmental problems is that humans should vanish from the earth, I wouldn't be giving the issue the thought it deserves, because in addition to being completely implausible, it isn't a position I stand behind. I wouldn't trade the people I love for a mythical world of wilderness untouched by man. Instead, we need to find a solution that is sustainable, ethical, and plausible.

It's hard! When you start trying to make sure that people, but *not too many people*, can visit nature, you are inherently gatekeeping. The first people to lose access to nature will be those who have less free time, less expendable money, less ability to negotiate difficult terrain. Yes, roads and even trails are harmful to ecosystems. But it's not a coincidence that the Civilian Conservation Corps—the program that built so many of our nature trails and roads—was created by our only president to use a wheelchair. It's easy to advocate that nature be just accessible enough to meet your own personal edge: *everyone less hardcore than I am doesn't care about the environment and everyone more hardcore than I am is ableist*. It was easy to say I cared about industrial tourism because of its effect on the environment—but wasn't it also that I didn't find the solitude I'd romanticized, didn't always get a photo where it looked like I was all alone at the waterfall, didn't find God because the park bathroom was too dirty and it didn't feel like nature at all, just another outpost of civilization?

Zipping through dozens of national parks, I began to suspect that the sustainable, ethical solution to overtourism involved traveling more slowly, spending more time in one place. Not only because traveling by bike or by hiking or, I don't know, by horse doesn't burn gas like road-tripping around the country, but also because staying in one place and learning deeply about it encourages engagement and understanding in a way that stopping in for a quick hike and an Instagram slideshow doesn't. And though I didn't see myself setting up semipermanent camp at Channel Islands National Park (I'd probably just spend all my time trying to win over Ranger Lucas), this was the kind of slow travel I now craved.

I COULDN'T FIND Ranger Lucas when the time came for me to grab my badge before my ferry departed for the mainland.

Maybe he was hiding from me, or maybe he had a job that didn't revolve around me and my Junior Ranger experience. Instead I walked up to a bro-y enforcement ranger wearing sunglasses and a gun. (An enforcement ranger is the answer to the question, "What if a park ranger were also a cop?") "Uh, excuse me," I said. "Do you know where Ranger Lucas is?"

The enforcement ranger let loose a barrage of your-mom style Ranger Lucas jokes. Once Lucas was well and truly roasted, he paused for breath. "Why are you looking for him?"

"Oh, I'm trying to get a Junior Ranger badge," I said.

"I can give you one of those." He led me behind an old outhouse, where there was a large metal locker. He gave my booklet a cursory flip through, occasionally making comments ("Lucas *would* love blue whales") and handed it back to me, then opened the locker and revealed a treasure trove of Junior Ranger badges. They glittered like gemstones; every heist movie I'd ever seen flashed before my eyes.

On the ferry ride back I grabbed a seat in the open air. Somewhere in the middle of the Santa Barbara Channel I looked to my left and saw a dolphin. Its long beak and smooth body appeared, disappeared, appeared again as it jumped through the water in parallel to the ferry. Then another dolphin joined the first. People started to come out on deck to look at them as another dolphin swam up, and then another. Soon there was a small pod springing through the waves in the ferry's wake. No one really knows why dolphins do this. The theory goes: it might just be fun.

The Southwest

15

See Trees While Trees Still Exist

IT GETS SO HOT IN THE SUMMER IN THE SOUTHWEST NOW that you can get third-degree burns from the asphalt. (Third-degree, if you're like me and don't know, is the worse one. First-degree burns are superficial; fourth-degree burns are what you get when you burn in hell for all eternity because you once dropped your house keys on your friends' chihuahua.) The Phoenix area in 2019 experienced 103 days where the temperature was in the triple digits. Large portions of California, Nevada, Arizona, and New Mexico have been experiencing the worst drought in twelve hundred years. I possibly should have thought about any of this before I planned my trip. Instead, after one last evening at Jose's after Channel Islands, I left Los Angeles in late July to begin an extremely ill-timed tour of the American Southwest.

It was hard to say goodbye to Jose and Patrick, even though they had already let me stay an incredibly generous five nights, long enough for me to forgo my usual meticulous tidiness for a new method called "a lot of piles." Before I left West Hollywood I sat down to plan the next leg of my journey. If I wanted to hit every park in the continental United States from which I didn't yet have a Junior Ranger badge, my trip was maybe half done. I'd need to swing through the Southwest, then up to Mammoth Cave in Kentucky and down through the Carolinas to the very tip of Florida, where I'd catch a boat or seaplane to Dry Tortugas National Park, seventy miles west of Key West.

(I'd already been to Everglades National Park two years earlier with Dad and my stepmom, Linda. At one point someone spotted a mama and baby manatee. It took me fifteen minutes to find them despite multiple family members pointing right at them, but finally I saw them: two blobs. "Majestic . . ." I whispered, snapping a photo. We left the park and pulled into an independently run airboating business. These outfits cruise through a part of the Everglades ecosystem that isn't protected, so you can go superfast and do donuts on a boat so loud you have to wear industrial headphones. Is it good for nature? Definitely not. Is it fun as hell? [Repeatedly dabs so intensely I fall off the boat and into the wide-open jaws of a manatee.])

From Dry Tortugas I'd drive up the Eastern Seaboard to Acadia National Park in Maine before turning east to scoop up urban parks like Cuyahoga in Cleveland and Indiana Sand Dunes, the park with *the* most views of power plants you've ever seen in your life—and that's a guarantee. It was a lot. I didn't think I had it in me. I loved seeing my friends and family scattered across the country, but I missed the ones who made up my life in New York. I missed standing on stages in Brooklyn and doing my little PowerPoints about men driving me clinically insane. I was fed up with spending so many hours driving, an activity that is both very high stakes and also *so* boring. I could have slowed way down to space out the driving, could have spent several nights in each park I visited, but already I felt so self-indulgent. This trip was the longest I had ever been on vacation, and it was making me twitchy. My dad once asked me if I, like him, ever felt guilty when I wasn't working, and I told him: "constantly." I didn't need to make money right away, but I was learning that I found it difficult to justify my existence if I wasn't being conventionally productive.

So I had agreed to take a part-time job that started at the end of August. I decided in Los Angeles that this next week or so would be the final leg of my trip: I'd visit the national parks in the Southwest, including Texas's Big Bend, which I'd heard was incredible, and then I would turn north toward home. I shoved my piles of shit back into the Prius and got on the road.

I didn't get far before I hit traffic. The hordes were trying to escape LA; the hordes were tired of constantly being sized up on the buzziness of their career; the hordes were afraid if they stayed here any longer they'd develop body dysmorphia; the hordes wanted to be somewhere where finding street parking didn't take forty minutes and involve at least some crying. As the outdoor temperature displayed on the Prius's thermometer crept up, the traffic slowed, until I was sitting still, idling. Nothing was moving, and idling cars are horrible for the environment, so I threw the Prius in park and pulled out some light traffic-jam reading, Susan Brownmiller's *Against Our Will: Men, Women, and Rape*. Finally cars started to move. I put my book down and began driving in earnest to Joshua Tree National Park.

I'd wanted to see this park ever since I learned that Joshua Tree is a real place and also a real plant, and not just a U2 album—an epiphanic experience shared by a shocking number of Millennials, I've learned. Once I knew about Joshua Tree, I saw it everywhere: friends in Los Angeles were constantly visiting and posting about it, and then, more improbably, friends in Wisconsin were too. But I had a more urgent reason for wanting to visit: the Joshua trees in Joshua Tree were dying.

In 2021 the NPS published new guidelines for managing the parks, which frankly stated that absolute preservation of the parks' ecosystems was by then impossible. The publication states that "it will not be possible to safeguard all park resources, processes, assets, and values in their current form or context over the long term." Joshua trees are one of those resources. Since the Industrial Revolution, human-caused climate change has led to the area protected by Joshua Tree National Park becoming hotter and drier. Under these changing conditions fewer Joshua tree seedlings are sprouting and surviving. Any trees that do grow are threatened by increasingly damaging wildfires, due to warmer conditions and invasive grasses that help spread fire between the trees. Scientists estimate that, under the highest emissions forecast, by 2099 all suitable Joshua tree habitat in the park will be eliminated. Joshua tree habitat across the entire Southwest will be reduced by 90 percent. In a few generations Joshua Tree really will be just a U2 album.

Joshua Tree National Park is not alone in losing its namesake. The giant sequoias at Sequoia National Park are also on the decline, due to climate change and to candy-ass Junior Rangers too scared to stop tourists from stealing sequoia pinecones. In 1850 there were 150 glaciers within Glacier National

Park; by the end of this decade there will likely be none. It was getting to the point where, if a national park had a noun in its name, you should probably start worrying about that noun. (Just wait until you hear about the precipitous decline in the population of Theodore Roosevelts.) My road trip was, in many ways, a See Trees While Trees Still Exist tour of America.

The temperature was in the 100s by the time I made it to Joshua Tree. Working the information desk of the visitor center was a young man in a great mood. He smiled and chatted with me as he gave me my Junior Ranger book. "Write down this email in case you need more information," he said, giving me the park's email address, which included the first two letters of each word of the park name: jotr. "That's just what they do for all public land," he said. "So for Lake Mead, it's *lame*." He laughed. It would be a long time before Lake Mead recovered from a burn like that.

I walked back to my car where everything was, once again, melting. I worried about my skin: I have the kind of Irish complexion where I don't tan, I don't sunburn, I just burst into flames wholesale like an extremely ancient vampire suddenly exposed to daylight. Given the weather conditions, the ranger told me, the most I could walk today without risk of dying was a half mile, so I drove to a nature trail and did just that. Every animal that wasn't a moron (me) was napping somewhere shady, so I didn't see a single mouse or lizard or even a bird. What I did see were plants, an astounding variety if your mental image of a desert is a barren place devoid of life. There were juniper trees and sage and Indian ricegrass and Mojave yucca—that plant I felt so happy to learn the name of and now saw varieties of everywhere.

And of course there were Joshua trees. They were unlike any

plant I had ever seen: as if a yucca were a tree but also, some-how, a woolly mammoth. For years these trees had seemed so far away, so strange, that I'd honestly doubted I would ever get to see them in person. It may have been four hundred thou-sand degrees outside, but I was elated to be where I was. I hoped I'd one day get my shit together enough to come see the trees in a cooler season, but there are no promises in this life. I was here now, and my trip was ending soon. I walked, pushing the human limits of "how long can you hike in the desert in July before starting to puke," appreciating every second.

I DRAGGED MY feet as much as I could getting to the Oasis Visitor Center at the east side of Joshua Tree. First I parked to take photos of a big chunk of granite called Skull Rock, then to take photos of a very tall Joshua tree called the Barber Pole. Instead of branching in all directions, the Barber Pole just shot upward for maybe forty feet. (Joshua trees branch off after they flower, so the tallest and most imposing ones have never bloomed—a metaphor, surely, for something.)

When I finally walked into the visitor center, the rangers on duty were complaining about idiot tourists who got lost hiking and how they deserved to pay for their own search-and-rescues. This conversation hit on two of my favorite topics—people nearly dying in national parks and workplace gossip—so I browsed around the gift shop eavesdropping un-til I had looked at every single Milky Way magnet and plush tarantula and copy of *Roadside Geology of Southern Califor-nia* and could no longer plausibly act like I was there to buy anything.

As the ranger at the desk flipped through my Junior Ranger booklet, he told me about the decline in Joshua trees, the decline in most living things in the park really, due to climate change. Desert tortoises were dying out due to habitat loss. As the climate warmed, bighorn sheep would need to migrate to higher elevations, cutting off populations from each other and leading to genetic isolation, which could make healthy reproduction impossible. Bird species already had suffered a 43 percent loss throughout the Mojave Desert. Worldwide there's been a 60 percent decline in vertebrate populations since 1970. Not as in 60 percent of species have gone extinct but as in: there are 60 percent fewer animals in the world. There were simply many, many more wild animals when my parents were kids than there are now. (And considering how much my mom hates camping, who knows if they even appreciated it?) The only animals whose numbers keep increasing worldwide are those we've domesticated and whose lives we immiserate: cattle, pigs, chickens, sheep. Together with humans these animals make up 95 percent of total vertebrate biomass on the planet. All wild animals make up only 5 percent. I am so tired of looking for animals on road trips and acting happy to see a cow (or if I'm very lucky, a horse).

The situation is similarly dire across the national park system. In May of 2019 a report by the National Parks Conservation Association said that 96 percent of sites run by the National Park Service experienced significant air pollution problems. Glaciers were melting not just in Glacier but in Yosemite and in North Cascades, where more than half the ice had disappeared over the past hundred years. Parks like Yosemite and Yellowstone, Lassen and Sequoia and others, were experiencing or would experience more frequent and more damaging fires, would see their rivers and streams become warmer and shallower, and would be affected by more invasive plants. I was used to telling people how much I had seen New York City change since I moved there nine years ago (the café that was some old Italian guy's living room but served the best iced coffee turned into another art supply store, ugh!). I wasn't ready to tell friends how many more trees Yosemite had a couple years earlier, how much stronger the river flowing past Arches had been, how you'd once been able to go outside at Joshua Tree for a full fifteen minutes.

The Park Service is doing what it can to avoid the worst outcomes. In Joshua Tree National Park scientists are working to identify "refugias" for the trees, higher-elevation habitats in the park that receive more rainfall and so might be able to sustain Joshua trees in the future. Once these areas are identified, rangers work to clear them of invasive grasses that spread wildfire, so that the trees have a better chance when the next inevitable fire rolls through. It was cheering to know that plans were being made and action being taken. But the refugias in the park will function only if warming is held lower than the worst-case scenarios. If it isn't, all the identifying and weeding will be for naught: a reminder that even "protected" land is not protected from climate change.

"Anyway," said the ranger. "What did you think of the guy working the info desk at the other visitor center? Did you think he was nice? Was he funny?"

I laughed. "Uhh, yeah. He was great. Very helpful."

The ranger probed for more. "Helpful how? Did you think he was hot?"

I heard a groan behind me and turned to see another park employee, a woman, straightening things in the gift store. "Sorry," she said. "That other ranger is my boyfriend."

I was caught in the middle of gossip *and* I was in nature: I could die happy. I said goodbye, filled up every water bottle I had, and set my sights for the Mojave Desert.

TECHNICALLY I WAS already in the Mojave, at its far southern edge, but the 225-mile drive north to Death Valley National Park would take me deep into its heart. Why was I driving two hundred–plus miles into "the heart of a desert" starting at like 4:45 p.m., you might ask? Great question. I was trying to find somewhere less hot to sleep, and my phone indicated that it might get cooler at night in Death Valley than in Joshua Tree. It seemed, at least, worth a shot.

The Mojave Desert absolutely did not come to play. It's the hottest desert in North America and the driest one too: it gets an average of four inches of precipitation a year. I passed a vast expanse with literally no plants at all, a dry lake bed where a company had built evaporation pools to extract calcium chloride, and the temperature ticked up. I passed a sign telling me there were no services for fifty-seven miles, and the temperature ticked up. I drove into the Mojave Preserve, and the temperature ticked up again. Now the Prius told me that outside it was 112 degrees. As far as the horizon there was nothing but desert. I had maybe passed two cars since Joshua Tree. I realized that, for the first time on my trip, if I broke down here I might actually die. Luckily I had shared my phone location with Jose so he could see where I was, and could, if not alert rescuers to my location, at least direct the coroner to my desert-mummified corpse. I turned off the car's air conditioning to try to save the engine.

FOR MUCH OF my life climate change felt like a problem looming in the future. I don't remember hearing about it at all when

I was a kid; instead people talked about the ozone layer and saving the rainforest. Once "global warming" became the acknowledged threat, it always seemed to be couched in language suggesting we had thirty or twenty or ten years to act on the problem. It wasn't something that was happening immediately. I've lived in the Midwest and the Northeast my entire life, places we liked to think might be refuges from the worst of what was to come. After all, our winters were cold, our precipitation consistent. Maybe years were getting hotter, and maybe the sea level was slowly rising, but for the most part it didn't affect us day to day.

In the Southwest it was very clear that the effects of human-caused climate change are already here and already serious. Climate change was doing a number on national parks, which are pretty much as protected as land gets in this country. Everything outside the parks was feeling it even worse. Friends who live in the Southwest told me they expect to have to leave the area within their lifetimes when it becomes uninhabitable. They anticipate something like "a *Mad Max* scenario," and not in the good way (women getting buzzcuts, people playing guitar on the front of moving vehicles).

This scenario isn't far off. Already drought and plant die-off have led to soil erosion, freeing desert sand that blows into dunes over roads and even buildings. Researchers estimate that in the next few decades, some parts of Arizona will experience days with temperatures above 95 degrees for half the year. The average flow of the Colorado River, which supplies drinking water to forty million people in the West, has declined steadily over the past three decades.

When my friends talk about abandoning the places where they live, they aren't being hyperbolic. According to Pro-

Publica, it's possible that by 2070 four million people in the United States will live in places no longer habitable by humans. Even more may need to move due to wildfires and drought. Rising sea levels may displace another thirteen million—a level of migration our country has never seen before. Fewer than four million "Okies" became climate refugees during the Dust Bowl, and we know how that went. We're looking at frankly unsustainable rates of *Grapes of Wrath* in the next five decades.

As usual, those with privilege will be able to insulate themselves from the worst effects of this mass migration. Those who can afford to move will; those who cannot afford to or who are elderly will disproportionately be left behind. The cities in California and the Northwest and the Mountain West where climate migrants relocate will be overtaxed and struggle to provide housing and services, and the communities that empty out in the South and Southwest will become even poorer than they already are. As I drove through the Mojave, the immediacy of this future—that it would likely happen in my lifetime and not that of the imaginary children I may agree to have only if my gorgeous husband promises to stay at home raising them—hit me full force. Hot air blew into my face through the open windows, I looked around at the bleak landscape, and anxiety washed over me.

AFTER MORE THAN three hours of driving through the desert, sometime past eight p.m., I saw the first animal I had seen in the Mojave: what looked like a skeletal, jet-black horse, staggering through the desert two hundred yards away. It looked like the animal that came to tell other animals they were about to die. It was a feral burro, descended from animals abandoned by prospectors, a population of which somehow still survive in the desert all these years later.

The sun had just set and the temperature was still over 100 degrees when I crossed into Death Valley National Park. *I'm not sleeping tonight,* I conceded. I followed my GPS to a dirt road, then crawled down its rocks and potholes for a mile before pulling to the side and parking. My beloved free-camping website told me I was allowed to sleep here, and even though free-camping generally isn't allowed in national parks, I didn't really care. If a ranger came to evict me at three in the morning, I'd be awake sweating anyway and could easily leave. Banking on the fact that this wouldn't happen, that I was a mile from the main road and unlikely to be disturbed, I took off all my clothes and lay on top of my sleeping bag on the passenger seat. Through the window I could see thousands of stars, maybe more than I'd ever seen, a number that felt miraculous. Then something that didn't expect a car to be where it was flew full-speed into the passenger door next to me, making a noise that sounded bat-sized. Minutes later it happened again. I let the thuds of the bats lull me slowly to sleep.

Eager to see what I could of Death Valley and hit the road before the worst of the day's heat set in, I did something that runs counter to everything I stand for as a person: I woke before the break of dawn. The visitor center didn't open until eight, so I meandered over there, stopping to walk a quarter mile up to a viewpoint of Death Valley's badlands at Zabriskie Point. A placard explained that Death Valley was originally protected not because of its stunning landscapes or its record-setting heat or its endemic species or the fact that it contains the lowest point in the United States but because . . . it served the economic interests of the Pacific Coast Borax Company.

The company owned land in and around what is now the park, but when mining slowed down in the 1920s, it decided the best way to continue monetizing the land was to open an inn there and encourage tourism. Christian Zabriskie, for whom the viewpoint was named, was a vice president of the Pacific Coast Borax Company. Only in America would we name a scenic spot in a federal nature park after a private company's VP. Not even the CEO!

FURNACE CREEK RANCH, just across a road from the visitor center, is where the highest air temperature ever recorded on earth was measured on July 10, 1913: 134 degrees Fahrenheit. Never again has a temperature that high been recorded, but the weather station—located near the visitor center since 1961—has recorded 130 degrees. (I think Rob Thomas and Carlos Santana have a song about just this kind of temperature.) The science behind what makes Death Valley so hot also explains why Phoenix and other cities retain heat: Death Valley is surrounded by steep mountains that trap heated air. Hot air rises from the valley and cools just enough to drop back down, unable to escape over the mountains. Back on the valley floor it gets compressed and superheated. The same thing happens with air trapped between tall glass buildings in cities. Seems like a good thing to try to avoid when urban planning, but I'm no expert, my only college degree is in "how to read a poem really hard."

The minute the visitor center opened, I and the handful of other tourists who had been hiding in the shade with me darted into the air-conditioned building: outside, it was already 107 degrees. I grabbed my Junior Ranger book, bought some salty snacks—essential when you're losing salt through sweat—and sat down to fill out my workbook. The first page asked me how Death Valley was similar to my home in New York City, and I wrote: it's hot, it's a tourist attraction, and it's a hard place to live.

Climate change is happening where I live too. I've noticed it in New York: storms have gotten heavier because warm air can hold more water, leading to more precipitation when it does finally rain. I've noticed it when wildfire smoke blows across the country and Canada all the way to NYC, eclipsing the skyline, turning the sun into a glowing orange ball, and making it unsafe to exercise outdoors (Blythe's cause of death: biking up the Williamsburg Bridge to take a photo of the weird smoke). I've noticed it when I visit my family in Wisconsin and the humidity is worse than I remember; extreme humidity will continue to worsen in states along the Mississippi River, making heat waves more dangerous. But what I didn't notice until I read about it is that forests are dying off. Like, the entire idea of forests. Because of warming and invasive species, fewer and fewer trees will grow back after logging or wildfires, so we will end up with more grasses and shrubs. Forests might soon become like portable CD players or the movie *You've Got Mail*: something younger generations call us old for knowing about. Forests: real '90s kids will remember!

I FINISHED MY booklet using things I had seen that morning, and though I normally would have gone on a hike first to save face before turning my booklet back in to the same ranger who had just given it to me, I decided it was too hot to faff around for the sake of my nonexistent dignity. Smiling sheepishly, I brought it back to the ranger, a man in his sixties. He was in the middle of making fun of me when I heard another voice.

"Hey, don't I know you?"

I looked over. It was Ranger Green, who had given me my Junior Ranger badge at Great Basin more than a month earlier.

I felt as if the fabric of space-time had ripped; I was elated. "Oh my God!" I squealed. "I've been thinking nonstop about how you told me my life is going to be all downhill from age twenty-eight!"

"Nah," he said, chastened. "That was just me."

We explained to the older ranger how we knew each other, and the three of us had a long, happy chat. I told Ranger Green about all the places I had been since I last saw him, rattling off parks one by one. When I asked him what he was doing in Death Valley, he told me he didn't even work at Great Basin: he'd just been there temporarily because they had a staff shortage, and was now back at his full-time park. I asked him and the other ranger how they liked working in such an extreme environment, and they told me that more and more days saw temperatures in the 120s. I told them about struggling to sleep in the heat and that I had free-camped a mile down a dirt road, and they assured me that it was allowed. Catching up with Ranger Green felt almost as good as catching up with Todd in San Francisco. And unlike when I saw the same road-trippers over and over in Utah, finding the ranger in two sparsely visited parks weeks apart didn't feel like a depressing reminder of my unoriginality but instead like a serendipitous moment, a gift. A part of me hoped he would be proud of my trip, would see I was a person who cared deeply about the national parks and not just some weird woman who didn't shower between going in caves.

The rangers flipped through my book, Ranger Green by now familiar with my limited drawing skills. Asked to draw a desert animal with unique adaptations, I had drawn a lizard that evolved to have a bucket hat. "I wonder if this lizard originally evolved to just have a baseball hat," the older ranger joked. "The rest of the brim came later." When I could no longer justify taking up their time, I said goodbye. And then I stepped outside, directly into the center of the sun.

A trip to Death Valley is not complete without a visit to Badwater Basin, the lowest point in the United States, at 282 feet below sea level. The rangers had told me not to stay outside my car's air conditioning for longer than fifteen minutes. Seriously, they told me, set a time for five minutes and then start heading back. I parked at the Badwater Basin lot, set my phone timer, turned off the car, and rushed to see what I could in three hundred seconds.

Badwater Basin is a dry lake bed that is now a salt flat—just a cracked white crust of salt crystals with no vegetation stretching for two hundred square miles. The eponymous bad water is a sad little spring-fed pool that sits atop the salt. As the story goes, a surveyor traveling through the area long ago tried to get his mule to drink from the pool, and the mule refused, saying, "Not today, Satan." ("Satan" is how all mules refer to all humans.) The heat on the salt flats was all-consuming; I felt like a pizza roll inside a miracle oven. I walked on the salt flats as long as I could before my phone chimed, then reluctantly headed back to my car. It wasn't the first time I'd prioritized "not dying" over "wanting more salt," one of the unifying struggles of my life, but that didn't make it any easier.

On my way out of the park I drove through an area called Artists Palette because the hills are a million crazy colors (celadon, Millennial pink, spicy beige) due to volcanic deposits. As I had felt many times before on this trip, I could not believe the earth just spit out colors like this and we could just roll through and enjoy them. The rangers had recommended more things for me to check out, but I felt bad for my tenacious little Prius struggling against the ungodly heat, and decided to head on my way, hoping to eventually arrive somewhere with more forgiving temperatures. But first, I would have to pass through Las Vegas.

HERE'S THE THING you have probably already noticed: I was being extremely complicit in climate change. Hello, I was driving around the entire country. The fact that I was driving a hybrid with good gas mileage only goes so far. According to an August 2021 article by Coral Davenport in the *New York Times*, "Gasoline-powered cars and trucks are the largest single source of greenhouse gases produced in the United States, accounting for 28 percent of the country's total carbon emissions." The burning of fossil fuels in general is responsible for 86 percent of carbon dioxide emissions. The only thing that can meaningfully stall climate change is breaking the stranglehold fossil fuels have on our world economy; it's hard to see how I was doing that while buying a tank full of fossil fuels almost every single day. Not only did fossil fuels give me mobility, they also enabled the existence of every job I ever had and the society I lived in. It didn't seem likely that a culture that ran only on the energy from wood we burned and food we ate would be able to sustain a woman like me writing jokes about my crushes and about weird plants I saw.

I tried to remind myself that ravaging the environment, putting greed above all else, worshiping at the altar of constant growth toward some imagined perfect future—none of these were inherently human nature but were instead the nature of capitalism. Then again, capitalism isn't some random thing aliens brought down to bum us out for all eternity: it's just a system we set up to the extreme benefit of a few and the extreme suffering of most.

There have been efforts to save the environment using the logic of capitalism. People trying to protect land have lately introduced the idea of "ecosystem services"—the amount of money saved by services the ecosystem provides for free, like trapping carbon, cleaning the air, and providing clean water. In one sense I support any argument that makes people understand how short-sighted it is to clear-cut or frack or mine. But it makes me queasy to enter these natural areas into the capitalist matrix, to accede to the idea that something can be allowed to exist only if it proves its monetary worth. The risk there is that if someone comes along who thinks they can find a way to clean the air cheaper than trees can do it, suddenly it's adios to trees and hello to Trï, the tree startup.

I crossed the border into Nevada and drove around a truck that was going slow. The driver stuck his hand out the window and flipped me off.

FOR YEARS I had assiduously avoided Las Vegas, as a personality trait. I was not a person who enjoyed gambling. I was not a person who enjoyed bright lights. I was not a person who enjoyed, for example, "having a good time." But I was twenty-eight and figured that by now people had gotten the point. I decided I could stop there for lunch without undermining my hard-won introvert clout.

Vegas is a city very clearly affected by climate change. Its raison d'être is "keeping one jillion lights on at all times." Its drinking water comes from the Colorado River, specifically Lake Mead, which is 130 feet lower than it was eighteen years ago. When I turned on the Prius after stopping in the city for lunch, the dash thermometer told me it was 114 degrees outside. Vegas stressed me out; I felt right in having avoided it. But it had some charm too. After almost two months of driving around the country, confronted by billboards telling me that HELL IS REAL and LUST IS A SIN and that I shouldn't abort my six-month-old, headband-wearing baby, it was refreshing to drive through Vegas, where the billboards promised to cure my erectile dysfunction.

The next national park on my list was Saguaro, in Tucson, southeast of me on a four-hundred-mile diagonal line that cut right through Phoenix. But given everything I knew about Tucson and Phoenix and Las Vegas, I doubted I would find anywhere I could free-camp on that route where evening temperatures would dip below 80. And actually, this is kind of a quirky thing about me, but my body requires sleep to sustain human life. So I made a hundred-mile detour to spend the evening in Flagstaff, a mountain city. As I drove, I thought about the heat and Las Vegas and the monstrosities we build for ourselves.

Humans built the capitalist system because, for at least some people for at least a little while, it worked. It came with dreams of linear progress, of constant modernization, and those dreams sounded sweet until they didn't. It's become clear that the system we built isn't working, for us or for the planet. Luckily we can build another.

It may be difficult, but that's okay: together we can do difficult things. It may cost money, but if the earth is no longer habitable we can't spend the money we saved anyway. It's time to work together toward what the anthropologist Anna Lowenhaupt Tsing calls "collaborative survival."

Throwing our hands up, saying it's too late and we're already screwed, isn't helpful. That kind of thinking is paralyzing. It's also just untrue. We can still work to prevent the worst outcomes. We can do more than minimize the harm we cause: we can have a positive relationship to the world we live in. We can view nature, in parks and public land but also in the cities and suburbs where we live, as not only providing "ecosystem services" and resources and opportunities for tourism but as valuable in and of itself, as sacred.

One way we can adopt this view is by returning public land to Indigenous communities. While Indigenous people of course participate in resource extraction and capitalism or have in the past overtaxed their environments, many Native peoples sustainably managed land and resources for a long time before Europeans came to North America. (Maybe, as scientist, professor, and enrolled member of the Citizen Potawatomi Nation Robin Wall Kimmerer has pointed out, this is because many Indigenous creation myths view earth as a gift given to humans to steward, while Christianity views earthly paradise as a fun place humans got to enjoy for like a week before irrevocably screwing it up.) Already forest managers have realized that many Native practices once widely dismissed, like setting controlled burns, keep ecosystems healthy. And studies have shown that when land is managed by Indigenous peoples, the forests and carbon stores on that land are more likely to be kept intact.

In *Braiding Sweetgrass*, Kimmerer describes having a give-and-take relationship with the land as becoming indigenous: "becoming indigenous to a place means living as if your children's future mattered, to take care of the land as if our lives, both material and spiritual, depended on it." Paying close and careful attention to the land we inhabit and the way all plants, animals, geological processes, and climate interact can aid us in cities too.

Before Anglos came through the Southwest and built brick homes with grass lawns and metal roofs, people lived in homes made of adobe with high ceilings and transom windows to help hot air escape. (My mom and I sat in an adobe building in New Mexico one July and remarked over and over for ninety minutes how nice the air conditioning was until someone told us there was no air conditioning; this was just how adobe buildings felt.) We can return to planning our communities in ways adapted to our environment. We can look for refugia to save existing species, and we can use technology to replace burning asphalt with "cool pavement" that reflects the sun's heat instead of absorbing it. We can protect more land from extractive industry and build corridors of protected land so that plants and animals can migrate to cooler climates as the planet warms. We can stop driving so much, we can stand with those defending their land and water rights, we can come together to dismantle the fossil fuel industry. We can't blow up pipelines, *legally*, wink. But once we decide to treat earth and nature as if they matter, and as if they exist for all of us and not just for a few white male billionaires with personality disorders, there's so much we can do.

I DIDN'T YET know how I would contribute to the solution beyond occasionally staying up all night spiraling about glaciers calving. I just knew that the part of my life when I saw climate change as an issue that was pressing but not urgent, right-this-second immediate, was now behind me.

At Walnut Canyon National Monument, just down the road from Flagstaff, it dipped down into the 50s that night, and I slept soundly.

16

Watching, Screaming

THE DRIVE FROM FLAGSTAFF TO TUSCON'S SAGUARO NA-
tional Park, including a sweltering breakfast stop in Phoenix, surprised me. This was a year before Arizona went blue
for Joe Biden, and I couldn't believe it when I saw Bernie
bumper stickers and bumper stickers calling for Trump's im-
peachment. *Wow,* I thought, *the country really is more purple
than we're made to believe. All kinds of people live everywhere.*
My reverie was interrupted by a semi truck with mud flaps
that said, simply, HEIL.

I was eager to get to Saguaro because as a Millennial
woman I had been fully indoctrinated into the cult of cactus. I
had multiple cacti in various states of health, many of which I
had continued to care for (read: overwater) months after they
were visibly dead. I owned a cactus necklace; I also owned a
shirt embroidered with tiny cacti; I even had a cactus tattoo.
If you love cacti, you have to love saguaros, the Meryl Streep
of cacti, the cactus you think of when you think about the

concept of cacti. It's the biggest cactus in the United States, growing to heights of fifty feet (the tallest ever recorded was seventy-eight feet tall, making it a full two to three times as tall as the men I usually date).

Saguaro National Park consists of two units flanking the city of Tucson. I had chosen to visit the larger east unit. The ranger who greeted me told me how to pronounce "suh-war-oh" and warned that if I didn't want to suffer from heat exhaustion, I absolutely could not be out of my car for longer than fifteen minutes at a time. He then handed me my Junior Ranger book—or so I thought until I glanced at its cover and saw that it was actually a <u>Not So</u> Junior Ranger book (emphasis theirs). It was like a Junior Ranger book but harder, made for people who were obviously too old to be participating in a kid's program. On one hand this made sense, as I was old as dirt; on the other hand I had never been so offended in my life. The ranger must have seen this on my face because he added as explanation, "Saguaro has a lot of adults trying to get Junior Ranger badges."

The day was only getting hotter and more likely to make me sweat out all my electrolytes and die, so I decided to hike straightaway. The ranger recommended a flat, paved trail where I would be able to walk for five minutes and then turn right around and go back to my car; I climbed in the Prius and started down the Cactus Forest Loop Drive to get there.

On each side of the drive were more cacti than I could imagine in my wildest dreams. There were saguaro, yes, but also prickly pear and cholla and barrel cacti. There were ocotillo and palo verde trees, which have green trunks that perform photosynthesis. I was in a houseplant lover's paradise; I stopped at every pullout just to see it all closer up. So *this* is what a cactus looks like without an anxious woman water-boarding it.

I glanced at the time before setting off down the flat Mica View Trail, making a mental note to turn around in five minutes, but despite my limited time I couldn't help but dawdle as I stared at the giant saguaro around me. They were so tall, with so many arms branching out, so imposing and so new to me: while I had been in and out of deserts for a month and a half by now, saguaros only grow in the Sonoran Desert. This was the first day of my trip I had actually seen any.

Saguaros don't branch until they are fifty to seventy years old and don't even bloom until they're about thirty-five, which, as a woman who is not yet thirty-five, I find encouraging to a degree that probably needs to be explored in therapy. If all goes well for a saguaro, it can live two hundred years. But in this day and age, very often all does not go well for saguaros. People continue to move to the Southwest in huge numbers despite its being, along with Alaska, the part of the country hardest hit by climate change. As cities sprawl, the saguaro loses habitat. Invasive grasses have spread across the region, outcompeting native plants for water and making it possible for fires to spread in an area whose plants have no natural defenses against fire. Drought and extreme weather make it harder for young saguaros to survive. And thanks to the same culture that had convinced me—a midwestern woman with no ties to any desert in my family history going back to the dawn of life on this or any planet—to get a prickly pear tattoo, the saguaro was facing a new threat: cactus theft.

The cactus market in the United States alone is estimated to be worth tens of millions of dollars, only about one million of which comes from me personally buying succulents.

Between 2012 and 2017 the market increased by 64 percent. Bitches love a cactus: that's just facts. The problem is, if you want a mature saguaro in your yard, you can't just plant a seed and watch it grow because after eight years you're still going to have a little shrimp shorter than most small rocks. The best time to plant a saguaro in your yard is fifty years ago; the second best time is forty-nine years and fifty-one-and-a-half weeks ago. Failing that, your only real option is to buy one on the black market. Because they're so iconic, they go for up to $100 per foot. The demand has led to people coming to Saguaro National Park and stealing cacti, like an *Ocean's 11* where the motivating force is not "getting back together with Julia Roberts" but "getting Instagram clout," where the thieves are getting one over not on Andy Garcia—problematic enough, to those of us who love Andy Garcia—but on the entire citizenry of the United States, which, let's not forget, notably includes Andy Garcia.

Cactus theft wasn't happening just in Saguaro, of course. I had seen PLEASE STOP STEALING THE CACTUSES :(signs in Big Sur, and I've read about similar theft happening everywhere from the Grand Canyon to South Africa. And it's not just big, slow-growing saguaros being stolen but also weird little species that are popular as houseplants. The problem with this is that stealing all the rare weirdo cacti to make them houseplants may lead to the eradication of these species, especially if you sell them to someone like me.

Saguaros are meant for more than just looking good in a front yard or symbolizing the American Southwest. I learned this on the quarter-mile nature trail I walked next. "A whole quarter mile?" I hear you exclaim. "Is that *safe*?" The ranger had told me I'd be pushing it but would probably make it back to my car alive. The Desert Ecology Trail leisurely looped off the park's main road, with little signs along the way educating whatever hiker or cactus thief might pass about the animals that lived in the Sonoran Desert. The Gila woodpecker and the gilded flicker, I learned, dug holes in saguaros' flesh to use as nests. When they got bored of those holes, decided to upsize, or became convinced their life would be so different if they just lived in, say, Phoenix (it might be different for a few months, woodpecker, but then you just have all your same problems in a different saguaro)—they abandoned the cavities, and sparrows and finches and elf owls moved in. Hawks build nests on saguaros where the arms meet the body. For other animals, saguaros provide food—nectar and pollen from their flowers feed bats, and all kinds of creatures, from birds to mammals to reptiles to insects, eat their fruit. Very thirsty deer will sometimes even eat the flesh of a saguaro cactus, needles and all. *Needles and all.* It was the best argument I had yet heard for not being a deer.

WHY WAS I so obsessed with cactus? Why was I so in love with the western and southwestern aesthetics in general? Can it all be traced to the 1994 Mary-Kate and Ashley film *How the West Was Fun*, in which the Olsen twins engage in hijinks on a ranch somewhere in the intermountain West and which I watched over and over as a kid? Is that why I have multiple western-themed tattoos, own two ranch blankets, have a giant gold cattle skull hanging ominously opposite my bed? There's a certain kind of white lady who really should not be wearing so much turquoise; I hoped I was not one of those white ladies.

To me one of the most foundational western women was

Georgia O'Keeffe. A print of one of her skull-and-mesa paintings hangs above my desk; I thought of her when I imagined living in the Southwest. But putting aside O'Keeffe's Anglo heritage, she wasn't even from New Mexico. Like me, she was from Wisconsin. Like me, she then moved to New York. There was a difference, surely, between cultural appropriation and being Georgia O'Keeffe—or was there? The first type of white lady rolls into the Southwest never questioning the history of violence against the Indigenous people who have lived there since long before Europeans arrived. That type of white lady buys jewelry and clothes and home goods inspired by Native aesthetics but not made by Native people. I had definitely bought some stuff like this in my life. I'd like to think there's a different way of being that involves learning about and respecting the place where one settles, its human history and its ecology. But maybe all white people who move to the West are chasing dreams of violent Anglo westward expansion even if we don't think we are, even if we specifically think we aren't. Maybe the draw of white women to turquoise is about a fantasy of being Native, being the original inhabitants of a land and thus the moral authority on that land's use. It's the fantasy of being free from the sins of settler colonialism.

IT'S ABOUT A six-and-a-half-hour drive from Tucson to Guadalupe Mountains National Park, nestled in the pointy, far western end of Texas, right on the New Mexico border. Speeding along the interstate across the bottom of Arizona and New Mexico the next morning, I couldn't believe I was driving while at that very moment Robert Mueller was testifying to Congress about his report on Russian interference in the 2016 election. After three and a half years as a researcher at a late-night show, watching party conventions and State of the Unions and confirmation hearings and anything else you could imagine live on TV, it felt illegal to not know exactly what was happening while it happened. It was so strange to suddenly be living a life that didn't involve sitting in front of a television and two computer screens, watching, screaming. It was, as guilty as I felt to admit it, a huge relief. So instead of watching testimony that would ultimately reveal nothing, I watched the pavement rolling under me at eighty-four miles an hour.

The sun was setting as I pulled into Guadalupe Mountains, located right off the highway. The escarpment had been visible for forty or fifty miles, rising out of the flat desert with a promise of intrigue and adventure. I couldn't make a camping reservation in advance, so I turned into the unassuming park and hoped that it held someplace for me to sleep. Luckily I found an empty walk-in campsite under a tree where I could set up my little Walmart tent and fall asleep to the sound of the moths who were trying to get inside with me, convinced that my phone was the moon.

In the morning I headed to the visitor center to pay my camping fee and get to the lay of the land. At this point I had entered the fourth and final desert zone of my road trip. There are four desert zones in the United States: the Great Basin, which I had encountered around Utah; the Mojave, around Joshua Tree; the Sonoran, home to the saguaros; and now the Chihuahuan Desert. The mountains around me were the highest in Texas, but I'd have to explore them later.

First I was swinging up to another national park: Carlsbad Caverns, just a forty-five-minute drive north. Who knew? Certainly not me, who had never even heard of Guadalupe Mountains National Park and almost forgot to add it as a stop on my trip. I hopped back on the highway I'd taken the night before, heading northeast past sparse vegetation of yucca and agave.

The gate to Carlsbad Cavern's natural entrance trail sported a new, bright yellow sign: CAUTION, it said, AIRBORNE RADIO-ACTIVITY AREA. And under a radioactivity symbol, for clarification: RADON. *Go ahead and try me*, I thought. *If this trip hasn't killed me yet, it's not gonna.* I sprouted a third arm and continued down the trail. A series of tight switchbacks led me to the massive entrance, into and out of which swarms of cave swallows were flying. And then I was in.

MUCH LIKE EVERY cave that has ever existed, Carlsbad Cavern was the most exciting place I had ever been in my life. Down and down and down I descended into the cave, sinking the equivalent of seventy-nine stories over a bit more than a mile. I paused to peer at columns dripping with rock and stalactites hanging precariously from the ceiling like daggers. At the bottom of the trail I entered the Big Room of Carlsbad Cavern—the largest single cave chamber in all of North America. Walking around just that one chamber is a loop of 1.25 miles. A frayed rope ladder from 1924 hung next to the trail, dangling into a seemingly bottomless pit. It was damp and a little cold and enormous and echo-y, sounds carrying farther than normal because of all the solid surfaces, meaning that I could hear each drip of water and each inane thing the loud middle-aged couple hundreds of feet from me felt the need to say at full volume.

The loud people made me think about how I'd been on the road for about two months now, alone for most of that time, and had completely lost the ability to moderate how I was being perceived by others. It struck me that I had spent the trip shedding identity markers: I wore whatever clothes were cleanest and weather appropriate, I generally kept to myself, I didn't even carry around a book, cover out, to let the people know what kind of reader I am, because I had replaced my hobby of reading with my new hobby of looking at the road while driving. For the past two months traveling around and visiting national parks had been just a thing I was doing. But when I got back to New York, I realized, all this would become a marker of who I was: the kind of person who went on a long road trip and hiked all over the country. (Put another way: I would be the kind of person who was like every single other person, somehow, on Hinge.)

When we travel to other countries where the culture is different or we don't understand the language, where we might end up at the tourist traps and where we make a Herculean effort to go to the wine bars that locals frequent, we're used to feeling out of place. In that kind of travel you are constantly reminded that you aren't from here, that you're away from home, that you're trespassing in a place where someone else's real life happens. But domestic tourism in America felt different, felt like I was doing exactly what the culture wanted me to do.

I wasn't putting down roots in any place I visited; in fact, I was coming and going so quickly that the pace sometimes depressed me. But I was shocked at the number of places where I was able to meet up with family or friends I had met while growing up or while in college: Milwaukee, Denver, Mesa Verde, Yellowstone, Cisco, San Francisco, San Luis Obispo, Los Angeles, and more to come. It seemed to me that not only was road travel in the United States canonical, but so was settling in a place for a few years and then dispersing. There's something uniquely American about wanting to be constantly on the move.

And taking a trip this long, across this much space, is not something you can do in every country. The United States is huge. When I talk about road trips in America to friends who live in the United Kingdom, they salivate: in Britain if you drive for twenty minutes you're in the ocean. It's almost impossible to get a sense of how big America is unless you drive around it, realize the sheer amount of car time between, say, Chicago and Michigan's Upper Peninsula. The differences in our country, the dizzying heterogeneity of thought and politics and basic acceptance of reality, also start to make more sense when you drive from Denver to southern Utah. It's not so far as the crow flies. But you drive from vegan restaurants and weed dispensaries over mountains, past resort towns I can't even afford to look at, into a desert, through towns oriented around camping and mountain biking and grungier forms of travel, past a ghost town that has become a toxic dumping site slash art installation, through beautiful canyons and past drilling leases, into a land so empty and unforgiving you're more likely to see a cow than a human.

Travel is a way to more deeply understand America, to grapple with its flaws, but also to see what is—don't cancel me—beautiful about it. Of course, that domestic travel might inspire patriotism has been an express purpose of domestic travel since the jump: Stephen Mather, the first Park Service director, wrote that the national parks would help people "love more deeply this land in which they live." That this was what *the man* wanted didn't take away from the fact that, over the past two months, I had been awed at the natural beauty of the country where I was randomly born. Neither did it take away from the warm glow of hanging with homies, both those I had long loved and now saw only rarely because of their geographic distance, and those homies I met on the trail and never saw again, or saw only a couple more times if we were in Utah and all acting out the same vacation.

Just then the loud tourist couple I wanted to murder walked up to me in the cave. "Can you take our photo?" the wife asked, handing me a camera. I smiled. "Of course," I whispered.

I'D LEFT NEW Mexico too late, and by the time I parked at the trailhead back in Guadalupe Mountains it was only about an hour before sunset. My park pamphlet told me I'd need probably an hour and a half but maybe as much as three hours to hike the loop trail to Smith Spring and Manzanita Spring. Already the escarpment was throwing a long shadow over the desert, and I worried that the gate to the ranch road I'd taken to the trailhead would be closed if I stayed out too late. But I had young legs, and visiting an oasis in the desert seemed worth the risk. I laced up my heavy hiking boots and power-walked up the trail toward the mountains.

The springs were, of course, so weird. From a scrubby expanse of creosote I abruptly stumbled into a world of emerald green: trees and moss and even a tiny waterfall. I gave myself a minute or two to gawk before racing the darkness back to my car as the sky turned a deeper and deeper blue. I rounded a corner and startled a mule deer. *Binch, what the hell are you doing out of your car so late?* it was probably thinking, and it wasn't wrong. But I was vibrating with happiness to be hiking at nightfall, watching the darkness spread over everything, seeing how, after a long, hot day, the desert came back to life.

DURING THE YEARS immediately before I went on the road, the president of the United States said racist things, bragged about committing sexual assault, passed orders aimed at making the lives of trans people miserable, and generally emboldened many people to openly express hatred that had long been embedded in the country's laws and norms. In those years I felt more and more ashamed of America. It didn't represent my values. I was wary of anyone who celebrated the country openly. To proudly wave an American flag or party uncomplicatedly on the Fourth of July or unironically belt out a song about being stoked to be an American, because at least I'm free—these things now felt synonymous with being a Trump supporter, with supporting racism and sexism and transphobia, abortion restrictions and kids in cages at the border and Black people murdered by the state.

But why does that type of person get total ownership of the concept of the United States? Why do they get to define it and ruin it? There are entirely different ways of being an American, ways that don't ignore how this country failed or sometimes actively terrorized anyone who is not a straight, white, rich man. Ways that take a clear-eyed view of this nation's past and its present, take seriously the ideas of freedom and democracy, and work to build a United States that lives up to those ideas. Instead of throwing up our hands and saying it's too late and letting the most hateful people define what it means to be an American, we can work together to make the country what we imagine it can be, for each other.

Being an American is complex! It's a blessing, and it also comes with a lot of baggage to reckon with and try to rectify. Criticizing the failings of the United States is not anti-American; I'd say it's patriotic to think rigorously about the meaning of what we stand for and the ways we're letting each other down. Especially when there is so much about the United States to love.

Looking out over the West Texas desert, I was floored by how beautiful—like, literally, aesthetically beautiful—America is. I was reminded of the first week of my trip when I drove all evening from Wind Cave National Park to Molly's house in Denver. I came over the crest of an unassuming hill, and suddenly what seemed like hundreds of miles of buttes and flatland and farm poured out to the horizon. "Jesus Christ!" I yelled out loud, for real, fumbling for my phone before realizing that I probably couldn't take a photo, drive downhill at seventy-five miles per hour, and take all this in at the same time. So, even though I was just one person and felt too small to appreciate the enormity of it, I just looked.

From that hill on the western edge of South Dakota I felt like I could see all of America. I'll probably never be back on that secret two-lane road again, but I'm happy I saw it once in my life. It reminded me how much I loved going on road trips, and this trip in particular, and how lucky I was to be able to do any of it. To live in a country with so much protected land, and so many people fighting for it. To find people I loved all across the country; to live in a country where strangers are weirdly so nice to each other; to know people who cared about being kind and making art and improving the places where they lived, and who engaged with the world via direct action and also via anarchist Gritty memes.

Joan Didion said it: "A place belongs forever to whoever claims it hardest, remembers it most obsessively, wrenches it from itself, shapes it, renders it, loves it so radically that he remakes it in his own image."

17

Okay, Marfa Slaps

DRIVING SOUTH FROM THE NEW MEXICO BORDER, I MEN-
tally prepared myself: today finally I would be cool. Today
I was going to Marfa, where the hip people go. I had wanted
to visit this town in far west Texas ever since I had seen it featured in *I Love Dick*, the TV adaptation of one of my favorite
books. *I* love dick! *I* love Kathryn Hahn! *I* wanted to visit
this town which was both a mecca for minimalist art and a
place where everyone dresses like a cowboy. And now I had an
excuse to make the very inconvenient drive: Marfa was on the
way to Big Bend National Park. I'd be spending the next two
nights with Austin, a new friend who lived fifteen minutes
outside Alpine, one town over from Marfa. In West Texas,
"one town over" is approximately a thirty-minute drive.

If states had ambassadors, Austin (the woman, not the
city) should represent Texas. Seeing Texas through her eyes is
what made me begin to love the state. We met by total fluke:
in 2019 I was booked on the lineup for an annual feminist

literary festival Austin had organized. The festival was canceled at the last minute, but I already had nonrefundable plane tickets. So I flew to Dallas anyway, where I knew no one and had no plans. Austin, beauty angel that she is, got dinner with me and then walked me over to the New Orleans–style jazz bar a friend of hers had just opened. There, everyone was dancing, in the bar and in the street, and they all seemed to know Austin. Here's how to describe hanging out with her: she can make anyone love Dallas. (When I meet anyone from Dallas and tell them I love it there, they invariably look at me with confusion and say, "Why?") I couldn't wait to see Austin's version of West Texas, a place that, unlike Dallas, people generally agree is actually enjoyable.

After a pit stop at a Marfa café that was also a newspaper— in a town of two thousand people, apparently you need diversified revenue streams—I sat with Austin on her porch, looking at the US Border Patrol station less than a mile away. Although Alpine is far from Mexico, Border Patrol is authorized to set up checkpoints anywhere within 100 miles of a border. This one sat about fifty feet north of where Austin's dirt road met the only road into town, meaning that every time Austin or one of her neighbors or any of their guests wanted to go to the grocery store or Tractor Supply or anywhere else in the entire United States—literally anywhere other than Big Bend National Park—they had to pass through Border Patrol. Unlike at an actual border crossing, where agents can legally search anyone's car or person without a warrant or even reasonable suspicion, Border Patrol agents here legally need probable cause to search your car. All they're actually allowed to do is ask you your residence status. Across the country, however, they routinely ignore this and conduct illegal searches and interrogations, leading to the nickname for anywhere within 100 miles of a border: the Constitution-Free Zone.

It hadn't always been this way, Austin told me. By the time I visited, though, practices at the border were cruel, inhumane, designed to subject already desperate people to further misery. Residents of the area did what they could: leaving jugs of water out for anyone migrating (even though Texas sometimes prosecuted people for leaving out food or water) or helping migrants get medical treatment. But the Chihuahuan Desert is huge and deadly, and it infuriated me to think about the United States government's lack of humanity. It threw into stark contrast just how easy traveling here had been for me.

Austin and I climbed into our separate cars to drive to Viva Big Bend, a music festival that happened to be going on in Alpine and Marfa that weekend. The Border Patrol agents waved Austin through. I stopped and rolled down my window. "Are you an American citizen?" the agents asked me. When I told them I was, they let me drive on.

AUSTIN WANTED TO show me a classic Texas night, so after we caught a set from her coworkers' Beatles tribute band (this should give you an indication of the kind of music festival Viva Big Bend was) we walked over to Railroad Blues, where a proper country-western band was playing. In front of the stage people were dancing in a lively way that involved a lot of footwork and spinning. Everyone was doing it differently, but everyone looked like they knew what they were doing. This, Austin told me, was two-step.

I later tried to research two-stepping on YouTube, but the problem is that everyone who uploads videos of themselves two-stepping is literally psychotic, twisting intricately and without pause, flipping their hair dramatically, doing full handstands on their partners' shoulders. I watched one video of a high school two-stepping team where dozens of teen boys dressed like the Texas flag twirled teen girls dressed like the Texas flag over their heads to a song about how superlative Texas is. Texans are off the deep end!

Almost immediately after we arrived a man walked up to me. "Would you like to dance?" he asked. I barely know where my limbs are at any given moment; I didn't think I could two-step for ten seconds without accidentally getting in everyone's way on the dance floor.

"I'm good, but thank you," I told him.

"I'll dance with you!" said Austin, and she and the man twirled out onto the floor, dancing beautifully even though they had just met.

When the song ended, Austin rejoined me. As we got our drinks she explained what's so great about two-step culture: everyone dances and it means nothing. You chitchat with a guy for one song, and when the song is over he says thank you and finds someone new to dance with. He doesn't creepily hover around you the whole night.

"By the way, that guy was named Harris," Austin told me. "That's the county Houston is in. Everyone in Texas is named after something in Texas."

We took our beers outside and met up with Christian, (name's relation to Texas obvious), a writer for *Texas Monthly*. On and on the night went as we roamed around Alpine, meeting up with friends and running into people. It felt like the whole town was partying and everyone, including people who didn't live there, knew each other. But I hadn't come to West Texas solely for vibes: I was there to visit Big Bend National

Park. Eventually I peeled off from the group so I could turn in early and head to the park at the crack of dawn.

I parked in Austin's driveway, got out of the Prius, and—on Austin's recommendation—looked up at the Milky Way. I couldn't believe I was surrounded by such natural beauty in a corner of the country that also offered art and cowboys and coffee and was full of welcoming, generous people who all knew really complicated dances. Staring at the entire galaxy, knowing I wouldn't see stars like this again for a long time and trying to really take it in, I was glad I'd be going home soon to my own corner of the world, where people knew me.

Travel is appealing because it lets you escape your responsibilities. You can leave them behind for a long weekend or a holiday break or, if you go fully insane and quit your job right before a pandemic, for months on end. Traveling to the wilderness feels like an escape not only from your own quotidian responsibilities but from the responsibilities of society as a whole. It gives you the illusion of relying solely on your own abilities and having no one rely on you. But we affect each other no matter where we are on the planet, and you can't really leave your responsibilities behind.

I slipped into Austin's tub to get the dirt off me. *We're all interconnected,* I thought (sleepy). I sighed and sank lower into the water. An ant, fully alive, swam out of my hair. "Sure," I said. "Nature is miraculous." Just kidding. I shrieked.

"YOU'RE GOING TO LONDON?!?!!?" This was the joke every single person made when I told them I was going to Big Bend. Ha! Ha! Ha Ha Ha! HA!!!!! No. I'm going to the Mexico–Texas border.

Big Bend is among the larger of the national parks and

among the less visited. It's not because the park is lacking in any way: it has desert, mountains, and dramatic canyons cut by the Rio Grande. (The river bends north here, wrapping around the park and forming that knob that makes up West Texas—that's how the park got its name). No, the reason the park isn't overrun is that it's such a production to get there. Alpine is more than two and a half hours away from the nearest airport served by major airlines; it is—and I say this with love because I would love to move there—the middle of nowhere. Austin's house was a fifteen-minute drive from the middle of nowhere. To get to Big Bend National Park's headquarters, you start fifteen minutes from the middle of nowhere and drive south into the desert for another hour and a half. There is no easier way.

So it was nine-thirty a.m. before I was talking to a ranger at the Panther Junction Visitor Center in the middle of the park. This was strike one against me. The ranger gestured to the clock hanging on a wall. "This is the desert," she said. "You should be *back* at the trailhead by ten a.m." Factoring in the time it would take to get my Junior Ranger booklet and drive to the trailhead, this would leave me a solid three minutes of hiking each way. I pointed out that I was planning to hike in the mountainous part of the park—shouldn't that afford me at least marginally cooler temperatures? The ranger refused to budge. She then looked at the two one-liter Nalgene bottles I was planning to fill up outside. "I hope you have more water than that," she said.

"I have three gallons in the car," I told her.

"Well, you need to drink a gallon—"

"A gallon per person per day," I said along with her. It was one of those decrees I had seen again and again at visitor centers and on park literature. "But I'm not going to be out all day." The trail I wanted to hike was 4.8 miles; there's no way I would be out for even three hours.

The ranger launched into a lecture about desert preparedness and hydration and rangers having to rescue people. I couldn't tell if she was having a bad day or just didn't like me. I was pretty sure I had acted fairly normal during our entire interaction; hell, I hadn't even asked for my Junior Ranger book yet.

"Well, I don't want to die in the desert," I said to appease her and because, well, I *don't* want to die in the desert. "I'll carry one of the gallons." The woman nodded, victorious but weakened by what it took to get here. "Also, can I have a Junior Ranger book, please?" I got the book and left the poor ranger to see how else Satan would test her that day.

THE CHISOS MOUNTAINS were in fact noticeably cooler than the surrounding desert. In the summer, the daytime temperatures there are usually twenty degrees cooler than those down by the Rio Grande. We're still talking desert temps, so twenty degrees cooler than "the actual freaking desert in July" is still hot, and Americans have proven they can find a way to die in nature at *any* temperature—it's one of the things that makes our nation great. But as I slathered on sunscreen at the Lost Mine trailhead, I felt good about my chances of surviving the next two and a half hours.

I looked at my water bottles. I *knew* I would be fine with two liters of water. I'd been hiking my entire life, including the last seven and a half weeks straight, and I knew my body. Two liters would be more than enough. But then I imagined somehow dying on the trail and being found by the annoyed

ranger. She would look around, see that I had only two Nal-
genes, and feel vindicated. She would take a picture of my
skeleton and post it to Instagram to warn others not to be as
stupid as I was. She would contact the Secretary of the Interior and have him formally revoke my Junior Ranger badges.
It wasn't worth the risk. I shoved a full gallon of water in my
backpack and set off.

The Lost Mine Trail came on Austin's recommendation,
and she was right: it was gorgeous. No actual lost mine was
involved, she warned, which was fine by me; as a kid you always assume the mine in question is full of gold or rubies, but
in my experience of the American West mines were usually
full of uranium, and I was not trying to become irradiated so
early in the morning. Every time I passed a cactus—there are
about sixty species found in Big Bend, more than in any other
national park—it was like seeing the real *Starry Night* after
living with a miniature magnet version on my fridge. And up
here in the Chisos, as the elevation rose, I found agaves right
next to colder-weather plants like juniper and pinyon, a fun
juxtaposition. Mainly I was thrilled with myself that I knew
the names of about six total plants.

The trail rose steeply, which normally would not present
me with huge problems but turned out to be very bad and in
fact horrible while carrying a full gallon of water in my backpack. Perhaps the mental image alone is enough to tell you
how much of an idiot I was. Hiking uphill in the desert carrying a full gallon of water is not a wilderness hack, it is some
torturous challenge they would make you do on *Survivor*. My
pace slowed, and I began to feel like I might actually puke
onto an agave. I chugged water to try to lighten my load, but
that barely made a dent in the liter I was carrying, and left the

gallon untouched. My situation was unchanged, except that now I kind of had to pee. Maybe I *would* die in the desert. Maybe my sun-bleached bones *would* end up on the Big Bend Instagram page.

Then I realized: I could just pour some of the water out. It felt sacrilegious, pouring out precious water in the desert, and I wondered if this one-time, quarter-gallon monsoon event would send a small patch of desert into complete climate chaos. But I did it: I dumped part of the gallon onto the side of the trail. Immediately the going was so much easier.

Lighter now by multiple pounds and fueled by vindication, I hurried to the summit. The views there, from a perch on the hard volcanic rock, were beyond belief. Mountains and canyons rolled away down into the Chihuahuan Desert and hundreds of miles south into Mexico. It was more than my brain could take in; I felt so lucky to be there. I tried to stay in the present as much as I could, but I knew that in a few weeks I'd already be missing this moment. This had been the whole point of my trip: to walk in the wild, to see enormous plants I'd never seen before, to sit on top of a mountain and take in the view. Back home my only view was of the old men who sit in the vacant lot across the street from my place and drink all day, and the "wildest" my walks got was when a rat crossed the sidewalk in front of me. There were things I was eager to return to, but I felt so grateful I had put myself here now.

LESS THAN AN hour later I took the park's scenic drive through the desert, past canyons and rock formations and historic ruins all the way to the Rio Grande. I parked at the Santa Elena Canyon trailhead and walked down to the river. "River" is a very generous term for what I encountered: on that hot late

July day, at this particular spot, the Rio Grande was more like something you'd find in a ditch by the side of the road. The river was so unimposing that it practically begged you to walk across it—and to prevent this very thing a stern-looking enforcement ranger stood on the bank, peering at all of us through his dark sunglasses. He peered at the people walking in the river. He peered at the people hanging out along the shore. He peered at me, peering at him. I instinctively turned away and started walking upriver, into a mudbank.

It didn't used to be like this. For years the entire surrounding area was one big community, with people from the United States and Mexico traveling freely back and forth. Santa Elena Canyon was an unofficial river crossing, and farther east in the park was another at Boquillas Canyon. (Just outside the park, fifteen miles west of Santa Elena Canyon, there was a third unofficial crossing at Lajitas.) People on either side of the river might work or sell things or hang out on the other side, and visitors to Big Bend might dip into Mexico for a few hours. But after 9/11 these crossings were shut down, cleaving the community in two. For years, if you wanted to cross the border from where I stood, instead of wading across a shallow stream you had to get back in your car and drive at least two and a half hours to the closest official port of entry at Presidio, Texas. Finally, after more than a decade of this, a port of entry was opened at Boquillas, though it was shut down again for a long stretch during the pandemic. It seemed so, so stupid that so much vitriol and violence went into making sure people didn't cross this sad little stream.

I hurried away from the enforcement ranger toward the mouth of the Santa Elena Canyon, one of the most iconic spots in Big Bend. I looked at the mud covering my shoes after walking forty feet and thought about how long it would take me to get back to the visitor center to grab my Junior Ranger badge and realized I didn't have enough time to do all that *and* extricate myself from a quicksand mud puddle *and* make it to Marfa for my evening plans with Austin. I turned back toward Texas.

On my walk to the Prius I ran into the ranger again and thought of the enforcement ranger who had given me my badge at Channel Islands. "Excuse me," I said, stopping him, and asked if he could similarly hook me up to save me the long drive out of my way back to the visitor center.

"Well," he said, again giving me a long hard peer through his sunglasses. "Did you do all the activities?"

"I did the preponderance," I told him.

"Ooh," he said, faux impressed. "'Preponderance.'" He did have badges, he told me, remarking that the park didn't get too many people my age doing the books. I let all this shade bounce right off me: after seven-point-five weeks in the sun I was baked to a hard crisp impervious to shame from cops slash park rangers. I just looked back at him impassively. His name tag, I noticed, gave his first initial and the last name Law.

"Is that your real last name?" I asked.

"No. I decided my old last name didn't work so well with this job, so I legally changed it."

"Whoa!" I said. "Really?!"

"No."

He flipped through my book, making sure I truly had done the preponderance, and I asked him if across the trickle of the Rio Grande really was Mexico. Somehow the river seemed too small, the entire scene so unassuming, that I felt like I must have gotten it wrong and turned up at some random stream in the desert. No, he said: this really was it, I really was looking at a different country. "I have to yell at people all the time who hop across the river. That's an illegal border crossing," he said, relishing the phrase too much.

Satisfied that I had done my Junior Ranger work, Ranger Law walked me to his car and handed me a badge. "One last thing," I said. "I noticed on the map that there's a dirt road from here right to the exit that looks like it would save me a lot of time. Am I allowed to drive on that?"

"Well," he said, in a tone that I already knew meant I was in trouble, though I didn't yet know why. "Technically, it's allowed. It will take you just as long as the other drive because it's dirt. That's if you even make it. Which you won't, in that little Prius of yours."

How he knew I was driving a Prius he did not explain.

"Now, you can ignore my advice if you want. But I'm gonna give you a fine if you get stuck and I have to come rescue you."

I was offended that he thought I would ignore his advice *and* immediately proceed to get stuck, but I didn't want to deal with his aggro energy any longer than I had to. Also, after trying to stunt-drink a full gallon of water I really had to pee, so I just said, "Yep! Sounds good!" and hurried away to the bathroom. When I emerged he was back at the river, policing our nation's border. I got in that little Prius of mine and drove the long way back to Austin's house.

THE NEXT STOP on Austin's tour of West Texas culture was the best restaurant in Marfa, which just so happened to be the restaurant where she worked. As soon as we walked inside, a half dozen people greeted her, servers and diners alike. We slipped into a table in a bay window to join Austin's friends, who had beaten us there. Together we ordered just about everything on the menu, then set about exchanging tales of our West Texas day. One person had either met or learned of a veteran who, as performance art, was walking between Border Patrol stations carrying a seventy-pound American flag to show what migrants had to endure. Another person at the table had heard a rumor that Kenny Chesney was in town to shoot a music video. Discussion of local and state and nationwide culture and politics was robust and thoughtful, the table crowded with progressive women born and raised in Texas who cared about the state and wanted to make it better. It was almost enough to make me forget that Ted Cruz was from there.

For more than a year before setting off on my trip I had lived alone. When I returned to New York I would continue to live alone. During covid, I would be alone so much that I would become mentally insane in ways I am only now beginning to understand. That I lived alone was something I could do only because I had the immense good fortune of selling a book while also working a full-time job, though in the years since quitting that job my financial ability to continue living alone has often been precarious. Living alone is a marker of adulthood or of having your life together, but it's also probably the thing in my life that has made me the most crazy.

In a way my trip felt similar. Extended solo travel was a luxury and a rite of passage, but the long stretches I spent alone were the times I felt most frustrated and unsure of my purpose. Later, when people asked me about my favorite parts of the trip, I did think about particularly huge trees or especially pointy mountains, but always my mind went first to the times I was surrounded by friends. Times like this night in

Marfa, with women I barely knew or was just then meeting, eating improbably delicious food in the middle of the desert. It reminded me of the times I'd fantasized about convincing all my friends to move to remote Montana or upstate New York or somewhere in the Pacific Northwest, to live in houses on the same street and just hang out and kiss each other, before realizing that what I was doing was, essentially, designing a cult.

From the restaurant we walked two and a half blocks to the Marfa Public Radio building, where a party or the beginnings of one was happening. People of all ages milled about and tailgated, including a middle-aged woman who passed us a plate of frosted sugar cookies in the shapes of cowboy boots and the state of Texas. Members of our group greeted friends in the crowd, and I chatted with one of the new faces. We went inside and found an even more random assortment of people who seemed to have wandered in off the street, except there were definitely not this many people wandering around the streets of Marfa. At the head of the table was a man wearing sunglasses and the biggest hat I have ever seen. This was Joe Nick Patoski, host of the Texas Music Hour of Power.

As you might expect from a show hosted by a man with two first names, the Texas Music Hour of Power ran, in fact, for two hours. (On his website Joe Nick explains that this is "because Texas spans two time zones and frankly, the music is too dang big to limit it to one hour.") Every Saturday night Patoski plays Texas music spanning genres from country to zydeco, rhythm and blues to Tex-Czech, swing to conjunto. Austin and I walked into the studio as Joe Nick announced into the mic that Marfa Public Radio would be hosting a dance contest *right now* for anyone who wanted to swing by. "If you come to the Marfa Public Radio station you can get loaded and go home with cash money, expressing yourself through music," he said. "Ain't nobody do that but us!"

Before we could be pressed into dancing ourselves, Austin and I and another woman in our group peeled off to walk to a third location, a friend's going-away party at a house nearby. In a living room dominated by a geometric, burnt orange rug and books elegantly piled along the floor, a man wearing only shorts lay across a folding massage table, getting a very meticulous stick-and-poke tattoo from a man in a perfectly distressed Metallica T-shirt. *Okay, Marfa slaps,* I realized. I could aspire for my entire life to be as cool as this one room at this one party and never achieve it, even though I couldn't tell if the random stacks of books and clusters of prayer candles were an intentional aesthetic or if the house's owner was just moving. We found the rest of the party in the kitchen, and the host explained the tattooing: he and the man on the table and the guy moving away were all getting friendship tattoos of bristlecone pines. I wanted to be friends with everyone at the party; I wanted to be home partying with all of my friends.

FOR THE PAST two months my life had been organized around seeing and doing new things. This was what I had craved when I took the same trains to the same office job where I compiled a Google document of research on another celebrity Monday through Friday, week after week. I wanted adventure. And on the road and in national parks and at random places along the way, I had found it. My friends and family and the strangers who followed me on Instagram felt like I had found it too, constantly DMing me that they were traveling vicariously through my trip, that I was doing what they had always wanted to do. But now, after seven and a half weeks away from home, I was excited to return to my community, to reconnect with the idea of staying in one place and taking care of that place and the people who lived there.

Mierle Laderman Ukeles, who wrote about the Death Instinct, also wrote about the Life Instinct, of "the perpetuation and MAINTENANCE of the species." You could have a revolution, sure, but Ukeles asked, "after the revolution, who's going to pick up the garbage on Monday morning?" She wrote a manifesto in praise of maintenance art. While creation and newness got all the glory, maintenance was needed to preserve what had been created, to "protect progress" and "renew the excitement." But maintenance was devalued and given low status because it was performed mostly by women and because it was, as Ukeles wrote, "a drag. . . . The mind boggles and chafes at the boredom." The scholar and activist Silvia Federici calls this kind of work—childcare, cooking, cleaning, taking care of the elderly—"reproductive labor," tasks that have to be done again and again.

Without maintenance workers, housewives, sanitation workers, and everyone who does reproductive labor, the economy wouldn't run and cities would collapse into entropy. Ideally people should be able to do both, to create new things *and* to protect progress, to go on road trips *and* come back to a community, to be a woman of heart and mind *and* have a child to raise. (If you don't want kids because you don't want them, that's fine. If you don't want kids because you're a woman and you can't see a way to both have kids and be free, that's a problem.)

The idea of staying in one place and taking care of it felt especially urgent to me in these climate crisis dystopian end times. Since the Industrial Revolution our economy and culture have been structured around newness and growth and creating more and more products to sell; it has now become clear that the mirage of limitless growth is killing our planet. Instead, we need to commit to maintaining what we already have, need to stop strip-mining the world of its remaining resources just to make new plastic clothing and cheap electronics and to make oil executives even more extremely rich than they already are. Because frankly, if we don't, there will be no point in going on road trips because there will be no glaciers and sequoias and forests and cacti to see.

VIVA BIG BEND was still raging, and we had paid for all-weekend wristbands, so after an hour we left the party—the same man was still getting the same incredibly detailed tattoo—and headed to the Lost Horse Saloon. I watched from the sidelines, sipping water, as everyone danced their asses off. One of the familiar faces walked over and asked me to two-step. This time I said yes. I had no idea what I was doing, but I twisted and spun and tried to figure it out.

I WENT ON the road because I love hiking and trees and mountains and waterfalls and all the stuff I can't get in New York City. But while the national parks were stunning—hello, I must have cried looking at a big tree or a large view at least once a week—they're not the only places where a person can go to connect to the natural world. There are federal lands and state lands and local public lands all over the country. I'm lucky enough to live within a ten-minute walk of two parks in Brooklyn, and while neither has glaciers or sea stars or wolverines or the swolest tree in the world, I interact with those parks far more often than I will ever interact with all the national parks combined. I'm not exaggerating when I say that my life changed the moment I decided to pay attention to the parks where I live. Something as simple as looking at a weird-looking tree with splotchy bark and wondering what the heck this alien thing growing all over my neighborhood *was*, led to trying to teach myself about all the kinds of trees nearby, and now when I look at a tree I really notice it. I still have no idea what I'm seeing most of the time, but the wondering grounds me.

The naturalist and author Aldo Leopold proposed a "land ethic," that views land not just as a commodity we exploit or the place where we build our community but as *part* of our community. "The land ethic simply enlarges the boundaries of the community to include soils, waters, plants, and animals, or collectively: the land," he writes. Under such an ethic, we would consider whether any action preserved the "integrity, stability, and beauty of the biotic community."

One of the great things about the United States, and the thing that made my trip possible, is that we're encouraged to think of the entire country as our community. The national parks are part of my community and the community of all Americans, and the fact that they "belong" to every citizen does, I think, encourage people to consider the health and integrity and beauty of the parks when thinking about climate change. But it's also important to think of ways we are in community with land closer to home. The parks I live near are part of my community, but so is Newtown Creek, the creek that separates Greenpoint and Queens. At the time of the American Revolution it was a beautiful waterway bordered by orchards and estates. But over time it became polluted with runoff and toxins and raw sewage and oil from the Greenpoint oil spill, first noticed in 1978 but caused by seepage over many decades—one of the worst spills ever recorded in the United States. (When the backstory to an oil spill involves "eventually getting around to noticing," you know it's going to be bad.) Newtown Creek is now a Superfund site and remains one of the most polluted places in the country. Thoreau said, "There is no hope for you unless this bit of sod under your feet is the sweetest to you in this world, in any world." Brooklyn was the bit of sod under my feet.

I appreciated the freedom I had to travel around the country. What was just as important—way more important, really—is the freedom of communities to live without fear of the ground and water poisoning us, of the sea rising and flooding our homes, of asphalt giving us third-degree burns. I mean, I know we are *capable* of operating every day in abject terror and dystopian depression, running around with our hair on fire as everything we know and love burns, but it kind of seems like a human right not to have to do that. That second kind of freedom we can't access on our own, only collectively.

I thought there was great value in women breaking free of the socialization that keeps us from having our own adventures—and I still think so! But I missed my life when I was on the road, and Trump was still president even if I wasn't staring at a screen for twelve hours a day tracking what he was up to. Alone on the road I realized there is so much value in relationships. Relationships were what made my trip possible! My stepdad lent me the Prius; my dad lent me all sorts of gear; my mom made camping reservations for me when

I was rushing to get somewhere and had no Wi-Fi; friends and family let me crash with them and defile their pristine showers with my dirt; complete strangers sent me thoughtful recommendations about what to do in corners of the country where I had never been. And all the while I knew that my community would be waiting for me when I got back.

Returning to the Toilet Women

BIG BEND WAS THE LAST PARK ON MY TRIP I HAD ACTU-ally dreamed about going to, and so, even though I was still days from home as I drove away from Alpine the next morning, I felt like my trip was over. I resolved to stay as much in the moment as I could for the next few days: after all, I still had one park left, Hot Springs. I was going there less because I wanted to and more because it was directly on the way back to Wisconsin, and what kind of American would I be if I didn't at least stop in and embezzle a Junior Ranger badge? But first I needed to drive across the entire state of Texas.

Driving anywhere in Texas takes forever, but it especially takes forever when you're starting in far west Texas and driving northeast. At that point you might as well give up the idea of ever seeing any other states in your lifetime: you're pretty much in Texas for the duration. The feeling you get on this drive is that if it's possible for humans to get out of Texas via motor vehicle, scientists haven't yet figured out exactly how.

Had my trip changed me for the better? I knew I was glad I had done it, and I wondered if the doing of it had made me realize how open I was to experience. My urge to go everywhere and see everything and get there by two-lane back roads was nothing new. What was new, what I had never realized before, was that this urge wasn't some unique thing about me, some personality quirk, something I came to sui generis. It was also because I'm a Sagittarius. (Just kidding.) (I mean, this is true, but it's not the main reason.) No: the desire to road-trip across America had been suggested to me by Jack Kerouac and Bill Bryson and the John Travolta–starring, canonical travel story *Wild Hogs* and all the narratives I gobbled up when my brain was still setting into its Jell-O mold. The desire came from listening to a hundred thousand emo bands singing about getting out of their small suburban towns, and to Joni Mitchell singing about road-tripping away from a failed relationship and toward a new one, and to Bruce Springsteen singing about cars as escape (songs he wrote before he even had a driver's license; when I learned this, it cured me of having imposter syndrome ever again in my life). The desire came from Walt Whitman poems about the open road and from every poem about being free, and from playing *The Oregon Trail* every day in computer lab in fourth grade. My desire to take a Great American Road Trip came from my curiosity about the world, the fact that the Internet was invented and that I was now aware of the existence of places of great beauty on public land in my own country, which I could see with my own little eyeballs if I could only get my ass over to them.

And now I had done it. Much like how I once wanted to be the kind of person who had tattoos and then I just got tattoos, I didn't feel very different afterward. But I had very badly

wanted to go on a road trip, I had very badly wanted the pleasure of seeing this country, very badly wanted to hike and to
connect with nature and to do things that put me in touch
with what's bigger than me. I had, simply, wanted to have fun.
And over the two months of my trip, I did. Sick, good work!

BY DEGREES THE landscape changed from wide horizons
of hills and creosote and one tarantula in the road to green
farmland and suburbs. At a certain point, Texas looks more
or less like the part of the Midwest where I grew up. If I remembered my geography correctly, things wouldn't change
too much between here and Wisconsin. I tried hard to remember the thoughts I'd had about appreciating nature in all
its forms, about deeply loving the place where you're from, but
sometimes it's hard to feel beautiful swelling feelings about
the universe when you're looking at corn. When I hit the ver-
dant grass of central Texas, I knew I wouldn't be seeing any
more novel and thrilling landscapes for the rest of my trip. In
that way too, the trip had already drawn to a close.

I stopped in Fort Worth to grab a late lunch at a vegan
diner. Walking to it from my parking spot, I ducked through
an alley where trash baked in the summer sun. The smell
of hot garbage hit me directly in the hippocampus. *Jesus*, I
thought, *it smells just like home.* I missed New York.

Did I find freedom through traveling, as I had hoped? I
don't know. [takes massive bong rip] Can any one human really be free? Personally I had become suspicious of the whole
idea of individual "freedom." We're all part of systems that are
entrenched and so much larger than us: economies and gov-
ernments, laws and narratives. Individuals can push against
them but not ever fully escape them. If you try, you end up

the Unabomber, attempting to use pistols to shoot airplanes because they were "too loud." (And also, you know, unabombing.) There were people who lived on the road full time, but I wasn't trying to do anything like that; I wasn't permanently pivoting to Van Life. I was just *On Vacation* by Jack Kerouac.

I would need to return to capitalism and a day job soon, but I hoped my trip had taught me something about the value of actually having fun for once in my life, of getting out of the city, of paying attention to nature—and the worth of those things in relation to my ambition, which seemed to me to matter less and less. We're alive one time, I thought. Who cares!

IN DALLAS, I stayed overnight at the first Airbnb I had ever booked. Usually when traveling I prefer to sleep on rocks and dust rather than shell out $150 because, well, *I don't have a job, remember?* But I needed to get some Wi-Fi–dependent things done. The apartment was decorated to pander to Millennial tastes: throw pillows on a couch, a potted succulent, and twinkle lights lining the bedroom window. I was charmed as shit. I put my bags down and turned around to see two posters on the bedroom wall. One said MAGIC IN THE DESERT above mountains and the words MARFA TEXAS. The other was a map of the US national parks. The rich, deep, meaningful trip I had taken over the past two months was, itself, a cliché of Millennial tastes.

I was mentally preparing to re-enter my life, where I would try to form relationships and try to get paid money for labor and, generally, try to build a future. In most ways going on a road trip had been an escape from being productive. Spending hours in the car, hiking up mountains with no cell service, camping far from Wi-Fi or even a place to charge my devices—all refused the minute-by-minute accounting of work. For most of the time I was on the road, I literally did not have the ability to be economically productive.

But on a very primal level, I did feel productive simply because I was moving forward. Getting where I was going each day felt like industry and achievement, even if all I was "doing" was putting my foot on a gas pedal and constantly scanning the horizon for cops. In *The Origins of Totalitarianism* Hannah Arendt talks about "the perpetual-motion mania of totalitarian movements which can remain in power only so long as they keep moving and set everything around them in motion." Has there ever been a more apt description of road trips? Movement for the sake of movement? If I think about this for even one more second, I may convince myself to never travel again.

In a wishful way, a way that wasn't yet in existence, I was being productive or hoped to be: like so many people I met on the trip, I was documenting my time in the national parks, hoping to make something out of it that felt both meaningful and, crucially, monetizable. For some that meant Instagrams or YouTube videos. For Professor Josh it was his movie, which he cut together and released directly online while I was writing the final chapter of this book. While I was on the road I thought about our collective efforts as some tic we were driven to by our capitalist conditioning. We'd been told from day one that our worth in America lay in our ability to be productive, that food and water and housing and health care were not guaranteed and could only be ours if we earned them with our labor. Of course we were trying to monetize our vacations!

It wasn't just some "Protestant work ethic." No, feeling like we needed to be working while on vacation was a trauma response.

But the more I thought about it, the more it struck me how much my documentation of my trip, and Professor Josh's of his, and all the kinds of documentation I encountered, were *not* some tic we did without thinking. For years before leaving my job I had thought about the trip, created elaborate Google Maps routes on CBS company time, had read travel books, and tried to figure out how the finances would work. What I was doing was very much considered and planned. It wasn't that I couldn't have fun hiking unless I was also performing some approximation of labor. It was that hiking was one of the things I found most pleasurable, most meaningful, and most purely enjoyable in my time on this planet, and I was trying to create a future in which I could do it as much as possible. For that to work, I needed to find a way to get paid for it.

I SET OFF late the next afternoon toward Hot Springs National Park. Arkansas was lushly alive, overgrown and humid and buzzing in a way I hadn't seen anywhere else in the country. Night fell and a thick wall of fog obscured anything more than twenty feet away, so the world felt liminal, like I was creating it with my own mind as I drove. Frogs covered the pavement and small mammals darted into the line of my headlights and then into the night on the other side of the road. I saw two possums, then a fox, then a mother raccoon with her raccoon baby. I saw what I thought was a third possum but was in fact an armadillo. I squeaked with glee—I'd never seen one before—and slammed on the brakes to watch the armadillo as it padded away. Then I called my mom to share the good news.

When I got to Hot Springs late that night, having run over enough frogs and mice to ensure a solid three hundred to four hundred years burning in Hell, I circled the park's official campground until—thank God—I found an empty spot. I reversed into it and turned off my music. Outside the cicadas were singing just as loudly.

THERE'S AN APOCRYPHAL story that goes like this: someone asks John Lennon if he thinks Ringo Starr is the best drummer in the world. "Ringo's not the best drummer in the world," John replies. "He's not even the best drummer in the Beatles." Hot Springs National Park was not the best national park I visited on my trip; it wasn't even the best hot springs.

It's an urban park consisting of a row of historic bathhouses fed by natural hot springs. For thousands of years Indigenous people had been coming to the area to quarry novaculite, a very hard and dense rock they used to make arrowheads and tools, and to enjoy the springs. (If there is one thing that unites humans across all cultures and eras, it is "thinking that hot springs are tight.") The springs came to the attention of Anglo settlers in 1804, when Thomas Jefferson sent an expedition to explore the area, which had just become part of the United States via the Louisiana Purchase. Word got back east about this magical place where you could chill out, soak your little bod, take a nice bath in the mountains, and generally have the time of your nineteenth-century life; soon the springs were a popular tourist destination. The national park was established in 1921.

I spent the afternoon there, walking past the springs and around the bathhouses. I could see why people who took baths here would advocate for the government to protect taking baths here in perpetuity. At a ranger program, I tasted the water (it tasted like hot water). I visited the Hot Springs Mountain Tower and viewed the Ouachita Mountains rolling away to the west. I read about how much Al Capone and Frank Costello and Bugs Moran loved Hot Springs; it was, to quote Coolio, a gangster's paradise. (I can imagine the tourism campaigns: "The stresses of bootlegging, gambling, and doing murders got you down? Come take a bath!") The criminal element continued to hang out and gamble in Hot Springs until the US government finally got around to cracking down on the whole deal in the 1960s. You know, forty years after the national park was established. I'm sorry to tell you that if your two passions are public land and high-stakes poker against mob bosses, you *just* missed your golden opportunity.

And then I walked down the stairs from the observation deck and found the trail for the last hike I would take on my road trip. It wasn't long—I had miles to go before I slept—but I wanted to savor it. I took a good long gander at all of Arkansas from a lookout point, then set off into the forest. I really listened to the sounds of birds, really looked at the dappled light leaking through the hickory trees. I realized that my trip had, in perfect poetry, come full circle: on June 4th, the day I set out, I had started my period, and during this last hike my period started again. (In the two months between, I had gotten my period only eleven or twelve times.) And then, 1.7 miles later, my hiking was done.

I went back to the visitor center, a restored old bathhouse. There were tubs for soaking, of course, but also a gym and an elegant music room complete with grand piano and stained-glass ceiling. I walked by a sign that said TOILET WOMEN and thought, ah, my squad. I returned to the information desk and exchanged my Junior Ranger book for one final badge.

"I've spent my summer traveling to national parks," I told the two women rangers as they looked over my work. "I started two months ago in Wisconsin and drove up to Isle Royale, then headed west, and now I've driven all over the country. I think I've been to about thirty parks by now. This is the last one of my trip. From here I'm heading home."

The women didn't even look up. "Okay," one said.

"You missed two pages in the book," the other told me.

I apologized, and they handed me my badge. I was officially a Junior Ranger.

THE STORY FROM there is just about driving north-northeast for 750 miles. I swung toward Memphis to have an early dinner with my brother. As I entered the city, I crossed the Mississippi on its winding way for the first time since I'd waded across the headwaters at Lake Itasca. There, it was eighteen feet wide; here, it was more than a half mile across, just huge. God knew how much of it was little boys' pee by now.

I swung up I-55 and stopped for gas in Blytheville, Arkansas, to check on my citizens. (Real community, in my opinion, is having a town named after me where I am the queen.) Just after sunset I made it to my final free campsite, somewhere in southern Illinois's Shawnee National Forest. There was an SUV already parked at the trailhead lot where I planned to sleep in the Prius, and I crossed my fingers that its owner wouldn't murder me in the night. Can you imagine? Surviving for two months only to get murdered on my very last night?

It would be the first line of my obituary; it would be engraved on my tombstone; it would be *so me*.

DRIVING AROUND THE country for two months, hiking and camping and visiting national parks, eating and crashing with family members and my oldest friends and new friends I was looking forward to knowing for a long time—all of that did feel like freedom. It was a blast. But the deeper freedom was in recognizing my own sovereignty and the ways that pleasure and action were in my control, while at the same time recognizing that the cult of the individual is in a lot of ways what's wrong with America, not what is special about it.

The monk Thomas Merton wrote, "The true solitary does not seek himself, but loses himself." I had set off on a Great American Road Trip in the Kerouac tradition, asking what if a woman could find individual adventure too—and found instead the collective. Anything beautiful, in the natural world or in the promises of what America can be, comes from collective action, I'd realized. It comes from a sense of shared responsibility and love. I know that's corny. Don't tell Jack Kerouac I said that.

Much of what I learned about the places I went to—that there never was such a thing as "uninhabited wilderness" in America; that an unsustainable number of people, including me, were having the exact same idea and visiting the parks; that *so many* plants and animals and glaciers were already seriously in danger of completely disappearing—made me feel like I might be damned for all eternity for my road trip, that maybe women *shouldn't* go on the road after all, that no one of any gender should do any of this ever again.

But then I thought about how looking at trees and seeing

my homies were my two favorite things about being alive, and I knew I wouldn't stop traveling altogether. Try as I might, it is not within my power to single-handedly correct all of America's sins. That is Bernie Sanders's ministry. (Just kidding. It is Gen Z's.) (Just kidding, it is all of ours, together.) Like Whitman, I tramp a perpetual journey. I would continue to road-trip and recreate, but I would try to do it more mindfully. And maybe I'd explore other ways to experience nature. I'd spend more time hiking closer to home. Maybe I'd take up backpacking. Maybe I'd get a touring bike and see America while simultaneously chiseling a high, tight ass.

In the morning I woke up to the chatter of four men who belonged to the SUV and who, in their beneficence, did not murder me. I took a short walk to a small waterfall, then forced the Prius up its last dirt road, tricky and washboarded but nothing too hard for my determined hybrid to navigate. I dragged out my day, stopping in St. Louis to grab lunch and buy books and eat ice cream. In central Illinois I drove past a series of signs saying CRIMINALS MENACING A LADY ALONE, DETERRENCE REQUIRES MORE THAN A PHONE, GUNS SAVE LIVES DOT COM and patted myself on the back for surviving a whole two months without the gun TB tried to buy me. I pulled into my dad's driveway, and my trip was over. I thought of a line not from Kerouac but that weird spiky little introvert, Thoreau:

> "I left the woods for as good a reason as I went there. Perhaps it seemed to me that I had several more lives to live, and could not spare any more time for that one."

Acknowledgments

WELL, THE POINT OF THE BOOK IS THAT THERE ARE SO many people who made the whole thing possible.

Dana, the best agent and perfect friend, who listened to me talk about how cool it would be to write a book about going on a road trip, and worked with me to figure out a way to make that book actually worthwhile. Kara, who did the same despite getting absolutely zero cut of the proceeds.

Sarah, who believed in this book and made sure to strip out the gratuitous references to my period and to my crushes until it stood alone from *How to Date Men*. Thanks for sticking with me as I figured out how to write an entirely new kind of book. Sorry I went fully insane from pandemic and breakups in the process!! Thank you also to everyone at HarperCollins who shepherded this book through the editing, printing, and publicity process.

The Home of the Brave artist residency, for giving me space to write and to think and to walk around the desert until I found a sheep skull. Eileen, you are a god and an inspiration. This book would not exist without you.

Emmy and Bart, Molly, Aunt Chris and Uncle John, Todd, Donna and Kevin, Patrick, Austin—thank you for letting me crash with you and for being a bright shining highlight of my trip. Thank you to "Brooke" at Yosemite, and to all the rangers and strangers I met along the way whose names I have changed.

Jose, my genius friend who let me bounce ideas off of him every step of the way. I'm so glad you wrote this book!

Jeff, for all the support and love and coffee and Ian's. Adolfo and Simone for the therapy. Fran and Harris for the TikToks about "which toilet would you shit hardest in?" Renée, Madelyn, Casey, Caitlin for the friendship. B–B——, whose Audi I hit in L.A. during this trip: thanks for never actually charging me for that repair! Sorry again!!

Mr. Krueger, one of the best teachers I ever had, despite the fact I never actually took a class from him, who made me believe my ideas were interesting and amusing, for believing in me so hard I felt like a shooting star too hot to catch.

And of course, always, so deeply, my family, whose support made the whole thing possible. Thanks for the car and the auxiliary logistical help and the phone calls and the long voice mails about how exactly the murder shows would cover my inevitable death. I love you all so much.

ABOUT THE AUTHOR

Blythe Roberson is a comedian, a humor writer, and author of *How to Date Men When You Hate Men*. She has written for *The New Yorker, Cosmopolitan, Kinfolk, Esquire, Vice Magazine*, and for the NPR quiz show *Wait Wait... Don't Tell Me!* Blythe was raised between Illinois and Wisconsin and lives in Brooklyn.